D1195392

DEAD
BEFORE
DEADLINE

To the staff at
Our Lady of the Elms —
Thanks for the wonderful
opportunity. Best Wishes.

Robin Yocum

10-27-04

Series on Ohio History and Culture

DEAD
BEFORE
DEADLINE

❏

*... and Other Tales from
the Police Beat*

ROBIN YOCUM

The University of Akron Press
Akron, Ohio

All inquiries and permissions requests should be addressed to the
publisher, The University of Akron Press, Akron, OH 44325–1703

Manufactured in the United States of America

First edition 2004
08 07 06 05 04 5 4 3 2 1

Library of Congress Cataloging-in-Publication Data

Yocum, Robin.
  Dead before deadline :—and other tales from the police beat / Robin Yocum.—1st
ed.
     p. cm. — (Series on Ohio history and culture)
  Includes index.
  ISBN 1-931968-15-2 (alk. paper)
  1. Crime—Ohio—Case studies. 2. Crime and the press—Ohio. I. Title. II. Series.
  HV6793.O3Y63 2004
  364.1'09771'09048—dc22   2004006300

The paper used in this publication meets the minimum requirements of American
National Standard for Information Sciences—Permanence of Paper for Printed Library
Materials, ansi z39.48—1984. ∞

Text design by Charles Sutherland

Dedicated to the memory of
Ned Stout and Ken Chamberlain—newspapermen

CONTENTS

LIST OF ILLUSTRATIONS

PREFACE

THIS WAS NEVER INTENDED TO BE A BOOK ABOUT CRIME. RATHER, it is book about a reporter covering crime for the *Columbus Dispatch*. I have tried to create a book that gives the reader insight into my life as a police reporter and my interactions with the accused, the convicted, the cops, other reporters and editors, and the eclectic characters who crossed my path during my more than four years on the police beat. I did not want this to be simply a regurgitation of old crime stories.

Therefore, I have tried to focus on stories that were appealing from a reporter's perspective—those with interesting twists or unique situations. Of course, I've included some stories simply because I found them humorous or sad or particularly intriguing.

I was a reporter with the *Columbus Dispatch* for more than eleven years. Four of those years were spent covering the police beat, which I have chronicled in this book. The book's title, *Dead before Deadline,* sums up my years covering the Columbus Division of Police and the Franklin County Sheriff's Department. Death was the determining factor in nearly every story: if there was no corpse, the most spectacular traffic accident was dismissed as unworthy of even three paragraphs. And deadlines dictated my life. It seemed that I was always struggling to grasp that last little nugget of information before the deadline. "It's a newspaper story, Yocum, not *War and Peace,*" Ned Stout once growled, growing impatient with the time I was taking to complete a story that he was waiting to edit. "Crank it out and get it in the paper."

Most of the stories included in this book occurred during my years on the police beat—1981–85—but I included other stories with a crime-reporter element. For example, my airplane trip with Governor Rhodes occurred before I started the police beat, but I included it since police reporters at the *Dispatch* were expected to cover natural disasters, such as tornadoes and severe storms. Also, I included segments from a series about teenage prostitution that I wrote just after I left the police beat.

It should be noted that some of these stories were not exclusively mine. Some had double bylines. In some cases, several reporters might have covered the same story over a period of weeks or months. For each of the stories included in this book, I did one or more of the articles. I do not want to diminish the efforts of other reporters.

In a few instances I have used only first names or no names at all. In a case like that of the juvenile who claimed to have been kidnapped, I found no reason to dredge up her name for something that occurred when she was fifteen years old. More than once, information that I gleaned never appeared in the paper. In those instances I have protected the source.

Obviously, as a reporter I did not write down all conversations verbatim. I have recreated dialog to the best of my memory, providing a substantially accurate representation of the conversations.

I would like to offer special thanks to Mike Curtin, president of the *Dispatch,* for his cooperation in my preparation of this book. The *Dispatch* granted me permission to reprint headlines and segments of articles, as well as the photographs that appear in this book. Also, special thanks to *Dispatch* head librarian Jim Hunter and assistant librarians Linda Deitch and Kathy Waxler for their help in tracking down photos and snippets of information that had disappeared from my files.

Also, I want to thank the University of Akron Press and its director, Michael J. Carley, for taking on this project. The relationship between a stubborn author and publisher can sometimes be tenuous. The process of getting this book into print was extremely smooth–bloodless, in fact. For this, I also wish to thank Production Coordinator Amy Petersen, Marketing Representative Marsha Cole, and copyeditor Nancy Basmajian, who did a skillful job of detail editing.

Ultimately, the only thing that bothered me was the fact that it did not bother me. . . . you cannot let it eat at you or you'll never be able to do your job. (Credit Larry Hamill Photography)

INTRODUCTION

SHE WAS JUST FIVE YEARS OLD AND HAD SUCH A BEAUTIFUL LITTLE face. In the photograph, she was sitting with her left hand atop the right. She was wearing a satiny top with lace cuffs and her hair had been curled, forming ringlets around her face. Just a few hours before her father handed me the photo, the little girl had been killed.

Her name was Regina Ruth Bell. She had been out with her ten-year-old brother, visiting some neighborhood friends. As they walked home about 4:30 P.M., she suddenly darted into Oakland Park Avenue. The brother tried unsuccessfully to grab her and yelled for her to stop. She ignored him and ran across the westbound lane and into the path of heavy eastbound traffic. The driver of the car that hit her, police said, simply did not have time to stop. Regina died an hour later at Children's Hospital.

It was December 20, 1982.

That evening, I knocked on the door of the family's north side home. The Christmas tree was decorated, but no one had bothered to turn on the lights. It probably didn't seem right. Under the tree were packages, wrapped and tagged for a little girl who would never open them. The father was obviously consumed with grief and could barely speak. How quickly the excitement of the holidays had dissipated from the small home, and how painful it would be to remove those packages and make plans to bury a child. Christmas, I thought, would never be the same for that family. Never again could they decorate a tree without the memory of their loss.

Part of me, the newspaper reporter, wanted to know what was inside the brightly wrapped packages. What had that little girl asked for when she sat on Santa's lap? Had the father gone out and personally bought the one special gift she so desired? The reporter in me wanted to know. It would have made for poignant reading. But the father in me could not ask the question. The little girl's dad had been kind enough to talk for a few minutes, and I knew the question would pierce a heart already broken. When he left to get me a photograph to run with my story, my eyes moved to a portrait of the little girl on a table near the Christmas tree. I wondered how her parents would ever go on with their lives, for certainly there would always be emptiness in their hearts.

I once had a grieving father tell me that it was, indeed, a comfort to have his other children around. He looked at me for several moments before saying, "But I'll never be able to replace the one that I just lost." The loss, the pain, and the void, he was saying, were permanent. I thanked the little girl's father for his time, said I was sorry for his loss, and left.

Despite the sometimes macabre nature of my job, I rarely had trouble doing it. In the great majority of the deaths I covered, the recently deceased had been begging for it. They had been driving drunk or messing with someone they should not have been messing with. In the most basic sense of news reporting, they were merely statistics. Their deaths were usually covered as basic record keeping—four paragraphs, no photos, few details. Those stories would get buried in the back of the local section, included in a briefs column with four or five items of equal note. It was the other deaths, that slight minority, that made the best stories and were the most difficult to cover—kids and the truly random victims. The drunk driver who plowed into a tree and killed himself was usually of little interest. However, when the drunk plowed into the mother of three and killed her, the interest level grew exponentially.

Emotionally, they were the most difficult stories to cover, but they made for the best copy. Most of my readers could not relate to someone who had been murdered in an alley over a drug dispute. However, all of them could sympathize with the husband and father of three who had just lost his wife to a drunken driver. It was my job to attempt to interview the husband, and it never failed to make my guts burn. Sometimes, I could hardly bring myself to knock on the door.

Knocking on the door. Ordinarily, it's such a simple, mindless task. But, in the life of a reporter, there is nothing more difficult than knocking on the door of a home where a loved one has just lost his or her life. No matter how many times you do it, it never gets any easier. I would often sit in the press car near the home and try to psych myself up to go knock on the door. Behind it, a family was enduring the most traumatic event of their lives. My job was to knock, introduce myself, and talk my way inside. It was impossible not to feel like a ghoul.

Still, the great majority of the time they let me in and I got the story. Most of the time, they wanted to talk. They wanted an opportunity to say something nice about the deceased. That did not make it any easier to knock on the door. The more I did it, however, the better I got at getting inside. I would introduce myself and tell whoever answered the door that I was doing a story on the death. "I would like for people to know a little bit more about him," I would say. "If you have just a couple of minutes, I promise not to take much of your time."

I never asked many questions during those interviews. Most of the time, I would say, "Tell me about your son. When people read this story tomorrow, what would you like them to know about him?" And then, I would simply listen and jot down an occasional note. They would tell stories. Share memories. No matter how despicable his life may have been, they would always think of the good. The last thing I would do before leaving was ask to borrow a photograph. Each time, as I left the house, I was consumed by a sense of both relief and accomplishment. And I hoped that I would never have to do it again.

But I would.

From May 1981 through August 1985, I was a police reporter for the *Columbus Dispatch.* The police beat is considered by most reporters to be the most distasteful job on the paper. You continually deal with death, every seamy element of society, and cops who view you as being only slightly above criminals in social status. As the night police reporter, I was responsible for covering all law enforcement agencies, fire departments, and the Ohio State Highway Patrol in Franklin and the contiguous counties. If someone called 911 for something other than a loud party or a grease fire, it was my job to know about it. Consequently, I spent a lot of time in neighborhoods that I would otherwise avoid. Suffice it to say that when the police get a "shots fired" call at 1:45 A.M., it is rarely in the high-rent district.

In the four-plus years that I covered crime for the *Columbus Dispatch,* I calculated that I covered more than one thousand deaths. I interviewed pimps and pushers, killers and child molesters. I went on drug, porn, and moonshine raids. I ruined so many slacks and shoes that I began wearing polyester slacks and cowboy boots; I needed something I could hose off.

There were times when I had to go home and shower in the middle of my shift. There were other nights when I stood in my backyard and turned the hose on my boots and pants before going inside. I tramped through cornfields looking for missing airplanes and missing children. I slogged through the county landfill with cops from the Juvenile Bureau looking for child pornography. I waded through a squalid home with knee-high trash and a flooded basement where a family of ducks had taken up residence. Nancy Nall, one of our general assignment reporters, once said, "If I had your job, I'd die of trash exposure."

In nearly every story, someone was maimed or dead. I covered murders, suicides, murder-suicides, fires, automobile accidents, motorcycle accidents, drownings, plane crashes, railroad crossing accidents, pedestrian-car fatalities, pedestrian-train fatalities, parachuting deaths, electrocutions, construction accidents, autoerotic asphyxiations. Some were flukes; some were deserved.

One man shot and killed a buddy in an argument over the amount of wine sipped from the bottle of MD 20/20 they were sharing. Another was impaled on the front loading tong of a garbage truck, and then run over by the irate estranged husband of the woman whom the impaled was dating. (He lived.) A Denison University coed was riding in the back seat of her father's car—on their way to a Parents' Weekend dinner—when a stray bullet from a drug battle a block away went through the open window of the car, under her uplifted arm, and hit her in the lung, killing her almost instantly. A narcotics officer was shot in the back of the head at point-blank range with a .22-caliber handgun during a botched drug raid; he was released from the hospital a few days later. A nine-month-old used a bucket of dirty mop water to pull himself up and then fell forward and drowned. A young man walked up to the police information desk with three inches of bailing wire sticking out of his forehead. He had drilled a hole through his skin to the skull and attempted to insert the wire in an effort to find his brain, which he believed had been stolen by aliens.

I was once in the middle of an interview with the husband of a murder victim when I thought, "You son-of-a-bitch; you killed her." I was in the middle of an interview with the father of a teenage girl who had been murdered when I thought, "You son-of-a-bitch; you killed her." In both cases, no one was ever charged. In both cases, I know in my heart that I was right.

The police beat was at times sad, morbid, and funny. It was sometimes pathetic, often ridiculous.

And it was intriguing beyond words.

There were never enough answers for my questions. I thought of that as I sat in a stark visitation room at the old Ohio Penitentiary near downtown Columbus, interviewing seventeen-year-old Brad Porter, who had murdered his devout Mormon parents in their suburban Columbus home. He had sneaked up behind his mother and shot her in the back of the head while she stood at the kitchen sink, fixing dinner. After dragging her body to the garage, he hid and waited for his dad to come home. He put a bullet from the same .22-caliber rifle through his father's eye. Why? I interviewed Brad for hours, but left without an answer. And I asked him . . . repeatedly. "Why did you do it, Brad? How did things get so bad that you felt you had to shoot your mother in the back of the head? What sequence of events in your life caused you to pick up that rifle? What was going on in your head in the days and weeks and months before you wrapped your finger around the trigger?"

Each time I asked, he just looked at me as if I were speaking an unknown language. He could not answer, because even he did not know. Rather, he said he missed being on the high school wrestling team.

I spent an equal amount of time in an interview room at the Ohio Reformatory for Women in Marysville, talking to a well-spoken, seemingly intelligent woman who had a road map of needle tracks up and down both arms. She also was scarred behind her knees and between her toes. "When my veins collapsed and I couldn't shoot up in my arms or legs, I'd inject myself under my tongue," she said, demonstrating with an imaginary syringe. The mental image this created was so vile that I wanted to curl up in the chair. She had allowed heroin to control and ruin her life. I wanted desperately to understand the addiction; try as I might, I could not. She said, "When I inject myself with heroin, it's like . . ." Her voice trailed off for a moment, then she refocused on me. "It's like drinking rocket fuel. I just couldn't get enough."

I'm sure I was staring at her with a slack-jawed look of disbelief. "You're going to have to help me out, here," I said. "I'm missing the attraction."

She continued in vain to explain the addiction, then finally looked at me and said, "You don't get it, do you?"

I just shook my head.

On one sweltering summer night, I interviewed an elderly robbery victim in her stifling west-side apartment. Earlier in the week, she had opened the door to a woman and her daughter who claimed to be selling Girl Scout cookies. Once inside, they rifled the apartment while the bony-thin old woman watched helplessly.

They must have been extremely desperate thieves. Otherwise, I cannot comprehend how they could have spent that much time in that rancid apartment.

On the floor were piles of German shepherd manure. Every surface in the apartment—furniture, floors, *everything*—was covered with dog fur. Hundreds—and I am not exaggerating—of cockroaches scampered across the floor and walls. It looked like rush hour on the cockroach freeway. I sat on the very edge of a chair, trying to keep as little of my butt as possible in contact with its cloth. The stench was overwhelming, and I was struggling with my weak gag reflex. Every time a cockroach scampered across the wall, which was constantly, I'd twitch. In the middle of the interview, the old woman frowned and said, "You're an awfully jumpy young man. Are you okay?"

"Yes, ma'am, fine."

"Can I get you a glass of lemonade?"

The thought of consuming something in that apartment forced me to fight back nausea. "Oh, no ma'am, no, thanks, nothing for me. I just need to get my story and go."

I left her apartment and went straight home to shower. I took my clothes off in the garage and wrapped them in a garbage bag before going into the house.

In the winter, I stood for countless hours in the freezing cold waiting for detectives to throw me a few snippets of information from a homicide. The cops knew I was waiting. The homicide detectives never much cared for me—we battled almost daily about the information that could or should be released about their investigations—and making me freeze was one way of exacting revenge for the irritation I caused them.

I had been at the *Columbus Dispatch* for a little more than a year when I learned I would be moving from my cushy job on the state desk to the city desk. I was ready. The better beats at the paper reported to the city desk—city hall, courts, and county government. I had enjoyed a good run on the state desk and believed I would be getting one of the primo city desk beats. I had no idea that I was going to be covering night police. I found out when another reporter, Kevin Kehres said, "I hear you're moving over to the city desk."

"Yeah."

"Night cops, I hear."

"Come again?"

"Night cops," he said. "I hear you're going to be doing night cops."

"No way."

"Oh, yeah. It's a done deal, I heard."

I wanted to punch Kehres in his smug little face for delivering such horrible news. The *Dispatch* was the afternoon paper in 1981 and the night police beat was considered the absolute worst beat. I would work 6 P.M. to 2 A.M., Sunday through Thursday. For the last four hours of each night, I would be the only reporter working at the paper.

The *Dispatch* had just gone through several unsuccessful attempts to fill the beat. This is not a knock on those reporters. I have known a lot of very good reporters who could not handle the police beat. They had weak stomachs. Or they did not like dealing with death. Or they were simply overwhelmed by the sadness that permeates the beat. Or their wives would not tolerate the hours. (There was an unwritten rule in those days that only male reporters did night cops. Supposedly, the paper's management did not want the liability of sending a female to the corner of Wilson and Oak at 1:30 A.M. to cover a drug shooting.)

It also meant working for Bernie Karsko, the *Dispatch's* demanding night city editor and dean of what reporters referred to as "Karsko's Night School of Journalism." Bernie once posed for the cover of *Columbus Monthly* magazine for a story on the meanest sons of bitches in Columbus, a designation of which he was quite proud. He had a flattop haircut and no-nonsense demeanor and was himself a former police reporter. Many excellent reporters developed their craft under Karsko's tutelage. But he could be brutal on young reporters.

Plus, there was no small amount of pressure to cover night cops. I would be the only reporter working after 10 P.M. Invariably, someone at the Camel Bell Bar on East Main Street would decide to shoot another patron at 1:55 A.M., leaving the night police reporter to follow the story to fruition. There were more than a few times when I was still sitting at a computer terminal when the day shift came in at 6 A.M.

I was introduced to the police beat by John Switzer, a veteran *Dispatch* reporter who had been covering night cops on an interim basis. I was terrified that I was going to miss a big story, and I sat at my desk at the police station pressroom, staring at the police scanner as if it were a television. Switzer, meanwhile, sat across the room and listened to a Cleveland Indians game on his transistor radio. "You're killing me here, Switzer," I said.

He waved a hand at me and said, "You'll be fine."

The central police station sat at the intersection of Gay Street and Marconi Boulevard at an angle, with the front doors facing the intersection. The back of the building faced downtown and most of the parking was located near the rear. Consequently, nearly all the foot traffic came through the back door.

The pressroom at the Columbus Division of Police—the "Cop Shop"—was an austere rectangle located just inside the back door and over the boiler, which kept the room at a toasty 86 degrees all the time. We had to operate the window air conditioner 365 days a year. I always assumed that putting us atop the boiler had been a calculated move by the police. The heat kept us miserable, and if the boiler ever exploded, a couple of reporters would be the first to go.

The pressroom had no such designation on the door. It was unmarked and the first door found by people wandering in off the streets. Thus, my office became the headquarters for a wandering band of misfits who found me by accident but apparently liked my company, because they kept coming back.

One of my regular visitors was a six-foot-eight, black transvestite-prostitute who called himself Monique and always referred to himself in the third person. He called me "Child," though I don't think there was more than a few years difference in our ages. The first time I ever laid eyes on Monique, he came charging into the pressroom with screaming red, two-inch nails, enormous hoop earrings, a miniskirt, and red platform heels. His considerable shock of hair was teased up on the top of his head, so from heel to hair he was standing about seven-foot-nine. "Child, do you know where can I fill out a police report?"

I thought it was some kind of gag. I wanted to laugh, but did not dare, fearing that I might get my ass kicked by a transvestite, which would do my ego no good. "Ah, yes ma'am, sir, ah, yeah, Room 100, right around the corner. They can help you out."

"Let me tell you something—if he thinks he can get away without paying Monique, he's got another thing comin', you know what I mean, Child? Monique will call his wife and tell her I been suckin' her husband's dick at lunchtime for two years. He'll wish to Jesus he'd paid Monique."

And out he went.

Of course, they would not take a report, and five minutes later Monique was back in my office demanding that I write a story about police discrimination, although he was not clear as to which of his unusual characteristics they were discriminating against. And, frankly, I was not about to ask. He did say that the client in question was a city hall employee who was two weeks in arrears in paying for Monique's favors. Despite my best efforts, Monique would not reveal the man's name.

Monique began stopping by the pressroom each time he was in the area. I once returned from making rounds to find him asleep on the psychiatrist-style couch in the pressroom. His legs dangled two feet over the bottom of the couch, partially blocking the doorway. "Where do you find women's shoes to fit those feet?" I asked. They were enormous.

"Monique has to buy slip-ons," he said. "Child, Monique is so tired. Now, don't make too much noise. Monique needs her rest."

"Really? Does Monique realize that he's sleeping in my office?"

"Shhhhhhh," he countered.

After that, I locked the door whenever I left.

Walter "Streamline" Green was one of the regulars who frequented the pressroom at the police station. His philosophy was: You have money. Give me some of it. (Courtesy of the *Columbus Dispatch*)

I never really warmed up to Monique, though he was funny. Frankly, it was just difficult to concentrate with a giant, chatty transvestite-prostitute hovering around the room. During one visit he squinted and said, "Child, you're not very friendly. Are you afraid of Monique?"

"Yes," I blurted a little too fast. "Well, no, not exactly afraid. But you, ah, you do make me a little nervous."

He giggled. "Child, there's no need to be nervous. Monique's just like you, 'cept I'm a workin' girl."

"Yeah, well, that's really a pretty big difference, actually."

He grinned and leaned toward my desk. "Are you married, sweetheart?"

I could feel the heat racing up my neck. "Oh, married, yes, very. Very married. Very heterosexually married."

He laughed and flitted out of the room. At one point, Monique was spending so much time in the pressroom that the cops began referring to him as "your friend."

Another of my frequent visitors was Walter "Streamline" Green. In his day, before alcohol took its toll, Walter was reportedly an accomplished jazz guitarist. It was not hard to believe. Walter was absolutely magnificent with that guitar, and it was obvious that a talent had long ago been wasted in alcohol.

Walter hated going to the homeless shelter because they had unreasonable rules, such as, "You must take a shower." Walter hated rules, and thus he wandered the halls of the police station—shuffling, filthy and smelling like feces, shoes untied, walking on his pants, squinting through a pair of yellowed, rheumy eyes, and carrying his guitar in one hand and his amp in the other. At night, after the police brass had left for the day, Walter liked to sit and play on the bench outside the detective bureau. If his smell was not too offensive, they would let him stay and even toss him a couple of bucks.

Walter would come into the pressroom to bum money. Walter did not want to be my friend; he just wanted my money. And "thank you" was not part of his vocabulary. Despite this, I liked Walter. There was no false pretense to him. His basic philosophy was: You have money. Give me some of it.

One day he came into the pressroom with his guitar, though it had no strings. "Walter, what happened to your guitar strings?" I asked.

He contorted his face in a show of disgust and said in his gravelly voice, "Over at the shelter, somebody stode 'em."

"They stode 'em, did they?"

"Yeah. You got some money so I can get some new ones?"

He was sitting on the bench in the back hall one winter day with a pair of sopping shoes, sans the laces. Walter never tied his shoes, anyway, but I asked, "Walter, what happened to your shoelaces?"

His response was the same. "Over at the shelter, somebody stode 'em. You got some money so I can get some new ones?"

Sometimes I would give Walter a couple of dollars just so he would leave because he smelled so bad that he made me gag. On his less odoriferous days, I'd offer to buy him something to eat rather than hand him money. Sometimes he'd take me up on the offer, other times he would storm out in disgust.

I was headed to lunch one day when I ran into Walter in the hall. He apparently sensed that I was headed to the grill in the basement of the police station, which was operated by a blind man named John.

"What's going on, Walter?" I asked.

"I ain't eaten in four days," he said.

"Really? Four days?"

"Maybe five. I lost count."

"Come on," I said. "I'll buy you something at the diner."

"How 'bout you juss give me a couple bucks and I'll get my own."

"Walter, if you want lunch, come on; otherwise, forget it."

He crinkled up his face, but followed me downstairs. I bought Walter a hamburger and a cup of coffee. As I was talking to John, with my back to Walter, he rewarded my generosity by stealing a bag of potato chips from the blind proprietor. When I turned around and saw him eating the chips, I asked, "Walter, where'd you get those?"

His brows arched, but without a moment's hesitation, he said, "I had 'em in my coat pocket when I came in."

"Really? Imagine that. A man who hasn't eaten in five days walking around with a bag of chips in his coat."

"Quit bringing that sonofabitch in here," John growled.

I paid for the chips and that ended the handouts for Walter.

Years after I left the police beat, photographer Mike Munden and I took a canoe trip down the Scioto River. We started in downtown Columbus and paddled to the Ohio River for a story for *Capitol,* the *Dispatch's* Sunday magazine. We docked in Piketon, Ohio, a small town about fifty-five miles south of Columbus, to pick up supplies at the grocery store. As I was cutting across town, I saw a familiar figure walking toward me. It was Walter. I had never seen him look so good. His eyes were clear; he was clean; his clothes were clean. "Walter, what the hell are you doing here?"

The Franklin County judicial system, Walter said, had grown weary of his frequent visits to court for any number of public nuisance violations, and he had been made a ward of the state. He said he was living in a group home in Piketon. "I hate it down here," he said.

I asked Walter if he wanted to go into the store with me, which caused him to contort his face in that familiar manner and say, "I'm not allowed in there." I remembered the potato chip theft and assumed that a similar indiscretion had caused him to be banished from the store. He waited outside while I did my grocery shopping. I picked him up a couple of pouches of Bugler tobacco, as I remembered that Walter rolled his own cigarettes and that was his brand.

"Walter, you look better than I've ever seen you," I said. "This place where you're living must be good for you."

"It's like prison," he growled. "How 'bout I go get my stuff and you take me back to Columbus with you."

I had already explained why I was in Piketon, but it must not have registered. "I'm not going back to Columbus, Walter. I'm in a canoe down at the river and I'm heading south."

"A canoe?" He thought about this for a minute, contorted his face, then turned and walked back toward the group home. "You're welcome for the tobacco," I said. He never turned back and I never saw him again.

One of my favorite pressroom visitors was George Jones, a tow truck driver for the Division of Police who looked like Popeye. Jonesy was everyone's pal—friendly, always laughing. When actor Nick Nolte and company were in Columbus shooting the movie *Teachers* at old Central High School, Jonesy earned a cameo role as, of all things, a tow truck driver who hauled away the car belonging to Nolte's character. When the premier was showing in Columbus, Jonesy was beside himself, hoping the scene had made it into the movie. "My debut role," he called it.

Unfortunately, Dennis Fiely, the *Dispatch* movie critic at the time, reported back to me that Jonesy's debut ended up on the cutting room floor. The next day, Jonesy came bounding into the pressroom. "Well, am I going to be a star?" he asked.

"Afraid not, Jonesy," I said. "They filmed the truck, but you can't tell who's driving."

Jonesy's head dropped. "I'm not going to get discovered?"

"Not in this movie."

Jonesy shook his head for a minute, then said, "Oh well, that's show biz."

Another character was "White Willie," a homeless man who had been arrested more than four hundred times. He carried the designation "White Willie" because there was another homeless man by the same name known as "Black Willie," who also had been arrested a few hundred times, mostly on a variety of public intoxication related offenses. The difference was, "Black Willie" was a mean drunk and a former boxer whom the cops hated arresting because it always turned into a brawl. "White Willie" was a sad, gentle little drunk and former salesman who couldn't resist the booze. He claimed to have once been a successful salesman with a wife and family. His alcohol consumption raged out of control, he said, while he was recovering from a bad automobile accident. The accident had left him comatose and with a severe brain injury. In fact, he insisted that I feel the hole-like indentations in his head where surgeons had drilled to relieve pressure on his brain. I resisted; he grabbed my finger, pushed it into one of the holes, and said, "Don't worry. It won't hurt me." Obviously, it was not the possibility of hurting him that I was concerned about. It was touching hair that had not been washed in months, or years.

"White Willie" read the papers and was quite intelligent. He once asked me my opinion on an impending income tax hike. I couldn't help but smile at the irony. "Willie, I don't want to be insulting, but is an income tax hike really of concern to you?"

He smiled, too. "No, not to me directly. But it is to the people that I hit up for money."

"Good point."

Willie would stop by and talk and bum money. It was a sad case. I dropped him off once on High Street in the Short North, where he hung out. He asked me for some money just before he got out of the car. "You're not going to buy booze with it, are you, Willie?"

"Oh, no sir, Mr. Yocum. I quit drinking. I've had enough of that. I thought I told you that."

"No, you didn't, but that's great news. Congratulations, Willie." He smiled and took the money. Of course, I knew it was a lie. But, just to see what he would do, I circled the block and watched as he headed into a bar.

I once did a story on Willie and his many arrests and told him to meet me at the White Castle on North High Street for our interview. "You want something to eat? Couple of burgers?" I asked.

"Oh, no thanks. Those things give me indigestion."

Considering the things Willie had put down his gullet, it was hardly a ringing endorsement for the burger joint.

Bobby and Tony, two of the police station janitors, also liked to spend time in the pressroom, hiding from their supervisor and smoking, but never cleaning.

Tony never said much, and only came around for a while, until he was charged with murdering his girlfriend in May 1982. He shot her once in the head with a 9mm handgun.

Bobby, however, was a regular visitor for years. He never did any work; he just liked to visit and smoke. Meanwhile, the trashcan overflowed and old newspapers and incident reports were stacked five feet high against one wall of the pressroom. "Bobby, do you think you could haul our trash out of here?"

Bobby would nod and wink. "I been thinkin' about gettin' to that."

His answer was always the same. After six weeks I said, "Bobby, this isn't brain surgery. How much thought does it take to empty our trashcans?"

He gave me a nod and a wink. "I been thinkin' about gettin' to that."

There were others—cops who liked to stop by and swap Cop Shop gossip; the obese woman from the parking ticket division who had a crush on one of the other reporters; narcs, accident investigators, and vice cops, with whom I always got along; and an assortment of oddballs who seemed to have a magnetic pull to the pressroom.

ONE

❑

The Value of Life

ALL LIFE IS NOT PRECIOUS IN THE NEWSROOM.

The value placed on a life in the newsroom is in direct proportion to the number of people who are likely to read a story about that death. I always thought of it as a story's entertainment value, although to utter those words in the *Dispatch* newsroom would have been heresy. It would have been seen as being too much like television news.

But it was true. During my years on the police beat, I looked for stories that would cause some guy to take the paper, shove it across the table to his wife, and say, "Jesus Christ, Margaret, read this story."

It has been said that every corpse has a story to tell. That is true. However, some corpses tell stories that are a lot more compelling than others. The death of a drug dealer who gets shot in a bar or of a homeless man who gets hit by a bus will rarely get more than a brief. They do not get detailed stories because no one cares. That sounds harsh, but it is true. (Okay, their mothers care, but beyond that . . .) If a drug deal goes south and one of the two business associates gets killed, does anyone outside of the immediate family care? No. In fact, if most people were honest, they would say, "Good. One less dope dealer on the streets."

Although they would never admit it openly, the cops worked the same way. I once asked a detective about the progress of an investigation into the June 1984 shooting death of David Scott, a fifteen-year-old leader of the Dozen Cousins street gang, who had taken a shotgun blast to the stomach, supposedly from a rival gang member. The detective gave me the standard response of continuing to interview witnesses and gather evidence, then said, "Off the record?"

"Sure, off the record."

We were standing on opposite sides of a barred window that separated the lobby from the detective bureau. He leaned closer to the bars, grinned, and said, "We don't want to solve this one too soon. We heard he might be planning to take out a few other members of the posse."

He was kidding, I think. But, the fact remained, just as the cops devoted less effort to some homicides, we gave less ink to those same deaths.

Thus, all lives are not equal.

Over the years, I had this discussion with people—usually the relative of a homicide victim—who argued that all deaths deserved equal and compassionate coverage. In other words, they believed that the death of a drug dealer deserved the same effort as the deaths of two high school track stars who were killed in a car crash on their way home from practice. I didn't buy it. The strangulation death of an eight-year-old girl who was abducted as she walked home from school, or a college student shot to death while driving down the street with her father, or a mother killed by a drunken driver was going to get more play. These were tragic stories about the deaths of innocent people. Readers are drawn to those stories. They want to know more.

Sometimes, the bizarre nature of a story—the entertainment

value—will draw readers in. A colleague of mine, Mike Norman, once wrote a story about a seventy-one-year-old man who had been shot and killed by his twin brother because they could not agree on which television show to watch. We're drawn to those stories the way we're drawn to the headlines in supermarket tabloids.

An easy way to determine the previous character of a corpse was to measure the comments made by his loved ones. If someone told me, "He was just getting his life back together," warning lights would go off all over the place. This was the standard comment about someone who had caused his family—it was always a "him"—an ungodly amount of heartache. However, since he was now dead, and in spite of the fact that his entire life had been the equivalent of a train wreck, they wanted a nice story about him in the paper.

It was okay to print those comments, but I always tried to do a criminal background check before running the story.

That, however, was not always possible. One of the difficulties of working the police beat was that I was usually working on deadline. In these instances, I was forced to rely on the word of witnesses or neighbors I was able to interview. I covered the murder of Byron Sprague, a fifty-eight-year-old fifth-grade teacher at South Mifflin Elementary School, who was found stabbed to death in his north-side apartment in January 1982. At the scene, neighbors described Sprague as a nice guy, a dedicated educator who spent his evenings tutoring terminally ill children.

By early indications, he was a great guy.

A day later, I found out that he had two previous charges for child molesting. In 1964, he was arrested for sodomy and assault on a minor and spent time in jail for the offense. In 1969, he was charged with sexual assault on a minor.

It's the nature of the business.

TWO

❏

The Death of a Child

Mark Anderson

JANET POTENZA COULDN'T THROW AWAY HER SON'S TOOTHBRUSH.
That was the one nugget that stabbed at my heart. Janet is one
of the strongest and most determined women I have ever met. She
sat through every minute of the murder trial of her son's killer—
Anthony D. Simmons. She went to the parole board to lobby suc-
cessfully against the release of Simmons's accomplice—Anthony
Green—at his first parole hearing. Three years later, when it seemed
apparent that Green would be released, she scheduled a meeting
with him at the penitentiary.

"I wanted him to know that Mark had been a real person and that
he was loved and he was missed," Potenza said. "I told him, 'I'm not
here so you can say something that's going to make me feel better. That's
not going to happen.' But, before he got out of prison and before he got
to go on with his life, I wanted him to know about Mark and the life
that had been taken from me."

Despite her iron will, she lacked the emotional strength to perform the seemingly simple act of pulling the toothbrush from the

Janet Potenza is a tough and determined woman. I admire her greatly for the courage she displayed after her son Mark was murdered. (Courtesy of the *Columbus Dispatch*)

holder and throwing it away. It hung in the bathroom for months after Mark Anderson was murdered.

"I just couldn't do it; I couldn't throw it away," she said. "I can't even tell you how many times I threw it in the trash, then fished it out and put it back in the holder. I thought that if I threw it away, I would be closing Mark out of my life. It was in the holder for months and months. It was one of the little things that people don't think about; I never thought about it until Mark was killed. Everyone understands making funeral arrangements, but when you've lost someone you love so much, and at such a young age, the little things eat you alive. For the longest time I couldn't throw away his old hairbrush because it still had his hair in it. His mail kept coming. I had to write 'deceased' next to his name on an income tax return. The dog—Speed—would go out and sit by the driveway every day for weeks, waiting for him to come home. It just broke my heart."

Mark Anderson was a good-looking kid, clean-cut and twenty when he was murdered. On a Sunday morning in April 1986, he was sitting in the parking lot of a Sister's Chicken with his girlfriend, Kelly. They were getting a cup of coffee and a biscuit before church. As they ate in the restaurant parking lot, Simmons walked up to the car, put a gun through the open driver's-side window and into Anderson's face. "Give me your money or I'll kill you," Simmons demanded.

Anderson had only a few dollars in his pocket, but he was not going to give it to Simmons. "You're not going to kill me," Anderson replied.

Simmons pulled the trigger.

He ran to a car driven by Green, who was just days from his eighteenth birthday, and fled. They were arrested a few days later.

Green pleaded guilty to involuntary manslaughter and aggravated robbery. Simmons was convicted of aggravated murder and aggravated robbery.

Janet will be eighty-eight years old before Simmons is eligible for parole in 2030. If necessary, she says she will go to the hearing in a wheelchair to keep him in prison. "He should be sitting on Death Row," she told me. "I don't think there's any need for keeping people on this earth who are capable of doing that. He's not sorry. The only thing he's upset about is that he got caught."

After the older of her two sons was murdered, Janet become active in a group for parents of murdered children and took a job at the Franklin County Prosecutor's Office in the Victim-Witness Assistance Division.

Janet is a tough woman and I admire her. She is one of the few people I interviewed that I have stayed in touch with over the years. For most people, I was a reminder of a horrific time in their life. Actually, I was part of the trauma. They could never see me without being reminded of how we met. Seventeen years after her son's murder, the heartache is still evident in Janet's voice. She cannot hide it. When she speaks of her son, the words leave her mouth with such effort and pain.

For a long time after Mark's death, Janet said there were times—just fleeting moments—when she would forget that he was dead. Something would happen and she would think, "When Mark comes home I need to tell him . . ." Then, the painful realization would return.

Mark was never coming home.

Laura Carter

The death of Laura Carter was one of the saddest cases I ever covered.

Carter was a freshman lacrosse player at Denison University, a small, private school located in the village of Granville, about twenty-five miles east of Columbus. On the third weekend of April 1982, her parents had flown in from Wayne, Pennsylvania, to spend Parents' Weekend with her.

At 8:15 on Saturday night, April 17, Carter, three girlfriends, and her parents were driving into Columbus to celebrate the women's lacrosse team's 11–1 victory over Oberlin College.

As they traveled westbound on Broad Street, near East High School, a drug deal was going sour on Winner Avenue.

Nancy Nall and I tag-teamed the story. We wrote:

As the group drove west on E. Broad St. near East High School, an argument involving four men, a world apart from the car yet only a block away, exploded into violence. With the sudden ring of gunfire, the two groups were drawn tragically together.

Three of the men began shooting at the fourth. One of the bullets traveled a block, sliding between buildings and trees, across an open lawn near the high school, and into the open passenger-side window of the Carter car. Laura had been leaning forward, talking to her parents. Her right arm was resting on the top of the front seat. The bullet went under her arm and into her chest.

Mr. Carter drove to St. Anthony Hospital, which was only a few blocks away, but it was too late. The bullet had damaged three major blood vessels in her upper chest and lodged in her left lung. Surgeons could not stop the internal bleeding.

She died at 9:50 P.M.

I often thought about the circumstances that placed Laura Carter at that particular spot on Broad Street at the very instant that the bullet crossed the same airspace. Had her father stopped at a yellow light to be cautious, or sped through one that was just turning red? Had he slowed or stopped to allow a pedestrian to cross the road? What sequence of events put lead and flesh at the same place at the same time?

I once interviewed a woman named Cookie Wilson, who, on a night in March 1982, was to meet her friend Michelle Granger at Gig's bar in downtown Columbus, where Granger was a bartender. The plan was for Wilson to hang around at Gig's while Granger helped close and clean the bar, then go home with her. However, Wilson got a flat tire on the way to the bar and never made it.

Laura Carter was a freshman at Denison University when she was killed by a stray bullet from a soured drug deal. It was one of the saddest stories I ever covered. (Courtesy of the *Columbus Dispatch*)

The next morning, the bodies of Granger, another bartender, Joseph Nebel, and a customer, Elton Shorter, were found by the janitor. They had all been shot in the head with a shotgun.

So, Cookie Wilson gets a flat tire and stays out of harm's way. Laura Carter, however, crosses Broad Street at the same fraction of a second as a stray bullet from a distant drug battle.

"She couldn't have been happier," Edward Carter said of his only child. "We had two happy days together. She was a terrific girl, cheerful, optimistic."

It would take the police years to sort out the events of that night and get convictions on the three men who were firing their pistols.

Singer Christopher Cross later wrote the song, "Laura", about Carter.

The triple homicide at Gig's was never solved.

Steven Boyer

When I drove away from my interview with Walter Boyer, I thought, "His life is over. He's sixty-one-years old, but his life is over." I could not in my wildest dreams imagine how he would ever recover from his son's death.

Walter lived in Lockville, a village in Fairfield County, southeast of Columbus. He was a pleasant man and he invited me into his living room and sat down on the couch across from my chair. He was very neat in a flannel shirt and slacks, his hair combed back with not a strand out of place. His eyes were red and moist, the result of too much crying and too little sleep over the previous two months.

It was February 1984. Two months earlier, the body of his son, Steven, had been found in the Pisgah National Forest in western North Carolina, near the Tennessee border. His body had been dismembered, the head and hands cut off in an attempt to conceal the identity of the corpse.

"It's been such a weighted load," Walter said, his voice eerily calm, as though he had accepted his fate as well as that of his son. "It seems like it's been a year since it happened."

As I interviewed him, Walter and his wife Ethel were packing for a trip to Haywood and Transylvania counties, North Carolina, where authorities hoped they were close to getting an indictment in Steven's murder.

Walter Boyer's son Steven was murdered in North Carolina when he went to visit his estranged wife and son. (Courtesy of the *Columbus Dispatch*)

After attending Rio Grande College for two years, Steven had dropped out to join the air force. He was a security officer when he met his wife, Ellen. They had a son, Jason, but had been married only a short time when the marriage broke up. By that time, Steven had left the air force and was working as a welder in Smyrna, Georgia.

Walter Boyer was not sure what caused his son's marriage to break up, but he knew it was not pleasant; the boy had told him that much. The elder Boyer tried to talk his son into moving back to central Ohio, but Steven did not want to be away from Jason. When the problems between Steven and Ellen intensified, she took the boy and moved to her parents' home in Haywood County, which adjoins Transylvania County.

On December 23, 1983, Steven Boyer left his roommate a note and said he was going to make the 250-mile trip to Haywood County to look for his ex-wife and son. He wrote that he anticipated problems with his former wife and in-laws. When he failed to return, the roommate contacted police.

Steven's mutilated body was discovered by two hunters on December 26, the eve of his twenty-sixth birthday. Ultimately, authorities determined that the body was within Haywood County. In 1985, Boyer's former father-in-law, Jimmy D. McElrath, was charged with Boyer's murder. McElrath was later found not guilty by a Haywood County jury.

No one else was ever charged in connection with the death of Steven Boyer.

Carmen Canale Jr.

I never parked my car directly in front of the house of someone I was going to interview. The *Dispatch* press cars were unmarked and much less conspicuous than the television vans, which had call letters and peacocks and such painted all over them. From my car, I watched the house in the rearview mirror. I looked at my watch and thought, "Okay, in two minutes you're going to walk up and knock on the door." Sometimes, two minutes came and went and I would still be sitting behind the wheel. Usually, however, I would meet my self-imposed deadline. It was a little game I played to summon the nerve to knock.

I needed to talk to Carmen Canale Sr. Earlier that day, Canale's seventeen-year-old son, Carmen Canale Jr., had been shot to death outside Knoxville, Tennessee, after stealing $21.06 worth of gasoline.

I learned about the incident from an Associated Press story and went out in search of his father. Carmen Canale Sr. answered the door at his small, Kenny Road home. It had been only a few hours since he had received word of his son's death.

The senior Canale seemed grateful for the company and invited me into the living room where he calmly spoke of the son he had, in reality, lost years earlier. He said he simply could not control the boy, who dropped out of high school and began roaming the streets. The only graduation his son had been involved in, the father said, was from marijuana to harder drugs. Canale Sr. had asked the police to lock up his son for his own safety. They refused, claiming the boy was not a threat to society.

On July 29, 1981, Canale Jr. and two buddies were on their way to Florida in a pickup truck. Canale Jr. had been charged with aggravated burglary and grand theft in Franklin County and was due in court later that week. His father said the boy was running to avoid the court date.

They had no money and stopped at a self-serve gas station in Knox County. With his two companions in the truck, Canale Jr. pumped the gas. When he was done, the driver pulled away and Canale Jr. jumped into the open bed. The station attendant, Fred

Lee McHaffie, ran out of the booth and squeezed off three shots from a .32-caliber pistol. One of the shots hit and killed Carmen Canale Jr.

McHaffie was charged with voluntary manslaughter. On December 1, 1982, he pleaded guilty to the charge and was given a sentence of one year's probation.

I always believed that the job of a reporter in these situations is to be a sympathetic ear, particularly because it is difficult for a grieving parent to be objective. Canale Sr. had just lost his son and was grasping for someone to blame. During the interview, he directed his ire toward the police for not locking his son up.

"I went down and told [the police] he had a drug problem and I couldn't handle him," Canale said that afternoon. "I told them I wouldn't take Carmen back until he acts like a man. They let him go and two weeks later he's dead. If they would have listened to me and put Carmen in jail, my son would be alive today."

Under different circumstances, I would have challenged Canale and asked him about personal responsibility. The young man's death was not the fault of the police department. It was the fault of someone who made the mistake of stealing gasoline from a man with a gun.

THREE
❏

Homicide Hated My Guts

Am I to assume that the folks in the detective bureau don't think you're so swell?

Richard "Dick" Radick
Columbus Police Accident Investigation Squad

Get out of here; get out of my office. I don't want to be called as a witness after Steckman shoots your ass. He's so pissed he'll probably shoot you, reload, then shoot you again.

Lieutenant John Tilley
Columbus Police Narcotics Squad

A few minutes after John Tilley made that comment, Homicide Sergeant Bill Steckman showed up at his door. When he saw that I was sitting in the office, Steckman turned and walked out, saying, "I'll stop back later." Tilley laughed, which he did often, glad that he was simply a spectator to the fray.

The battles I had with the detective bureau—the homicide

squad, in particular—were legendary. I know they all fantasized that some night they would pull up to a homicide scene to discover the corpse was a particular *Dispatch* reporter. I always imagined that the lead investigator would look at my body and say, "Hmm, we've got a dead reporter. Six bullet holes in his back of his skull. There's a guy standing over the body with a smoking .45. Yep, looks like a clear-cut suicide to me. Let's go get a beer. Oh, and you with the .45, you come too. I want to buy you a drink."

I held no such animosity toward them, particularly Steckman, who was a hell of an investigator. I understood that we each had a job to do. They did not hate me because I was a bad person; they hated me because I was a pain-in-the-ass reporter. I could live with that. If you take it personally, you'll go crazy.

This particular ruckus with Steckman occurred during the homicide squad's investigation into the downtown murder of accountant Jean Shrader. Steckman had ordered a news blackout of the case and prohibited his detectives from talking to me about it. During these news blackouts, the homicide squad would put out press releases that were so barren of any significant news that they might as well have read: "There was a homicide tonight. No other information will be released, now or ever. Go away. The great and powerful Oz has spoken."

The night before I found myself in Tilley's office, Steckman had issued a release stating that he would be the only one issuing statements or answering questions; then, he proceeded to avoid me all night and went home without returning my phone calls. So, at 2:15 A.M., I called Chief of Police Earl Burden and got him out of bed, complaining that his second-shift homicide sergeant was avoiding me. Ten minutes later, after receiving a call from an irate Burden, Steckman called the pressroom. He was highly upset and highly uncooperative, which I had anticipated, so I had about thirty questions for him; he would give me nothing more than a terse response to each. Usually it was, "I can't reveal that. It could jeopardize our investigation."

I wanted to ask him what he had for dinner, just to see if the words "burger and fries" would somehow jeopardize the investigation, too.

Steckman and Tilley had worked in the detective bureau together and were buddies. Before I made rounds and arrived at Tilley's office, Steckman had already been there once to vent. " 'You know what that son-of-a-bitch Yocum did? Called the chief to complain about me,' " Tilley said, still laughing as he quoted Steckman from their earlier conversation.

I'm sure that was the mildest thing Steckman said. Tilley was protecting me from the rest.

The problems with the homicide squad stemmed from the fact that they wanted to work in absolute secrecy. That way, I reasoned, they would not be held accountable for their screw-ups, of which there were many. In fact, they rarely solved the biggest cases. Of course, they loved to blame it on the press. We were releasing too much information to the public and harming their investigation was their favorite complaint. It was an ongoing battle. If detectives had spent as much time trying to solve homicides as they spent trying to identify my sources in the detective bureau, they would have been way ahead.

However, once the battle lines had been drawn, I was not totally innocent of trying to annoy the detectives. Years before I began covering the police department, the detective bureau was open on the second floor. You could walk around from robbery to burglary to homicide to sexual abuse. Eventually, they blocked off the main entry where a receptionist sat behind the desk and buzzed detectives through the door. They said this was done to separate the detectives from someone who might walk in off the streets. In reality, it was done to keep reporters out of the detective bureau. The only other way into the bureau was through the private elevator, for which you needed a special key.

When a buddy of mine retired from the juvenile squad, which was on the fourth floor, he gave me his key to the police elevator. I immediately went out and had ten copies made. I waited until I had an appointment in the robbery squad before I used it. I showed up at the robbery squad door and no one said anything, assuming that the receptionist had buzzed me in. However, about the third time I stepped off the elevator, Captain Harry Dolby saw me and demanded to know where I had gotten the key. Of course, I would not tell him. He also demanded that I give him the key, which I delighted in peeling off my key ring and turning over to him, realizing how furious he was going to be when he learned that I had more than one. I turned over several others, too.

Insecticide Needed

In 1985, my stories were causing such heartburn in the detective bureau that the bureau commander, Captain Antone Lanata, ordered an investigation into news leaks in the bureau, which included a sweep of the detective bureau for an electronic bugging device.

This was the ultimate compliment.

It was not the first time they thought I had wired the place. An investigator once tore the intercom system off the wall in homicide, believing that I had found a way to eavesdrop through the system. (This was laughable, considering how acutely inept I am at anything electronic or mechanical.)

The debugging investigation began October 25, after I broke a story quoting unnamed sources who said that eighteen-year-old Wesley B. Compton had confessed to the October 23 slayings of Melody Smith and her eight-year-old stepson, Nathaniel.

Sgt. Jim Carr was put in charge of the investigation, which included interviews—some quite extensive, I was told—of about forty detectives. This, of course, led to a lot of internal accusations and finger pointing.

They found neither an electronic bugging device nor the perfidious detective they believed to be among them.

During these days when I was squabbling with the homicide squad, there was a succession of captains who took over the detective bureau. One of my sources was a detective bureau sergeant who had been in the department too long and had grown bitter. He despised the police leadership. From my perspective, this was a good thing because he was happy to pass along detective bureau gossip. He slipped me information continually. His motivation, he said, was simple. "I don't do this because I'm some big fan of the First Amendment. I just like to be within earshot of the captain when he reads your stories and the top of his head comes off."

Riverside Homicides

On Friday, December 30, 1983, two Riverside Hospital research assistants—Patricia Matix, thirty years old, and Joyce McFadden, thirty-three—were found stabbed to death in a cancer research laboratory where they worked.

I was out of town when the murders occurred and began work on the case when I returned early the next week. From the beginning, police were baffled by the murders. McFadden's body had been discovered just after 5 P.M. by Dr. Devi D. Munjal, the physician with whom the women conducted research. She had been stabbed nineteen times. Matix's body was discovered by police in a small, refrigerated room where tissue samples were kept. She had been stabbed sixteen times. They both had been bound and gagged with tape. Police said there was no sign of a struggle.

The murder weapon, a wide-blade knife, was never found. Lead after lead proved worthless.

Although no one was ever charged in the case, police are now confident that they know who was responsible for the crimes—Patricia Matix's husband, William. Shortly after the murders, Mr. Matix left his Delaware County home and moved to Florida.

On April 11, 1986, Matix was involved in the deadliest firefight in FBI history. Matix and Michael Lee Platt were suspected in a series of brutal bank robberies in Florida. Authorities were looking for them on charges of suspicion of bank robbery and murder. When FBI agents attempted to apprehend them, a four-minute gun battle ensued. Matix and Platt both were killed. Two FBI agents—Benjamin P. Grogan and Jerry Dove—were killed and five other agents were injured.

In the aftermath of the Riverside murders, no one wanted to work in that laboratory. It was subsequently made into an office for the hospital chaplain.

"Come with us, Mr. Yocum"

A week after the Riverside homicides, we had been unable to land a substantial interview with Dr. Devi D. Munjal. My city editor, Bernie Karsko, told me to go to the hospital, sneak back to where Munjal worked and get an interview. Of course, Karsko knew as well as I that this would be next to impossible. Riverside had dramatically tightened security and the hospital was crawling with detectives, special duty cops, and security guards. Munjal hadn't returned any of my numerous phone calls to the hospital and his home. I had even left a handwritten note on the door of his home requesting an interview, but to no avail. So I had serious doubts that he would talk if I suddenly showed up at his office.

Nevertheless, I did as ordered. And I elected to hide in plain sight. I ran home and put on a suit, grabbed a leather notebook, my Cross pen, and my Ohio State Highway Patrol press pass. Reporters often give themselves away because, frankly, they dress like reporters. The suit was part of the disguise. I wore the State Patrol press pass around my neck on a chain, photo side out. No one ever looks at identification badges. As long as you have one visible, they assume you are legitimate. The Cross pen replaced my Papermate and the leather notebook replaced the spiral pad that reporters often carry in their hip pocket. I was trying to look as if I belonged in the hospital. When I walked through the main lobby, I pretended to be writing in the notebook. There was a throng of law enforcement types guarding the door through which I needed to pass. I did not slow down as I neared the door; I lifted my head and nodded to the officers, giving them a brief wave with the Cross pen in my hand. They nodded back and let me into the offices and lab area. No one gave me a second look.

A minute later I found the doctor's name on the wall and walked up to his secretary's desk. "Hi, I'm Robin Yocum with the *Dispatch*. I'd like to talk with Dr. Munjal. Would you tell him I'm here, please?"

You can tell a lot from the look on someone's face. And, at that instant, her face was telling me that I was in a lot of trouble.

She excused herself and disappeared into his office. I assumed that this was *not* to set up my interview. The sounds I heard next were not unexpected—the jangle of keys and a fusillade of footsteps. The door opened and a phalanx of red-faced cops and security guards entered the room.

"Hi, boys," I said.

"Come with us, Mr. Yocum," one said. And, surrounded on all points by a half-dozen security personnel and special-duty Columbus police officers, like a condemned man being walked to the chair, I was marched to the office of Marilyn Marr, who was head of public relations for Riverside and who had by this time been informed of my stunt. I sat in her office, one of the security guards standing at my side, while she called Karsko. I felt as if I had been summoned to the principal's office and she was calling my parents.

"Bernie, this is Marilyn Marr at Riverside Hospital. Robin Yocum is in my office. We just caught him back in the office of Dr. Munjal . . . this is not funny, Bernie . . . no, it most certainly is not."

Frankly, I had to agree with Marilyn on this one. Before I had entered the hospital, I knew I was not going to get an interview with Munjal. We were making a game of trying to get to the doctor. Meanwhile, Marilyn was dealing with the crisis of having two co-workers butchered a few feet from her office.

Getting nowhere with Karsko, she scolded me for another ten minutes before sending me out with the security escort. Not content to leave me at the door, he marched me to the parking lot and stood there until my car had pulled out on North Broadway. When I walked back into the newsroom, Karsko was laughing.

"Yeah, like you didn't know that was going to happen," I said.

"I think we had to take the chance."

We obviously weren't going to agree on this one, so I let it drop.

Suzanne Cozad

This is a good place to introduce Suzanne Cozad.

For eighteen years, Suzanne was the office administrator for Franklin County Coroner William R. Adrion. She also was a registered nurse who intimately understood the office operations and served as spokesperson for the demure Adrion. In fact, her nickname was "Mrs. Coroner."

Not only was she a sweetheart of a human being, but she was absolutely the best source I ever had in my career.

As a reporter, you develop sources in a number of ways. Some people give you information because they believe it is important for the public to know. This is rare, but it happens. Others give you information to spite someone else. This is common. Disgruntled employees can be wonderful sources, especially if they have been passed over for a promotion or two. They become anxious to sabotage the efforts of those who were promoted ahead of them. I was never overly concerned about their motivations, as long as I could verify the information. Others will give you information simply because they like to keep things stirred up. And still others will give you information because you have built a rapport and sense of trust. Ultimately, that develops into a friendship.

This was rare on the police beat, because most cops do not want to be friends with newspaper reporters. It causes other cops to look at them with suspicion. During four years on the police beat, I developed relationships with only a few people I considered friends— Lt. John Tilley; Pat Dorn, who was a narcotics officer; civilian polygrapher Randy Walker, whom you'll read about later in this book; vice cop Mike Martin; Accident Investigator Richard Radick; and Suzanne.

Suzanne and I hit it off the first time we met. She had a great sense of humor and loved off-color jokes. I always made sure I had a few to share. Once or twice a week I'd pop in and spend an hour in her office, usually just talking. After a while, I quit asking her for information. There was no need. If something was going on, she would make sure that I knew about it. When the homicide bureau was conducting electronic sweeps of its offices trying to find the news leaks, the source of information was almost always Suzanne, who received copies of all the detective bureau files.

On several occasions, she fed me some information, then called the homicide detectives and tipped them off that I was snooping around about one case or another. "That *Dispatch* reporter Robin Yocum just called me and asked me about . . ." The detectives thought she was looking out for them, when in reality she was just covering her tracks.

In one particular instance, she called Homicide Sergeant John Cherubini and told him that I was working on a case. I waited ten minutes and called him.

"Sarge, it's Robin Yocum. Hey, I'm working on a follow-up on the . . ."

"I know what you're working on," he said, smug in his tone.

"How do you know?"

"I've got sources, too."

It was great fun.

One of the best tips I ever received from Suzanne was during the Riverside homicide investigation. The police had executed a search warrant on the home of a maintenance worker, then had the warrant sealed to keep it away from the press. Two homicide detectives were at the clerk's office after getting it sealed by the judge. They gave me the "screw you" smirk. When I got back to the newsroom, the first call I received was from Suzanne. "Have you heard about the search warrant in the Riverside case?"

"Yeah, they had it sealed."

"So I heard. Want to know what's in it?"

"I'll be right up."

They had searched the home of a maintenance worker who had been at the hospital the day of the homicides. My guess was that a background check of people working at the hospital that day turned up someone with a criminal past. One of the items they were looking for was a pair of bloody work boots.

My fear, however, was that Suzanne would give herself up. There were only a few people who could have known the contents of the search warrant, and the cops might figure it out by process of elimination. The city editor, Bernie Karsko, was on vacation, so I went to our managing editor, Dick Otte, and explained the situation. It was late on Friday afternoon. There was no way for the *Citizen-Journal* to beat us on the story. They did not know the contents of the search warrant and would be unable to find them over the weekend. This gave me a three-day buffer to protect my source. Otte agreed.

One of the assistant city editors, however, did not. This led to one of the ugliest arguments in my eleven years at the paper. I am generally not a screamer. But this ended up in a fist-on-the-desk-pounding, finger-pointing, snot-bubble-blowing confrontation that I ultimately lost. I was ordered to write the story for the weekend.

To help cover my tracks, I asked our court reporter, Mary Yost, to start working the story from the prosecutor's office. She had access to the judge, the prosecutor and other county officials. By putting a double byline on the story, it might deflect scrutiny from Suzanne. Mary was a terrific reporter and an absolute gem to work with. Over the years, we used this tactic on several stories to help protect each other's sources.

(Suzanne always told me that I could reveal the fact that she was my best source after she had died, though I'm sure she expected to live more than fifty-one short years. After I left the police beat, Suzanne had a falling out with the coroner and left in 1985 to take a job as a nurse with the Ohio prison system. Suzanne suffered from a nearly lifelong liver problem, stemming from medication she took as a child for a skin malady. The last time I spoke to her, in the early summer of 1989, she was very tired; the illness was draining her. A few weeks later, her daughter Cheryl called to say that Suzanne had entered the Cleveland Clinic for a liver transplant. She never recovered from the operation and died on December 5, 1989. Cheryl asked me to speak at Suzanne's memorial service and I considered it an honor.)

Rubber Hose

After Mary and I started writing the story about the Riverside search warrant, I called the homicide squad to get a comment. Sergeant Cherubini was livid that I already had the contents of the search warrant.

About ten minutes later, I received a call from Clarence Sorrell, who was a homicide detective working on the case. "Can you come up here for a minute? We want to talk to you."

"Sure," I said. I never passed up a chance to talk with one of the homicide detectives. Sorrell ordered the secretary to buzz me through the door and I followed him back to an interrogation room, where we were joined by Sergeant Cherubini. It was a small room with a table, three chairs, and a two-way mirror. I sat on one side of the table; they sat on the other side, in front of the mirror. I assumed that the rest of the homicide bureau was crowded into the next room, peering in through the mirror.

After a few pleasantries—I could sense the cops were straining to be nice and make small talk—I asked, "So, what's up, boys? You're obviously upset about the search warrant story. Are you going to work me over with a rubber hose?"

They failed to see the humor in my comment.

"We want to know who your source is on the story," Cherubini said. "That warrant was sealed. We had it sealed so you couldn't put it in the paper. An hour later you know everything that's in it. Who told you?"

"Okay, let me make sure I've got this straight: You want me to give up my source?"

Sorrell nodded. "We can't have this stuff getting in the paper."

I couldn't believe they were asking me to give up my source. Never in my life had I given up a source, nor would I. I would have gone to jail before revealing a source. As a reporter, your sources must trust you. If you give up a source, you'll never get another one. Consequently, I went to great lengths to protect them. There had been many times when I held a story, as I had tried to do with this one, because I was afraid of burning a source. So, I found their questioning a little amusing. "If I tell you who my source is, you'll fire him."

"No, we won't," said Cherubini. "I promise. We'll just move him out of the detective bureau—put him on patrol."

I wanted to ask, "What planet are you from?" I refrained.

"I'm not sure that you guys understand how this whole newspaper reporting thing works," I said. "But, you see, I *need* people to give me information, particularly since it so rarely comes from official channels. You guys won't tell me dick, so I have to rely on other sources. If I tell you the name of my source, you'll treat him like a pariah and banish him to third-shift patrol. If I lose my source, I can't write stories. If I can't write stories, Bernie gets pissed. When Bernie's pissed, my life is miserable. And, if that pattern continues for any length of time, I lose my job. Which I'm sure would make you all happy, but I need the work."

"We're trying to solve homicides here. We just can't have people in the bureau leaking information like this," Sorrell said.

"Information like what? It's a lousy search warrant. You already conducted the search. The guy whose house you searched certainly knows you searched it, and he certainly knows what you were looking for. What's the big deal? You didn't have it sealed to protect your investigation; you had it sealed to screw with me."

The questioning went on for another fifteen minutes. At one point, Sorrell asked, "So, what's your story going to say?"

"It's going to say that you guys executed a search warrant on the home of a former Riverside employee who was seen leaving the cancer lab just before the bodies were found. He was apparently in the lab during the time period that the coroner says the murders occurred. A janitor saw him leaving the lab. You believe robbery might have been a motive for the murders and the former employee has a record of theft offenses. And, a couple of days after the murders, he was arrested for carrying a concealed weapon and was sentenced to eighteen months in prison."

"Really, that's what you're going to write?" Sorrell asked.

"Basically. Unless you'd like to add to it with some more details."

Neither man smiled. "Well, go ahead and write it," Sorrell said. "That's all wrong." He forced a laugh. "I'm not worried about that. I thought you had good information."

"My information's wrong?"

"Yep. All wrong."

I stood to leave. "Fine, but I don't believe that. I'm going to write it, anyway."

"Sit down," he growled.

I smirked, realizing I had called his bluff. He had hoped to make me doubt the veracity of my information, which I knew was solid. They made one more attempt to learn the name of my source. I refused and they showed me the door. I had no intention of giving up my source—who, by the way, wasn't even a cop—but it was a fun game to play.

Set Up

During one of my tiffs with the homicide squad, one of the homicide detectives caught me near the parking lot behind the police station and started dressing me down. In fact, he questioned my heritage and suggested that I perform a few physical impossibilities. As I returned a few comments about his investigative skills, or lack thereof, Harry Dolby, the detective bureau captain, walked out the back door.

The detective was facing me, his back to the captain. I looked at the captain with a scared look on my face, then back to the detective, then back at the captain before turning, lowering my head, and walking quickly to the parking lot.

From my car I could see Captain Dolby's red face just inches from that of the detective. Obviously, the captain believed that he had discovered my source, which was exactly what I hoped he would think.

It was one of the few times in my life when a great idea did not come fifteen minutes after the incident.

Lies, Lies, Lies

People lie to reporters all the time. Sometimes they do it on purpose. Other times, people have told the same lie so many times that, to them, it has become the truth.

In the early '80s, I was doing some stories on a Clark County minister who was embroiled in a fight with county officials because he wanted to operate a group home in a residential neighborhood. He claimed that none of his neighbors had complained about the group home until he brought in a black boy. Suddenly, he claimed, his racist neighbors did not want a group home in the area, and the county was trying to shut him down.

He seemed genuine enough and he believed passionately in his cause. I had written several stories about his ongoing battle with the county. He called me one day and asked me to come over, promising that he had a fantastic story to tell me.

Fantastic, it turned out, was the operative word.

The previous week, he claimed, he had gone to the Clark County Courthouse for a meeting with a county official. He said he remembered entering the conference room before he apparently blacked out. "I believe they drugged me," he said. "When I awoke,

I was in a Columbus motel room, naked, with a prostitute. She said they had taken pictures of us together."

"Have you seen the photos?" I asked.

"No."

"How do you know they exist?"

He was getting angry that I was not taking his words as gospel, so to speak. "She told me they existed. They paid her to pose nude beside me. Now, you listen to me. This deed was perpetrated by those who oppose me and God's work. If they have photographs of me and a prostitute in bed, I can only assume that they plan to use them as blackmail to force me to close down my group home."

I had questions. "Which motel were you in?"

"I don't remember."

"How can you not remember?"

"I'd been drugged, remember?"

"Were your clothes in the room?"

"No."

"What did you wear home?"

"I called a friend who brought me clothes and took me home."

"Who was that?"

"I don't want to drag him into it."

"Did they take your wallet?"

"I wasn't carrying one that day."

"Why?"

"I just wasn't."

"What was the prostitute's name?"

"I didn't ask."

"What did your wife say?"

"I don't want to drag her into it."

"How did they get you out of the courthouse without being seen?"

"I have no idea. I was unconscious."

"How did they get you into the motel without being seen?"

"I have no idea. I was unconscious."

I could only assume that either the good reverend had a fantastical imagination, or he had been into some serious hanky-panky and some embarrassing photos were about to surface, for which he needed an alibi. Of course, he wanted me to perpetrate this whopper by plastering it across the front of the *Dispatch*. I had a habit of tilting my head and squinting my left eye when something did not seem quite right, and I was at full squint at that moment. He sensed my disbelief.

"It's the gospel," he said, holding up his right hand. "Every word. As Jesus Christ is my witness."

I closed my notebook and headed toward the door. "Reverend, you better get him down here to back it up, then, because that's the only way that story is ever getting in the *Columbus Dispatch*." His battle with the county went on for months after that day, but I never wrote another story.

Another time, early in my career at the *Dispatch,* I received a call from the director of the Ohio Masonic Home in Springfield, who wanted me to write a story about one of the home's residents—a gentleman who was about ninety years old and who had played professional football and baseball in the early part of the century. He had been a member of the Columbus Panhandles, an early NFL team made up primarily of railroaders, and a member of the Cleveland Indians World Championship team of 1920. The resident claimed to have been spiked by Ty Cobb during an Indians game against Detroit and knocked unconscious by Jim Thorpe during a football game. I love sports and couldn't wait to do the story.

I spent an entire afternoon with the gentleman. He was bright, nattily attired, engaging, and funny and told grand stories. I loved it. He said he had played college football at Ohio Wesleyan University for the legendary Fielding "Hurry Up" Yost, who later gained fame as the coach of the Michigan Wolverines. He was confused on some of the dates, but he was almost ninety, so I was willing to give some ground. I asked him to tell me about the time he was knocked out by Jim Thorpe.

"I was playing for the Columbus Panhandles," he started. "We were playing the Canton Bulldogs and I was back to receive a punt. I called for a fair catch and that's the last thing I remember. The next thing I know, I wake up in a hospital bed and standing beside my bed is the great Jim Thorpe. Oh, Thorpe was a grand man, I'll tell you. And, Thorpe, he's crying like a baby. He says to me, 'I'm so sorry, pal, but I didn't see you call for that fair catch.'"

By this time, I had already invested several hours in the interview. And I was thinking, I've read an account similar to this in a book somewhere. And it did not involve this guy, and it did not involve a fair catch.

"Let's back up a minute," I said. "What year was this?"

"1922, or thereabouts."

Uh-oh.

I was not sure of the exact year that the National Football League instituted the fair catch rule, but I knew it was at least two decades beyond 1922.

When I returned to Columbus, I called the Cleveland Indians, who put me in touch with Bill Wambsganss, who had been a second baseman on the 1920 championship team and lived in Lakewood, Ohio. As I started to explain the reason for my call, he interrupted and snarled, "Did that nutcase get you to write a story about him, too?"

"Not yet, he hasn't."

"Well, I don't know who he is, or who he thinks he was, but I can tell you this: he never played for the Cleveland Indians," Wambsganss said. "You're probably the third reporter to call and ask about him."

And I bet he never played for the Columbus Panhandles, either. Oh, and I did a little research about his claim of playing for Hurry-Up Yost at Ohio Wesleyan, a private school in Delaware, Ohio, just north of Columbus. Yost coached one year at Ohio Wesleyan, 1897, which would have made my little storyteller about six years old when he was allegedly playing college football.

I think he was just a lonely old man who wanted some attention and someone to talk to, and he did it by making up great stories. He could spin a good yarn. Some of the stories he told—one of the others was about playing golf with a young Jack Nicklaus had some elements of fact. I think he had read the accounts of athletes and simply inserted himself into the stories.

(Obviously, I did not write the story. I called the director of the home and said I was not going to write the story because all the events were simply products of a vivid imagination. "I'm sure he believes that they're all true, but they aren't," I said. About a month later, the story appeared on the sports pages of a competing newspaper and was picked up for national distribution by the Associated Press.)

In December 1984, I wrote a story about the year's unsolved homicides. The next day I received a call from John Giuricich, a resident of Columbus's south side, who said that I had omitted the October 7 murder of seventy-one-year-old Angela Biskic. Biskic was a Yugoslavian immigrant who had arrived in Columbus in 1950. She and Giuricich had been neighbors and friends for thirty-four years.

When I first received Giuricich's call, I did not even recall Biskic, so while he was on the phone I went through my files and found a brief story that I had written about her death. The police had been called after Giuricich found Biskic's body lying on the couch in the ransacked front room of her home. According to the police, they suspected that she had apparently died of a heart attack after surprising a burglar. Although she probably wouldn't have had a heart attack if the burglar hadn't been in the house, investigators said it wasn't a homicide. The story quoted Homicide Sgt. John Cherubini as saying, "It's possible she could have died of a heart attack during the burglary. She was apparently a heart patient. There was no gun, no knife, no signs of beating." The police press release said the cause of death was "unknown."

I went back to the telephone. "John, I found the story. You know, I think whoever did this should be guilty of murder, but I didn't include it in my story because, technically, it wasn't a homicide."

"What do you mean, it wasn't a homicide?"

"The cops say she surprised a burglar and died of a heart attack."

"A heart attack!" he sputtered. "She most certainly did not die of a heart attack. She was murdered—strangled."

I promised Giuricich that I would follow up, and I called Suzanne and asked her to pull a file for me. "The night this happened, Cherubini said this woman died a nonviolent death. He said she probably surprised a burglar and dropped dead—possibly from a heart attack. I just got a call from one of her former neighbors who says she was murdered. What do you have?"

"Cherubini said it was nonviolent, huh?"

"He said she had a history of heart problems."

"Well, that may be, but I'm looking at photos of an elderly woman lying on a couch with her hands bound with a telephone cord and a bloody rag stuffed in her mouth like a gag. She's got a cord around her neck. According to the autopsy, she was strangled. And, she's got a nice-sized bruise under her nose. This certainly isn't what I would call a nonviolent death."

Cops often did stupid things, but I had a hard time trying to figure the motivation for this one. Her death occurred during a time when I was slugging it out with the homicide detectives on a regular basis. Perhaps, Cherubini thought if he said it looked like a death from natural causes, I would not give it much attention. And, he was right. However, now things were going to get ugly. I relished the call to Cherubini.

"Sarge, Robin Yocum, here. Do you remember the death of Angela Biskic—old lady on the south side who you said died of a heart attack when a burglar surprised her?"

"I remember."

"Do you remember you also said it was not a violent death?"

"Yeah, she had a heart problem."

"Well, my question is, why would you say she died of natural causes when it was obvious that she was bound up, beaten, and had a cord around her neck?"

"Who told you that?"

"Nobody told me. It's in the autopsy report."

"The autopsy report? How'd you get that?"

I stared into the receiver. "It's public record. Anyone can get it."

"Autopsy reports are public record?" He must have turned to one of the homicide detectives, because through the receiver I could hear him ask, "Are autopsy reports public record?" This was followed by a brief silence before he said, "Really?" He finally came back to our conversation. "So, what do you want?"

It was a classic example of catching someone in a lie and off guard. He was now on the defensive and his next comments did him absolutely no good. "I don't feel that just because she was bound that it was a violent homicide. At that age it doesn't take very much [to kill someone]."

When I took my evidence to Cherubini's superiors, they tried to defend him. "You know, Robin, John sees a lot of homicides worse than this. This probably didn't seem that violent to him," said Lt. Ralph Casto.

I liked Casto—nice guy, good cop. At that moment he was doing his best to defend his sergeant. But, in his heart, he knew Cherubini had screwed up. Casto had brought the investigation file to the meeting. I plucked a photo of the slain woman from the table, held it toward the lieutenant, and asked, "Lieutenant, if this was your mother, would you consider it a violent homicide? Because I sure as hell would."

He gave me a tacit nod.

Cherubini got skewered in the *Dispatch* and received a written reprimand for the tale. I had always had a decent relationship with Cherubini, whom I liked personally. When there were no other cops around, I called him "The Big Ragu." Suzanne had tipped me off that he liked that nickname and I used it to butter him up. It was, however, going to take more than a nickname to repair this rift. He refused to talk to me for months.

Police eventually charged Rodney R. Reese with aggravated murder in Biskic's death. He had been only fifteen at the time of her death and nineteen when he was convicted in July 1985. Reese was allowed to plead guilty to involuntary manslaughter in exchange for testimony against his accomplices in a string of robberies and burglaries. He was sentenced to twenty to a hundred years in prison and will be eligible for parole in 2012.

FOUR

❑

More Help from Suzie

The Grateful Jaywalker

WHEN SUZANNE CALLED, SHE NEVER SAID HELLO; SHE JUST
started talking. "What's the most unusual reason you've ever heard
for tipping a cop off to a murder?"

I had to think. "One guy confessed after they bought him a
pizza."

"This one might be better. The boys in homicide are about to
solve an '81 case because they didn't give a guy a jaywalking ticket."

It took me a minute to digest the sentence. "Okay, you've got my
attention."

It was July 1984.

Suzanne said that, from the investigative report she was reading,
in July 1981, Wesley Hampton had bragged to some associates in
crime that he was quite adept at stealing cars. This skill was important to the associates, a husband-and-wife team planning a series of
bank and restaurant robberies in Columbus and South Bend, Indiana, as they were in need of getaway cars.

"Well, apparently Mr. Hampton wasn't nearly as good at stealing cars as he was at *talking* about stealing cars," Suzanne said.

"Sort of like, 'I don't know nothin' about birthin' no babies,' huh?"

"Exactly," she said. "So, they've apparently got these robberies all planned out and they're supposed to meet at an apartment over at Tenth and Cassady. But Hampton shows up empty handed, which apparently didn't sit well with the husband. So, he killed him— shoots him three times with a .38."

"That'll do it."

"It did, and they buried Mr. Hampton in a wooded area of Krumm Park. Then some time later they got worried that the body would be discovered, so they employed the help of our jaywalking friend to rebury it—somewhere over around Twenty-fourth and Joyce. I guess there's a vacant lot over there by the railroad tracks."

"It's always good to get as many people as possible involved in a murder cover-up, don't you think? So, how does the jaywalker play into this?"

"All right, a year after the murder . . ."

"1982?"

"Right. This guy gets stopped for jaywalking. When he does, the cops find out he has an outstanding warrant for resisting arrest. So, they take him to jail on the warrant, and just give him a warning for jaywalking. I guess he thinks this is a big deal and he's so grateful that he tells the uniformed cop where he can find a murder victim. He tells the cops that he knows where the body is because he helped bury it. And he leads them to the body and gives the cops the name of the killer."

"That's it? He leads them to a corpse, which he helped bury, because he dodged a minor misdemeanor?"

"That, and he wanted $250 cash so he could get his car fixed and leave town."

"He'll have to leave town. If that guy killed Hampton because he couldn't steal a car, I don't think he'll have any problem killing a guy who ratted him out on a murder."

"Apparently that's not a problem. The shooter is in the federal penitentiary on other charges."

"It's been almost two years since they found the body. Why did it take them so long to get to this point?

"It's taken them that long to get the body identified. It was just a skeleton by the time they found it, so obviously we couldn't get any fingerprints. The cops just started asking around, trying to find out who hadn't been seen in a couple of years."

"Why didn't they ask the jaywalker?"

"They did. He didn't know."

"I suspect that he didn't want to seem overly interested in the corpse that he was helping the killer bury."

"Exactly."

"Man, that's a good one, Suzie. Anything else?"

I could hear her flipping through the pages of the investigative report. "Yeah, here's another nugget. They found the murder weapon in the police property room."

Again, it took a minute to process the information. "How did they know it was the murder weapon?"

"I guess it got traded around until it ended up in the hands of some guy who got into a shootout with the police in December of '81. He lost and the police ended up with the gun."

"Sure, because you'd never want to get rid of a perfectly good murder weapon. You want to keep those babies in circulation. What did he do, kill Hampton, then swap it out for a bag of Doritos?"

Suzanne laughed. She laughed easily, always welcoming a little humor into days spent working with corpses and grieving relatives. "Hey, I've been at this a long time," she said. "Criminal stupidity has solved a lot more homicides than good police work."

"So, the cops have the murder weapon in their property room, but they don't know it's the murder weapon until . . . when?"

"Some informant tips them off."

"So, it was common knowledge on the street that this was the same .38-caliber pistol used to kill Hampton?"

"Someone knew."

Alfred Warren, who was in the state penitentiary in Michigan City, Indiana, and his wife, Fanny Hill Warren, who was in the U.S. Army stationed at Fort Carson, Colorado, were both indicted for aggravated murder and a series of robberies in Columbus and South Bend.

Alfred Warren pleaded guilty to a reduced charge of voluntary manslaughter and is currently serving a seven-to-twenty-five-year sentence. Charges were later dropped against Fanny Hill Warren.

Mahfoud Bouldjediene

The Algerian community in Columbus was mourning the loss of twenty-five-year-old Mahfoud Bouldjediene. For a week after his August 1982 death, Columbus Algerians had been distraught and outraged, vowing to me to avenge his death. Bouldjediene's friends believed that a Middle Eastern sect with a loathing of Algerians had been responsible for his murder.

A man picking berries along I-71, just north of Cooke Road, had discovered Bouldjediene's charred body. A police officer who arrived at the scene said Bouldjediene had suffered "massive blunt force injuries to the chest and neck." Police believed that after beating Bouldjediene to death, perhaps with a baseball bat, his attackers had set his body on fire. Whether the body was torched to destroy evidence or as a sign of the attacker's hatred of Algerians was unclear.

Oddly, although police believed that Bouldjediene had been

dead for several days, his car was found nearby, the engine running and the lights on.

A day after Bouldjediene's body was found, I interviewed one of his roommates, Rachid Ouari, who quoted Bouldjediene as saying, "I think someone is trying to blow my head off." Ouari said Bouldjediene, who worked at a Wendy's restaurant but held a mechanical engineering degree from Ohio University, also had been upset over a recent breakup with his girlfriend. I wondered if there was a connection between the two. The death had been particularly violent, and the fact that his body had been set on fire indicated that it could have been a crime of passion.

Several days after Bouldjediene's death, Suzanne called. I was already working on another story.

"Hey, your friend Mahfoud . . ." she said, again not bothering to introduce herself.

"What about him?"

"Are his friends still rattling their sabers and talking about avenging his death?" she asked.

"The last I talked to them, they were."

"Well, they better put the swords away. I just got the preliminary results back. It was a suicide."

"I'll be right up."

Suzanne liked to sit behind her desk and taunt me with the paperwork, peeking at it and giving me the information in dribs and drabs, making me try to guess how the deceased came to be that way.

"The breakup with the girlfriend must have been bothering Mr. Bouldjediene a little more than he had been letting on," she said. "We found a suicide note in his pocket."

"Are you sure *he* wrote it?"

She nodded.

"Okay, he had blunt force injuries, but obviously didn't beat himself to death."

"No. The internal injuries didn't kill him. Those came after he was dead, or very nearly dead."

Suzanne grinned. She loved playing these games with me. She wanted my best guess. "Okay, here you go. He was with his girl-friend," I theorized. "He wanted to get back together, but she said no. So, in protest, he pulled off the road, doused himself with gaso-line and set himself on fire. The girlfriend is so horrified that she panics, tries to drive away for help, but accidentally hits him with the car. The car was still running when police arrived because she ran away."

"Oh, good guess, Dr. Watson, but not even close."

"I give."

"He was electrocuted. Apparently, he had pulled off the side of I-70, climbed a power pole and stretched across the high-tension wires."

"Ouch."

"Exactly. The injuries to his neck and chest were sustained when he fell to the ground. The power lines ignited his body, which is why it was charred and police thought someone had set it on fire. It was a logical assumption that he had been beaten to death, particularly after the cops interviewed his friends, who said someone had been trying to kill him."

I let all this sink in for a moment, then said, "I've got to tell you, Suzanne, as suicides go . . ."

"Oh, definitely, this would be a bad way go. There would be lots better ways of doing yourself in than stretching across some power lines."

FIVE
❏

The King and the
Caped Crusader

Dying for Elvis

LINDA MARSICK'S LIFE WAS A THIRTY-YEAR, FANATICAL DEVOTION to Elvis Presley. It ended on September 23, 1977, a little more than a month after the death of the King of Rock 'n' Roll. Marsick's body was found slumped in a bedroom closet of her north-side apartment. She had been strangled. A scarf was wrapped and knotted around her neck.

The question surrounding her death was: Was Linda Marsick the victim of murder, as her parents believed, or a sad suicide, as Columbus police and the Franklin County coroner believed?

It was one of the most strangely fascinating stories that I had ever covered. I was contacted by Marsick's parents, Bruce and Ruth Walkup, in the winter of 1985, more than eight years after her death. Essentially, the Walkups wanted me to do a story on what they considered to be the incompetence of Franklin County Coroner William R. Adrion, who had ruled their daughter's death a suicide. That ruling, however, was overturned in Franklin County Common Pleas Court more than seven years after Marsick died. The cause of death was changed from suicide to homicide. The Walkups were bitter over their extended battle to have the cause of death changed. Marsick's parents believed the police botched the investigation and that Adrion had covered up their incompetence by ruling their daughter's death a suicide. They said Adrion should have independently changed the ruling from suicide to homicide years earlier.

Marsick's death occurred when I was still in college and nearly three years before I arrived at the *Dispatch.* Thus, I was unfamiliar with the case. After receiving the phone call, I agreed to meet with the Walkups in their home. They were wonderful, caring people who were raising their two granddaughters. They did not want the girls to grow up believing that their mother had committed suicide.

Based on the information provided by the Walkups, I began work on the story. My first stop was the Franklin County Coroner's Office for a meeting with Suzanne. "Linda Marsick?" she groaned, as if an old demon had just crawled out from under the bed. Her head tipped back, her mouth dropped and her eyes rolled to the top of her head as she feigned a seizure. "Please, don't tell me you think it was a suicide, too?"

"Maybe I do," I said.

"Well, you won't after you read the file." She fetched it from a file cabinet and spread it out on her desk. "It wasn't murder; it was death by Elvis."

After spending weeks reviewing the coroner's investigative file, and state and county records, it seemed obvious that the ruling should never have been reversed. There was overwhelming evidence to support Adrion's conclusion of suicide.

Linda Marsick's parents believed their daughter was murdered. My investigation revealed a troubled woman who likely committed suicide over the death of Elvis Presley. (Courtesy of the *Columbus Dispatch*)

- Marsick's body was found after personnel at her apartment complex forced their way into the apartment, which had been dead-bolted from the inside. All the windows were locked. She had been dead six to ten days.
- Marsick was found in the closet, but none of the clothing had been disturbed. There was no sign of a struggle in the apart-

ment. Police said it appeared as though she had just sat down and died.

- Her body had no bruises or scratches.
- There was no bruising to the underlying tissues of the neck and the hyoid bone had not been crushed. When a person is strangled in an attack, the tissues are bruised and the hyoid is nearly always crushed. The absence of these injuries indicated to Adrion that Marsick had died by her own hand. She had tied the scarf around her neck tightly, slowly cutting off the flow of oxygen to the brain until she passed out and died a slow death. As suicides go, one detective said, "This would not be a pleasant way to go. It would be slow and painful."
- Taped to the inside of the closet door were two notes in Marsick's handwriting. One was to her estranged husband. It read, "Petula Clark Album for Gary Marsick in paper bag—top shelve [sic] of living room closet. Please see that Gary gets this album." The second note was written to a John Shea of Alexander, N.Y., whom police identified as her boyfriend. The note listed his work phone number and stated, "starts work at 7:30 P.M." Also found inside the closet was a tape recording of Marsick reciting the Lord's Prayer and singing a mournful rendition of Shelley Fabares's 1962 hit, "Johnny Angel."
- A friend of Marsick's, Laura Porter, told me that Marsick had considered suicide and had called a suicide prevention hotline several times.
- Letters that she wrote to friends and relatives in the weeks after Presley died show a woman despondent over the death. In a letter to "Uncle Bob," dated September 9, 1977, Marsick wrote:

When I heard Elvis died it really tore me apart. It's been three weeks since he was buried and I haven't stopped crying yet. I don't think I'll ever get over it. His death is the hardest thing I've ever had to face in my whole life. I've hardly eaten or slept since he died. I've lost at least 12 pounds. I guess I never thought in terms of Elvis dying and I just can't handle it. I don't understand why he had to die. He meant so much to me. I'll never be the same again. This is the most painful thing I've ever had to go through.

(The letters were part of the Ohio Victims of Crime Compensation Program case file at the Ohio attorney general's office.)

Considering what I thought to be overwhelming evidence that Marsick's death was a suicide, I began looking into the events that led to reversing the ruling. It was an odd chain of events that began with two seemingly minor mistakes in the original autopsy.

- The first mistake stated that Marsick hanged herself. She did not. That was a misunderstanding between a homicide detective and the forensic pathologist. The detective stated that Marsick's death was an apparent suicide by strangulation. The pathologist incorrectly assumed it was a hanging and recorded that information on the autopsy.
- The second mistake centered around a towel that was found clenched in the front of Marsick's mouth. The autopsy stated that the towel was "blood-soaked." It was not. Further examination by the coroner's office determined that the pink fluid on the towel was not blood, but body fluid that had leaked from her nose and mouth.

The Walkups took the autopsy to their daughter's personal physician, Dr. F. C. Schaeffer, who, without the benefit of the crime-scene photos, wrote a letter stating that the towel might have contributed to her death. (In other words, couldn't Marsick have suffocated when someone stuffed the towel down her throat? This was highly unlikely. When Marsick's body was found, the towel was barely in her mouth. It was clenched in her front teeth and one investigator speculated that she used it to keep from crying out during a painful death.)

The Walkups then took Schaeffer's letter to the Ohio attorney general's office, requesting compensation from the crime compensation fund. Since the fund does not pay on suicides, Attorney General William J. Brown contacted Hamilton County Coroner Dr. Frank P. Cleveland and asked for an independent ruling in the case. Cleveland, without benefit of the photos and without ever contacting Adrion or the Columbus police, made a ruling of homicide based on the two points in the flawed autopsy report.

Cleveland's ruling was not binding and Adrion refused to change his. The Walkups then filed suit in Franklin County Common Pleas Court, requesting that the suicide ruling be reversed.

During the hearing on the suit, an assistant Franklin County prosecutor who was days from retirement essentially fumbled the ball. Cleveland's ruling was entered into the court records, yet the assistant prosecutor produced not a shred of the overwhelming evidence supporting Adrion's ruling of suicide. Without the contradictory evidence, the judge reversed Adrion's ruling and ordered Marsick's death categorized as a homicide.

My story on Marsick's death ran in two parts, January 8–9, 1986. The first story ran under the headline:

DID LINDA MARSICK DIE FOR ELVIS?

The Walkups felt that I had pilloried them and their daughter and betrayed their trust. I did not, of course. I just reported the full scope of the case. They were loving parents who did not want to believe that their daughter had taken her own life. But the fact remained that the evidence pointed to suicide. After the second day, they had to rush Mrs. Walkup to the hospital with chest pains. Mr. Walkup called me at the paper. "We had to take my wife to the hospital because of your vile stories," he said. "If she dies, I don't know what I'm going to do to you, but it won't be pleasant."

About a week later I received a postcard from Mrs. Walkup. It read:

> *Your brutal article that reeked of sensationalism and half-truths put me in the hospital. My daughter's children are further burdened with trying to live down the reputation you created for their mother. I hope you are satisfied.*
>
> *Ruth Walkup*

I was not satisfied. I was just glad the story was over. I never again spoke to the Walkups.

The Caped Crusader

I cannot begin to tell you the countless hours of my youth that were lost trying to explain this simple premise to my brother, Matthew: Batman could be real; Superman was fiction.

"I don't understand why you don't get this, Matt," I would say. "It's simple. A rich guy could dig out the bat cave, buy a cool car and fix it up, and take karate lessons and become Batman. It could happen. There's no way some guy could fly and stop bullets with his chest. Understand?"

"Maybe if he came from another planet where they fly, he could," Matt would counter. "You're just jealous because Batman can't fly. He shouldn't even call himself Batman if he can't fly. Bats can fly."

It was useless to continue. There's no reasoning with a Superman fan. Despite the Caped Crusader's inability to fly, I don't believe there is any argument that he is the greatest superhero of all time. With this belief firmly entrenched in my psyche, imagine my delight when the one true Batman—Adam West—was scheduled to come to Columbus—with the Batmobile—to make a personal appearance at the Autorama in January 1985.

Celebrity interviews were the bailiwick of the features department, so I went down and asked—fully prepared to beg—if I could *please* interview Batman. I thought I would have to take off my shirt and wrestle someone for the rights to the interview. The features editor shrugged and said, "Sure. Go for it."

I met West, who was in his Caped Crusader costume, just before he went out to sign autographs for a throng that extended well into the back of the hall. He was great with the fans and said he spent half of his weekends each year on the auto show circuit with the Batmobile. West signed autographs and shook hands, easily outdrawing Morganna, professional baseball's buxom kissing bandit, who was signing autographs just a few hundred feet away. And I thought, could Superman outdraw Morganna? Not in my lifetime.

Said West, "I don't care if anyone in Hollywood looks down on car shows. Where else could you get a forum this large? It's not me they're coming to see, it's the character. Batman is ageless, timeless. When the film crumbles into dust, Batman will still be part of film history. Batman gets such immediate feedback that it's a pleasure to get out here and meet these kids. [Note: Some of the "kids" were easily in their mid-thirties.] They need heroes, they need to come out here and get this attention, the love. And, this gives me a chance to do a service. Some actors go out on stage and get feedback, emotional response. I get it from playing Batman. I've had more fun playing Batman than any other role."

It was the only time in my career that I asked an interview subject for an autograph. He signed my reporter's notebook: Best Wishes. Adam "Batman" West.

He asked me to send him a copy of the article, which I did. A week later I received a letter from West, who took issue with one paragraph of my story, which read: He still wears the cowl and cape, though the material now stretches a little tighter across the girth and they say the hair is now gray under the cowl.

He wrote: "Under my famous crime-fighting cowl my hair is not gray. But is thinner than Redford's. A little."

Taped to the upper right corner of the letter was a lock of brown hair.

Terrific, I thought. I've pissed off Batman.

Actually, the letter was complimentary and toward the bottom he wrote: "You should go into journalism."

SIX

❑

Reporters, Editors, Shooters, and Counsel

Ned "The Colonel" Stout

NED "THE COLONEL" STOUT'S LIFE WAS ONE OF WRETCHED excess—cigarettes, booze, and newsprint, mostly. His life was certainly no model for how I would want to live mine, but he was a hell of a newsman, reporter, and writer. He had the most incredible command of the English language of anyone I have ever met. And he was an acerbic, chain-smoking, horrendous alcoholic who consumed more beer and gin than any human being I have ever known. He was a caricature of the old-style newspaperman in suspenders and a necktie loosened around a starched white shirt.

Ned loved a well-turned phrase and despised the sanitizing that stories often underwent on the *Dispatch* copy desk, which he condescendingly referred to as "Romper Room." Here's a portion of a note he once slipped into my mailbox about a murder story I had written.

Ned Stout was the consummate newspaperman. As the night police reporter, I drove Ned home on nights when too much gin prevented him from performing the task. (Courtesy of the *Columbus Dispatch*)

Yocum

Bee-you-te-ful!
Under stern injunction, I attempted to cut it as I would my
own—before submitting it to the insensitivities of Romper Room.

Ned was, and I am probably being generous, only about 5-foot-4 and if he weighed much over a hundred pounds I'd be surprised. I was something of an expert on Ned's weight because I had carried him into his house stoned, coma drunk on more than a few occasions. Part of my job as night police reporter was to serve as a taxi service for Ned when he was too drunk to drive.

Bernie Karsko would call and ask, "You got time to run Ned home?" I always said yes. "Okay, he'll be waiting in front of the building." It took about five minutes to get to my car and drive the few blocks from the police station to 34 South Third Street, the *Dispatch* building. By the time I pulled up, Ned would be leaning against the building, a rolled up paper tucked under his arm, fighting to keep his eyes open.

"Did you call for a cab, buddy?" I would ask.

He would stagger toward the car and respond, "I certainly did."

It was our regular greeting. Most days, I would get out of the car and open the back door for him. I started doing this after he once miscalculated the height of the door opening and smacked his head so hard that for an instant I thought someone had rear-ended the press car. I was amazed he remained conscious and feared that we were heading for a trip to the emergency room.

"Ned, are you all right?"

After holding his head in his hands for several moments he said, "Goddamn. That'll sober you up."

After I got him inside the car, I'd inquire, "How you doin', Ned?"

"Ah, young troop, I have consumed great quantities of gin."

Invariably, by the time I got to his home in German Village, he would be slouched in the back seat, out. If I could get him to stand, I would walk him to the door. Generally, it was easier to throw him over a shoulder and carry him inside. I even knew the security code for his burglar alarm.

The first time I took Ned home, I did not know he had a security alarm. I was standing in his living room, holding him up like a little marionette with my left hand while frantically punching in the security code with my right as he struggled to remember the sequence.

"Four . . . two . . ."

He drifted off; I shook him awake. "Dammit, Ned, wake up! Four-two what?"

"What? Oh, ah, four-two, uh, seven . . ."

The thing kept beeping until he eventually spilled out the correct sequence. I felt as if I had disarmed a bomb just seconds before detonation. If the alarm had gone off and the cops had shown up, there was no way Ned could have vouched for me. I committed the code to memory for future missions.

Nancy Nall, one of our reporters, once said of Ned: "One of these days he's just going to die, that's all, he'll just be dead. They'll say he died of "Ned." They'll do an autopsy and his insides will look like a jar of pickled eggs that have been sitting around for 100 years."

Early in my career, Ned was the man whose name I most wanted to see on a police homicide report. He was brutal on young reporters. I would work until 2 A.M. and get to bed around 3:30. Ned would call me every morning—every morning—at 6:10 A.M. with questions about my stories.

When I started on the police beat, Ned was past his reporting days and was helping coordinate the flow of stories on the city desk. He would call with questions about my stories before he began reading them. If I could not answer his questions, I had to get on the phone and start making calls, waking other people who also had just gone to bed.

It took quite a while for me to appreciate that the calls were not total harassment—though he did glean some delight from them—but an effort to make me a better reporter.

Ned took great joy in typing out little notes on copy paper, praising or chastising reporters for good work or miscues. Here is a note that was attached to a map of Franklin County and left in my mailbox by Ned after I incorrectly placed a crime scene on West Broad Street when it was, in fact, located on East Broad Street.

Robin:

Eso es un mapa.
That is a Spanish phrase. It means: This is a map.
Maps are helpful.
They help us if we are lost.
We can find streets on maps.
We can find cities on maps.
We can find counties and townships and states on maps.
Countries are on maps.
So are oceans.
In fact, the whole world is on maps.
Except, maybe, for inner parts of Patagonia and maybe subur-
ban Pataskala.
Maps should be consulted when we do not know where we are.
Maps are our friends.
Use them.

NCS

By the time I moved to dayside cops—6 A.M. to 2 P.M.—Ned
and I had become good friends. I always checked in at the city desk
before heading to the police station. By the time I got there, Ned
would be furiously working at his computer, three beers in the tank
and wearing sunglasses to protect his eyes from the fluorescent lights
of the newsroom.

As he was editing stories, he would occasionally rub his temples
and say, "The question isn't, 'Why do editors drink so much?' The
question is, 'Why do we drink as little as we do?'" And he would
pick up the phone to awaken another reporter.

One morning I was working on a bad traffic accident. An elderly
man and woman had driven across the median of I-70 and crashed

head-on with a tractor-trailer. The woman was dead at the scene; her husband had been taken to the hospital, but was not going to live.

"The woman's dead, and the nursing supervisor says the old man is in surgery, but he's not going to make it. He'll be dead before deadline."

"Awfully decent of him," Ned replied.

Soon after I moved to dayside, Ned gave up a forty-year, several-pack-a-day cigarette habit. He had taken to such horrible coughing spells that he would stagger crimson-faced to the conference room and lie on the floor to catch his breath. There were a few times when we did not think he was going to pull out of it. His face would get red, then maroon, and then purple. It was painful to watch. He went cold turkey on the cigarettes and replaced the oral fixation with plastic swizzle sticks, which he gnawed. As he intensely worked on editing a story, a line of drool would run out of the open end of the stick and down into the keyboard, of which he was totally oblivious.

He was successful at giving up the cigarettes, but giving up alcohol was beyond Ned's abilities or desires. He relayed a story to me of a visit to his doctor, during which the physician asked, "Ned, how much gin are you drinking a day?"

"My intake is considerable, but it varies, depending on the amount of beer I consume."

"Ned, do you think you could quit drinking?"

"Doc, and I say this with all sincerity, I could quit this instant."

"Ned, that's great."

"I have absolutely no intention of doing so, but I could if I wanted."

His drinking antics were legendary. As a reporter, he sometimes was too hung over—or still too drunk—to type. He would track down the information for his story then, hiding behind one of the large pillars in the newsroom, he would get an outside line and call the paper's copy desk—about thirty feet away—and dictate the story to an unsuspecting copy editor.

Following one of the summer clinics, which were held at a company-owned property known as the Wigwam, Ned was so drunk that he confused the sidewalk for the road. As he tried to drive out of the property on the sidewalk, he wedged his car between two trees so tightly that they had to cut down one of the trees to free the vehicle. On another instance, he and photographer Glen Cumberledge hit a tree and Ned went through the windshield.

He suffered a serious head injury and doctors determined they had to put a steel plate in his head. Cumberledge, who escaped virtually unscathed, was with Ned at the hospital as they were preparing to take him to surgery.

Now, during all the time I knew Ned, he lived in Newark, Ohio, on weekends with his wife and children, and in German Village with his girlfriend during the week. According to Cumberledge, following the accident Ned was lying on the gurney calling out for his girlfriend, Kay.

"Oh, Kay; oh, Kay," he moaned.

Meanwhile, his wife had been called and was walking down the hall toward them.

"Stout, shut up," Cumberledge said. "It's your wife. Shut up."

"Oh, Kay. Kay. Oh, Kay."

"Stout, it's your wife. Shut the hell up."

"Oh, Kay. Oh, Kay."

His wife walked up to the gurney, took his hand, patted it and said, "That's right, Ned, it's going to be okay. It'll all be okay."

"Stout was the only sonofabitch in the world who could have pulled that off," Cumberledge said.

Ned once told me that, as a reporter, he was in a running battle with the captain of the detective bureau. The captain was telling people he had evidence of illicit behavior by Ned, which he planned to take to the owners of the *Dispatch* to have him fired. "I'm going to pull the package on that little sonofabitch," he bragged.

Ned, all hundred pounds of him, went to the captain's office, closed the door and said, "If you're going to pull the package on me, you tell me what you've got, other than I drink too much, I fuck too much and, occasionally, I talk too much. And my employers already know that. Now, if you've got anything else, I'm sure my employer and myself would love to know about it."

That ended the big talk by the captain.

Ned kept a flow chart of Columbus crime that included everyone from the mob to the Columbus Tenants Union, which he called a "bunch of subversive, commie bastards." Ned was an air force veteran and, if nothing else, a patriot. He once left me a note about an antidraft protest in which he referred to the organizer as a "snot-nosed, fairy-voiced, draft-dodging little son-of-a-bitch."

While some snickered at his attempt to show the commonality of Columbus crime, it was amazing how many times he could take a crime or suspected criminal of which I was writing and make a connection to something that had occurred twenty years before.

When a story did not pan out the way Ned had hoped, he would grumble, "I hate it when the facts get in the way of a good story."

After I wrote a story in 1983 about attempts to keep a convicted killer off Death Row, Ned wrote me a note that read: "Man is the only animal which attempts to preserve the unfit of its kind."

He lamented change. He refused to call the *Dispatch* library anything but "the morgue," which is an old newspaper term for the clip file room. He grumbled that newspapers began a downward spiral when editors began referring to them as "products" instead of "newspapers." "We don't deliver a product, we deliver a goddamn newspaper," he said. And he insisted that this phrase appear in his obituary: *He did not suffer adversity well.*

Ned died on September 3, 1986. He was sixty, though it was not the years, it was the mileage. He had been hospitalized after he broke a hip during a tumble at home in April. While in the hospital, they discovered he had cancer and the poor rascal had nothing to help fight it off. In his obituary, reporter Steve Berry printed Ned's most famous newsroom quotes:

> *A beautiful young woman once walked through the* Dispatch *newsroom, prompting Ned to declare, "Now, there's a winsome lass."*
>
> *A few minutes later, a woman considerably less attractive walked past and Ned said, "Win some, lose some."*

Botched Suicide

A north-side man attempted to commit suicide by hanging himself from the Agler Road bridge. However, he did not get the rope secured to the bridge. He put the noose around his neck and jumped, but instead of hanging himself, he simply fell to the rocky shoreline, knocking himself unconscious and ending up in Riverside Hospital with a severe head injury. I wrote a straight lead.

When I arrived the next day, Ned had written an alternative lead and left it in my mailbox:

> *All of his life, things have never seemed to go quite right for Arthur.*
>
> *Not even his attempt to end it.*

Ken Chamberlain

Kenny was my favorite shooter—newspaper slang for a photographer. He worked the night shift, too, so we spent many evenings

Photographer Ken Chamberlain and I spent many nights cruising the streets of Columbus. He understood the news business and was great at picking up tips at crime scenes. (Courtesy of the *Columbus Dispatch*)

and nights together. On nights when he had finished his assignments and I was not tracking down a story, he would swing by the police station and we would go out cruising the city. This was the newspaper version of a fishing expedition. You might not get anything. On the other hand, you might make it to the scene of breaking news. The key was to cruise the areas with the greatest propensity for violence.

Kenny always picked me up by walking into the pressroom, taking a quick peek at the *Citizen-Journal* reporter, then waving me out into the hall as if it were an urgent matter. It was just a game. I would go back into the pressroom, grab my stuff and take off. Of course, the *C-J* reporter was left to sweat the possibility that he had missed something big.

Kenny knew the city better than anyone at the paper, maybe better than anyone in the city. When I first started cruising with him, I took along my *Graphic Street Guide of Greater Columbus*. This just made him laugh. When something came over the scanner, Kenny listened for the address and then drove right to it. He knew the city so well that we would sometimes beat the cops and paramedics to the scene.

In April 1982 we pulled up on a barricade situation on the east side while shots were still being fired inside the house. We parked in a nearby alley when I heard the first shot go off. This was followed by screaming and another blast. I pressed myself flat behind a maple tree across the street. There was more screaming going on inside the house and uniformed officers were approaching. Ken said, "I'm going to get closer and see what I can get."

I said, "You be my guest. I'll be right here."

Ken always carried a .22-caliber pistol in his camera bag. I never doubted for a second that he would have used it, if necessary. The *Dispatch* management surely would have frowned on Kenny for carrying a revolver, but considering some of the places we ended up at night, I was just fine with it.

The cops entered the house about a half-hour after the last shot. The man had committed suicide by shooting himself in the stomach. (Earlier in the week, Kenny and I had been to a barricade situation on the east side. The man called police and said he had barricaded himself in his house. He had no weapon and no hostages. So, essentially, he had locked himself in his house and was not coming out. The media—television particularly—ran on these things as if they were five-alarm fires. I always had a hard time understanding why they warranted coverage. But if television had it, I needed to have at least a few paragraphs or I would get a 6:10 wakeup call from someone on the city desk wanting to know why.)

Ken and I were once a block away from a shooting when the call came over the scanner. It was early evening and still light. When we arrived, the shooter was standing in the front yard with the pistol in his hand. The shooter was screaming at the victim, who was gut shot and curled up in the front yard, moaning and squirming around. Several women were standing nearby crying.

"Kenny . . . Kenny . . . KENNY!" I finally yelled, pointing. "The guy who is doing all the damage is RIGHT THERE!" The press cars were Ford Fairmonts and they looked like the cars the detectives drove—clunky, ugly, and with antennas hanging all over them. I cannot say for sure that the shooter glared at us before he ducked back into the house, but that's the way it appeared to me.

He surrendered to police almost immediately. Ken got some good shots of the medics working on the victim and the shooter being hauled away in handcuffs.

Kenny was the photographer for the Mifflin Township Fire Department and the Gahanna Police Department, where he also was an auxiliary sergeant and a past president of the Fraternal Order of Police Auxiliary. Consequently, he knew every cop and firefighter in the county. The day after we had covered a story, I would always find a stack of photographs in my mailbox. He would attach delivery instructions for each. I would take the black-and-white prints to the appropriate cops and firefighters. No matter what people say, everyone loves having their photograph taken. I'm sure there are hundreds of Kenny Chamberlain photographs hanging in dens and family rooms around Franklin County. This was instrumental in helping me develop sources because it gave me a way to approach the cops and firefighters without needing something.

Covering a story with Kenny was like having another reporter to help. He was not just a photographer; he understood news. And he knew so many people and was so trusted that he always tracked down bits of information for me at crime scenes. He would be walking around, his camera bag slung over one shoulder and a pipe bouncing between his teeth, snapping photos and looking for someone to slip him some information.

Kenny retired on August 1, 1996. I went to his going-away party and took him a book on classic Ford Mustangs. Kenny had restored several of the cars and had plans for more tinkering once he retired. Sadly, he died of a massive coronary February 2, 1997, just six months after he retired. He was sixty-four.

Bernie Karsko

Bernie Karsko was the night city editor when I started the police beat. He was the last of a breed that was already disappearing from newsrooms. He worked in shirtsleeves and his tie was always askew. He had a no-nonsense flattop haircut; he smoked cigarettes, but just as often chewed on the plastic tip of an unlit cigar.

Bernie hated excuses. If he gave you a story, he expected it done. If something happened on your beat, you had better not miss it. And he did not much care how you got the story, as long as you got it. For example, I once left a note for Bernie to have the dayside police reporter check a rumor that a councilman who had been raising a stink over the number of unpaid parking tickets in the city had four unpaid tickets himself. Bernie was territorial and did not want the dayside reporter to track it down. He wanted it done by a nightsider. When I reported to work the next day, the note was back in my mailbox. At the bottom, Bernie had typed these instructions:

> *Cry, cheat, screw an ugly woman—do whatever necessary to get the story.*
>
> *Bern*

It was probably a bit of an exaggeration. I do not think Bernie actually would have expected me to cry.

(Note: Bernie Karsko died of a heart attack in October 2003, just as I was working on the final rewrite of this book. Michael Curtin, president and associate publisher of the Dispatch, *may have best described Karsko in the obituary when he called him "a standard-issue, old, old-school newspaperman," and said, "He was all about, 'Just get the story, get it all, and don't give any excuses for not getting it all.'")*

Grady Hambrick

It was the third time in six years that someone had tried to rob Miguel Mora's jewelry story in the Northern Lights Shopping Center. This time, however, Mora disarmed the would-be robber and shot him.

We knew that much from the traffic over the police scanner. I went to the scene with general assignment reporter Graydon "Grady" Hambrick. The first day I met Grady in the newsroom, he had a Styrofoam coffee cup in one hand and a cigarette in the other. As we spoke, he flicked the ashes of his cigarette into his coffee, then continued to drink it. He watched me watch him in amazement, then said, "The ashes don't hurt anything; they settle to the bottom."

It was in the low twenties on the afternoon that we went to cover the jewelry store shooting and, as usual, it was taking the cops a long time to sort out the story. Of course, they were not in a big hurry because the wind-chill was not nearly as bad inside the jewelry store as it was in the parking lot. As the sun dropped, so did the temperature. While we waited for the cops to come out and give us an interview, Grady and I split up. I canvassed one side of the parking lot for witnesses and Grady covered the other. I was freezing. I never dressed warm enough. I wore cowboy boots, but they did not keep my feet any warmer than regular shoes, and I did not wear hats because they messed up my hair. I was always a little vain when it came to my hair.

After forty minutes of walking around, my feet and fingers now frozen numb, I could no longer see Grady. I called back to the newsroom, but no one had heard from him. He was not answering his two-way radio. The township chief of police came out and gave us some basic information. They had arrested thirty-seven-year-old William Littlejohn in connection with the robbery. The chief said that after Littlejohn pulled his gun, Mora attempted to set off the burglar alarm. Littlejohn jumped the counter and grabbed Mora by his necktie. In the scuffle that followed, Mora took Littlejohn's gun and shot him in the leg.

I was waiting for the police to clear out to get an interview with Mora when, several doors away, on Grady's side of the parking lot, I spotted the bar. Mystery solved. I went in and there he was, coat off, sitting at the bar with a beer, laughing and joking with the rest of the patrons—his new best buddies.

"Grady!" I felt as if I were scolding one of my kids. "I'm outside freezing my ass off and you're in here having a beer!"

"No. Well, yeah, I am, but I'm interviewing these guys, seeing if anyone saw anything."

I could feel my left eye starting to squint. "Grady, please!"

"Yeah, that was weak, wasn't it?" he said, tossing down the last of his beer. "Okay, let's go."

Bob Ruth

I loved working with Bob Ruth. Actually, if you got teamed up on a story with Bob, you just tried to hold on while he ran through the walls.

If the *Dispatch* staff had been a football team, Bob would have

Bob Ruth remains the most tenacious reporter I have ever known. If you teamed up with Bob on a story, you just tried to hold on while he ran through walls. (Courtesy of the *Columbus Dispatch*)

been our fullback. He approached news stories like a fullback hitting the line—relentless, head down, straight ahead, full steam. Years earlier, someone had given Bob the nickname "Chainsaw" for the way he pursued his stories. It fit. He was a bull in short-sleeves.

Bob was covering city hall on an interim basis for a period when I was on the police beat. We were walking back from lunch one day when Bob spotted Columbus Mayor Dana Rinehart walking up Gay Street toward us. Bob said, "Crap, it's the mayor. What can I ask him?" He started rapping his forehead with his knuckles. "Think, Bob, think. Oh, I got it." He looked at me and said, "I'll catch up with you later." As the mayor and his entourage neared us, Bob broke away and began following the mayor up the street, peppering him with questions. Bob never missed an opportunity.

Bob never took it personally that people hated him. In fact, he could not have cared less. He was grateful to the *Dispatch* for the opportunity to work as a reporter. I was sitting next to Bob when he was on the phone working on a story about a homicide. He was doing his "best buddy" routine, in which he pretended to be an understanding, sympathetic friend. I heard him say in a maudlin tone, "Oh, I know, it's tragic, just tragic."

I looked at Bob and rolled my eyes. This is a fact: If bodies had been stacked thirty-feet high in the middle of Broad Street, it would not have fazed Bob Ruth. I sometimes wondered how he pulled off that lame sympathetic friend routine; he must have sounded a lot more convincing on the other end of the telephone than he did when you were sitting next to him in the newsroom. But it worked.

I was sitting near Bob the day he was dogging Columbus Councilman Jerry Hammond about the closing of his jazz nightclub, The Major Chord. The club had opened in the Short North section of Columbus, just north of downtown, to great fanfare. Bob had written a series of stories that revealed that Hammond had financed much of the club by selling $10,000 limited partnerships to attorneys, developers, and other businessmen who regularly appeared before Hammond and city council on issues, such as zoning.

I assume that Hammond was already upset about having to shutter his club. Add to this the fact that he was a Democrat and already sensitive to what he considered to be negative publicity from the Republican *Dispatch*. On this day Bob was the object of his wrath.

He screamed at Bob, "You're a whore, Bob. You're a whore for John F. Wolfe [the paper's publisher]. I want to make something of myself, but you'll always be a whore." I knew these were Hammond's words because Bob was holding the phone a foot away from his ear and I could clearly hear every word. Bob looked at me and smiled, patiently listening to Hammond's tirade, which lasted several minutes. Then, when Hammond stopped to take a breath, Bob went right back to his questions. "So, Jerry, would you say your club failed because . . ."

Soon after Rinehart was elected and took office as mayor, one of his first acts was to call Jack Snyder, who was head of the municipal garage, and order him to call an all-hands meeting in the garage's main floor.

Snyder did as he was told, and at the appointed time Rinehart showed up in a golf cart. He pulled to the head of the throng, stood up on the golf cart and announced that Jack Snyder was no longer head of the municipal garage. Beginning immediately, the mayor said, his brother Paul, better known as "Skip," would be head of the municipal garage. I understand patronage and politics. I was more scalded by the classless way he did it than by what he had done, which was to replace a qualified manager with his brother, who had no such experience.

I also had a personal interest in the story. Jack Snyder was my father-in-law.

If a reporter ever tells you that getting revenge was never motivation for doing a story, he is lying. That was my only motivation in suggesting to Bob Ruth that he might want to take a look at the qualifications of the new municipal garage director and explore his plans for the future of the operation.

Bob cackled. He couldn't wait.

He came back to the newsroom laughing upon completing the interview. After spending quite a while with "Skippy," as the younger brother was known in the newsroom, Bob was winding down the interview as the two walked through the parking lot toward the younger Rinehart's car. Bob said the final dialogue of the interview was similar to this.

Bob: Now, Skip, where did you go to college?
Skip: Ohio State.
Bob: Okay, and what was your major?
Skip: Pre-med.
Bob: Whoa. Pre-med? Man, you're a lot smarter than me. I was lucky to get through journalism. I could have never majored in pre-med.
Skip: Oh, yeah. It's a tough major.
Bob: When did you graduate?
Skip: Oh, I didn't finish.
Bob: Really? So, you're a dropout?

I would have loved to have seen the expression on Skip's face. Knowing Bob, I am sure he had spent the previous two hours gushing and playing impressed, only to set the hook with the final question of the afternoon. It was at that point, no doubt, that Skip realized he was not going to be the recipient of a puff-piece feature.

Glen Cumberledge

Glen Cumberledge was a reporter's photographer. He was a wonderful asset because he could talk his way into any place, any situation. He was such a likable guy and he had a great gift for talking.

On the night that Jean Shrader was murdered in a downtown parking garage, police sealed off the garage while they conducted their investigation. After a couple of hours, they opened one elevator and allowed people to get their cars. To get out of the garage, drivers had to drive past the murder scene where detectives and the Crime Scene Search Unit were still working.

One of our reporters had a car in the garage, so we used that as a way of getting up to the fifth floor. Cumberledge accompanied the reporter to her car and as she was driving down and past the homicide scene, Cumberledge pulled out his camera and began snapping photos.

Of course, the cops were furious and started yelling at the reporter to stop. She did and Cumberledge was apologizing before the detectives could get to the passenger side window.

"I'm sorry, I'm sorry, I'm sorry," he said. "I didn't want to do that. My night city editor made me do it. I knew it was wrong; I knew we'd get in trouble. I'm really sorry." He held the camera up and opened the back. "Here, I'm sorry. Take the film. Here, it's out and it's ruined. I'm really, really sorry."

They confiscated the film, scowled, and let them go. When they got to the *Dispatch* parking lot, he took his other camera—the one that actually contained the photos of the murder scene—out from under the front seat.

He was a gem.

John Zeiger

John was our corporate attorney and made a nice living just keeping me out of jail. He defended me in four libel suits, all of which were thrown out of court on summary judgment. I was getting hit with lawsuits with such rapidity at one point that City Editor Bernie Karsko put a copy of a libel suit in my mailbox with a note that read:

Robin:
You did it again.
Drop a copy (of the suit) at Zeiger's Monday morning.
Bernie

Before John took over as the *Dispatch*'s attorney, the paper had a reputation for settling libel suits. Thus, the paper was always getting sued. In the nearly twenty years John has represented the *Dispatch,* the paper has not paid out a dime in libel suits.

John's biggest case concerning the *Dispatch*—from my perspective —was a battle with Fairfield County Sheriff Jim Peck, who sued us for $7 million after Ted Wendling and I wrote stories linking him to drug dealers and gamblers.

John spent hours practicing with me to take the deposition. "Only answer what you're asked" was an admonition I heard many times.

During the beginning of our deposition, the opposing attorney asked for the names and ages of my wife and children. John asked what that had to do with the case and when she could not supply a satisfactory answer, he said, "Mr. Yocum's wife and children are not at issue here. Don't answer the question."

The opposing attorney was a young woman and, I assume, felt that John was trying to bully her. An argument ensued in which John calmly asked, "Would you like to call the judge and see what he says?"

"Yes, I would," she responded.

It was a masterful bit of deception on John's part. The case had been assigned to a judge in Cuyahoga County, who had to leave a trial in his courtroom to take the call. John introduced himself, explained the situation, and said, "What do Mr. Yocum's wife and children have to do with it? I don't know, your honor, you'll have to ask her." He then handed the phone to the opposition attorney and said, "He wants to talk to you."

I'd never heard so many contrite "Yes, sirs," in one brief conversation.

John had baited her into calling, knowing it would place us in the better light with the judge. I did not have to give the names and ages of my wife and children.

When Ted and I began writing the stories, we were ordered to keep all our notes, since it was likely that the sheriff would file a lawsuit. Ordinarily, I pitched my notes as soon as I finished a story. I did this because I did not want to get subpoenaed on a case a year after a story had appeared and be forced to interpret my scrawl. In this case, John wanted us to keep the notes to demonstrate how much work had gone into the investigation.

I had a habit of taking notes on whatever scraps of paper were within reach, including the back of incident reports from the police station. When we turned in the notes, we copied both sides of the paper. Thus, Peck's attorneys spent hours trying to determine the value of the worthless incident reports.

When John deposed Sheriff Peck, the air conditioning was broken in the offices of Peck's attorneys. It was stifling in the room where he took the sheriff's deposition. Everyone in the room had their jackets off and ties loosened, except John. He looked the consummate professional, peppering the sheriff with question after probing question. He never smiled, never took a break. All I could think of was, "Man, am I glad he's on my team."

Peck's case against the *Dispatch* was dismissed by the court.

SEVEN
❑

The Cops

Dick Radick

RICHARD L. "DICK" RADICK WAS ONE OF MY FAVORITE COPS. When I began covering the cops in March 1981, Radick was working the afternoon shift in the Accident Investigation Squad, the police unit responsible for investigating traffic fatalities and hit-skip accidents.

Like Suzanne Cozad, Radick became my friend before he became a good source of information. I liked his easy-going manner. Radick loved life. He took his job seriously, but not himself, and he had a great sense of humor. (Some would argue that it was morbid, but humor is subjective. I enjoyed it.) Radick prided himself on his ability to get people to confess to their involvement in hit-skip accidents. In many cases, Radick knew who was responsible for committing a hit-skip but lacked the physical evidence or the witness needed for a conviction, and thus he set out to trick suspects into confessing.

Occasionally, he would use me to help out in his investigations. One of his favorite tricks was to seat a suspect and his lawyer across from his desk, then come get me out of the pressroom. I would walk into the office with Radick, frown at the suspect for a few seconds, then nod to Radick and say, "That's him." We would go out in the hall, where he would work to quit laughing, then go back in. More often than not, the attorney assumed, quite incorrectly, that I was an eyewitness to the hit-skip and was then ready to offer up a plea.

Other times Radick would type up totally bogus but extremely detailed and incriminating eyewitness accounts and leave them on his desk where the attorney could find them. He would excuse himself for a couple of minutes, giving the attorney time to read the documents and discuss the consequences of a hit-skip conviction with the client. Again, the defense suddenly became much more amenable to a plea bargain.

My favorite Radick trick, however, was the Accident Investigation Lie Detector Test. The "test" was administered only to suspects with IQs rivaling cement blocks, and who came in for questioning without an attorney. "If he comes in alone and he's got a cigarette in one hand and a Mountain Dew in the other, he's generally a prime candidate," Radick said.

After the suspect had denied his involvement, Radick would look over the file and say, "We've got some eyewitnesses that say it was you driving the car."

"It wasn't me, I swear."

"Let me ask you this. Would you be willing to take a polygraph exam?"

"A what?"

"A lie detector test. If you pass, you can leave. If you fail, you've got to cop to the hit-skip," he would offer.

He would then take the suspect across the room to the copy machine and have him place both hands on the side of the machine. He would then look into the suspect's eyes and say, "Now, you have to be perfectly still. Relax. Breathe steady. If you move we won't get an accurate reading. You understand that you don't have to do this, correct? You're under no legal obligation to take this test." He would get a nod from the suspect, then, in a deadly serious tone, ask, "Were you driving the brown pickup truck that hit a blue 1978 Ford at the intersection of Sullivant Avenue and Nashoba Avenue at 8:30 P.M. last Tuesday?"

"No. I never did."

Having preloaded the copy machine before the "polygraph test," Radick would then hit the copy button and out would spit a sheet of paper that stated, "You're lying."

"Damn. Okay, it was me."

"God, I love this job," he would say after tricking someone into a confession. "Here's a tip. Don't ever confess to anything. If some cop wants to charge you with spitting on the sidewalk and he saw you do it and you're standing there with slobber hanging from your chin, deny it. If it weren't for confessions, we'd never solve anything."

Radick also ran the Accident Investigation Squad death pool. For five dollars you could get into the pool and guess how many traffic fatalities there would be in the city during the year. Sgt. Larry Bigler, who ran the squad, found out that Radick had let me into the pool and ruled that no outsiders could play. "Bigler says you're out," Radick told me, handing me back the five-dollar bill.

"Keep it," I said. "He's going to change his mind."

"I don't think so."

I went back to the pressroom and typed up the lead to a potential story that read:

Accident Investigation Squad Sgt. Larry Bigler approved and oversaw a "death pool," in which officers under his command paid $5 to wager on the number of people who would lose their lives in traffic accidents in Columbus this year.

"Show him this and tell him it's the lead to the story I'm going to write if he doesn't let me back in the pool," I told Radick, handing him the paper.

Radick laughed aloud. He could not wait until the next day to give Bigler the paper, which he would do with a straight face, deadly serious. When I saw Radick the next afternoon, he said, simply "You're back in."

(Bigler was not one of my bigger fans, particularly after I wrote a brief about a run-in he had at a Columbus fire station. He had parked on the lot and later noticed a scratch on the driver's-side door of his Oldsmobile. He went into the fire house and accused firefighter Paul Wright, whose Cadillac was parked next to the Olds, of putting the scratch on the car. Wright told me that Bigler got "very belligerent. He was kind of hot, very rude and very unprofessional." Bigler then called out his accident investigators to examine the scratch. Sorry, they said, but the scratch hadn't come from Wright's Cadillac. Of course, Radick was the one who tipped me to the story.)

Although they both dealt with death, accident investigators were much different from homicide detectives. Homicide detectives marked off an area with their yellow crime scene tape and you did not dare cross the tape. Accident investigators were much looser and gave me the run of their accident scenes, occasionally asking me to help with measurements or to hold a flashlight beam on the face of the deceased while they shot a Polaroid.

"Hold this," Radick had said, handing me the light while he snapped on a pair of disposable rubber gloves, preparing to grab the corpse of a pedestrian who an hour earlier had lost a head-on collision with a sedan near Georgesville Road on the west side. The deceased had been crossing an unlit road, heading to a local carryout, when he stepped in front of the sedan. Radick searched the body for identification, then adjusted the corpse to get a clear photograph of the face. There was a puddle of blood on the asphalt from a gash in the back of the man's head. His face was largely unmarked, though his eyelids were slightly open and he still had the "Oh-shit, where-did-that-car-come-from" look on his face. The corpse reeked of alcohol.

"Looks like he was heading to the carryout to refuel," Radick said, aiming his Polaroid. "Keep the flashlight beam right on his face. Okay, buddy, smile," he said to the corpse, snapping the photo. He then walked over to a uniformed officer, gave him the name and address on the driver's license, and sent him off to notify relatives.

Radick was working the Sunday night that I was called out on my first traffic fatality. I had been dreading this, afraid of how I might react. The accident occurred May 17, 1981, in the westbound lanes of I-70, just east of the Route 33 split. Elvin King Jr. was driving while highly intoxicated and with his three kids in his yellow pickup truck. He was eastbound on I-70 when he crossed three lanes of traffic and the median and crashed head-on with another pickup truck with a camper on its back. The camper virtually disintegrated on impact and was strewn over several hundred yards. The pickup with the camper spun around and hit another westbound car head-on. King's pickup truck began flipping down the westbound lanes. Along with the debris from the camper, pieces of pickup truck and bodies littered the asphalt.

Nine people were injured and two were killed.

Two of King's children were taken to Children's Hospital in Columbus, a magnificent facility of which the medics said, "If you can get them to Children's alive, they'll make it." King and his eight-year-old daughter, Elita, were dead at the scene. Radick walked over to the smaller body with me. "You don't have to look at this one if you don't want to," he said. "It's pretty bad."

"I'm all right," I told him, and he peeled back the sheet. She was wearing a yellow-and-orange plaid dress and she had no face. It was gone. From an inch below her hairline down, it was nothing but red pulp. No eyes, nose, or mouth. I nodded and he covered her up.

We stepped over several mounds of debris until he stopped and pointed ahead to a pair of black skid marks. "He came left of center and hit the other truck right there," he said, pointing to a spot in the westbound lane. "Killed himself and the little girl."

"Where's his body?" I asked.

One side of Radick's upper lip curled. "You're standing on him."

"Christ, Radick," I yelled, jumping back. Technically, I was just standing on the sheet, though it was close enough to give me a jolt and him a chuckle. "You did that on purpose."

"Of course."

I covered the story as though it were a council meeting. I had always wondered if I would have nightmares from covering homicides or fatalities. I did not. Ultimately, the only thing that bothered me was the fact that it did not bother me. I assume that I had a surge of adrenaline pumping through me. But, like the cops, you cannot let it eat at you or you'll never be able to do your job. I often thought of the fact that to me it was a story that had to be covered. To the mother and wife of the people in the yellow pickup truck, it was a tragic, life-altering event. Somehow, we were both connected, but with far different perspectives. I would go home and eat a sandwich and drink a beer. She would go home and make plans to bury her husband and child.

Gary Petzinger

Gary Petzinger worked in the police Identification Bureau. He was a short, powerfully built man with an easygoing demeanor, unless you crossed him, which I did while covering the murder of Jean Shrader.

In the early 1980s, the *Dispatch* relied heavily on crime news to fill its pages. Bernie Karsko was running the night city desk. He was a former police reporter who demanded follow-up after follow-up on the big stories. And the Shrader homicide was a huge crime story. It had all the elements—a young and beautiful victim, a husband as the chief suspect, a witness who saw the body being dumped in the stairwell of a downtown garage. It was big. Thus, the pressure was on to come up with new stories each day.

The homicide detectives had asked Petzinger to check the parking ticket found in Jean Shrader's purse for fingerprints. He mentioned to me that the fingerprints on the ticket were not Jean's and intimated that they might be those of her husband. I tried to act as though I were unconcerned about the information, but once I left the Identification Bureau, I bolted for the Detective Bureau to try to get the information confirmed. I used the information as the basis for the next day's story.

The detectives on the Homicide Squad ran right back down to Gary and accused him of trying to jeopardize their investigation by leaking information.

He was waiting for me to stop by the Identification Bureau. He turned his back to me and said, "Come on. Come pull the knife out of my back."

I panicked and tried to deny what I had done, which infuriated him. I thought he was going to come up out of his skin. His lower jaw jutted out and his finger was in my face.

It was, in part, the nature of the beast. I was a reporter. It was a juicy tidbit. I couldn't ignore it.

I felt bad about getting Gary in trouble because I genuinely liked him. If it had happened again, would I still have tried to find a way to get it in the paper? You bet. I just would have been more careful to protect the source.

Jim Cottrill and the Black Sheep

The Juvenile Bureau—Juvie—was a great place to hang out and troll for stories. You didn't have to ask them for anything. They were a loose bunch and if you just sat and listened, you would get your ears full. The afternoon shift was headed by Sgt. Jim Cottrill, who at the time had registered the most kills in the Columbus Division of Police. Cottrill's last shooting was in, of all places, a donut shop parking lot. One of his officers did an imitation of him at the shooting. Holding up a finger like a gun, he would squeeze off a couple of imaginary rounds: "Blam, blam . . . yeah, gimmie a couple of those jelly filled donuts . . . blam, blam . . . a cream stick . . . blam, blam, blam . . . ooh, and one of those bear claws . . ."

"That's good. Have you ever shown him that imitation?" I asked the officer.

"No. I don't think he'd much appreciate it."

Cottrill loved being a cop. He loved guns and was a skilled knife maker. He started making the knives as a hobby and turned it into a cottage industry. One Monday, I asked him if he had watched a big football game over the weekend, at which he scoffed and said, "The Cottrill Family Credo is, 'If I can't eat it, fuck it, or shoot it, I'm not interested.'"

He also liked to say, "There is no law against stupidity . . . but there should be." He believed in the three-strikes-and-you're-out rule. In some states, the rule means if you get three felony convictions you spend life in prison. Cottrill believed that three felony convictions should earn you the death penalty. And he wasn't kidding.

Cottrill had inherited an oddball bunch of cops that the reporters called "Cottrill's Black Sheep" or "Cottrill's Raiders." The nickname "Raiders" was adopted after Cottrill began organizing summer raids of city parks looking for open container violations.

During one such sweep, "Cottrill's Raiders" came back with an extremely intoxicated fifteen-year-old. I was in the juvenile bureau when a couple of the officers helped the drunken teen to one of the holding cells. He was screaming and generally not happy. I watched all this from Cottrill's office. While I could see out into the bureau, Cottrill's view was blocked by his office wall.

After the boy was placed in the cell, he started yelling at Fred Reed, an African American officer and a former marine. The kid hurled every racial slur imaginable at Fred. He screamed, shook the bars of the cell door, drooled, and screamed some more. This went on for at least ten minutes, nonstop. Finally, Fred, who up to this point had shown amazing restraint, took a breath, smiled, and said in an eerily calm voice, "I think that young man needs to be re-strained for his own protection." He grabbed a couple of plastic ties that were used as disposable handcuffs and headed toward the holding cell.

Fred unlocked the cell door and the encounter that followed took, maybe, three seconds. Fred attempted to grab the boy and a very brief struggle ensued; the boy got dropped on his head and it split wide open. When the boy came walking out of the cell with Fred, his face was covered with blood. His stringy blond hair and T-shirt were soaked. I had never seen so much blood come from someone who was still conscious.

Cottrill, still blocked from seeing the ruckus, looked at me as he used a small knife to clean the spent tobacco from his pipe. "Well . . . ?" he asked.

I shook my head. "I don't think you're going to be particularly happy with this one."

Cottrill, who didn't rile easily, nodded and continued to work on his pipe, making no move to get up until a contrite Fred Reed appeared at the door. "Sergeant, we have a little problem here."

By this point, the boy had changed his tone. Not only did he appear suddenly sober, but he was everybody's friend. Perhaps it was the sight of a gallon of his own blood pouring out of his head that caused him to change his ways. I hung around until they got him cleaned up and a couple of the other officers took him over to the hospital to get him stitched up. After he was gone, I said, "That's enough excitement for one night. See you boys later." And left.

I am sure they were discussing whether I was going to write a story about the incident. Cottrill called me a while later and asked, "When you were up here tonight, did you see anything out of the ordinary?"

"Sarge, just about everything I see in the juvenile bureau is out of the ordinary. Was there anything particular I should have been looking for?"

"How about if I ask it this way: Is there anything I should be concerned about coming out in tomorrow's paper?"

"Nope. But if you hear of anything, give me a call."

I had no intention of writing about it. First of all, the kid eminently deserved it. Second, it truly looked like an accident. And third, writing a story would have done me more harm than good. The Juvenile Bureau was fertile ground for stories. If I had written an article, I would have had a good, page-one story for one day, but I would have burned an entire bureau worth of sources. By not writing it, I ingratiated myself with all the officers and preserved a rich source of stories.

Besides, the kid deserved it.

Merry Christmas

One Christmas, the overnight juvenile sergeant, Dan Wood, put up a nice Christmas tree. Cottrill's troops kept screwing with it— one day they took all the ornaments and hung them on a single limb, another day they adorned it with paper cutouts of male and female genitalia—until the lieutenant sent word down for the afternoon shift to leave the night shift's tree alone. So, the next day Cottrill's boys put up their own tree. It was hideous, a scrawny thing with bare and broken branches that they adorned with condoms, soda cans, the paper cutouts, broken ornaments and lights, automobile parts, and a garland of toilet paper.

They were putting on the finishing touches as I walked into the bureau. Officer Trafford Ream turned to me and said, "Oh, Tiny Tim, isn't it beautiful?"

Child Porn

Cottrill and his band believed Paul Christopher Kruger may have pitched several hundred pornographic photographs of young girls after he learned police were investigating him. This occurred, juvenile officers believed, after the former Columbus police auxiliary officer had been arrested for exposing himself to three elementary school girls.

Cottrill thought Kruger had pitched the material in a garbage bin behind a Kroger store. They isolated the section of the landfill where they believed it had been dumped, and Mike Berens, another *Dispatch* police reporter, and I found ourselves in knee-deep garbage at the county landfill with Cottrill and four of his officers, looking for kiddie porn.

We found no pornography during a two-hour search.

I ruined my boots.

Wanted—.38-caliber Service Revolver

Not long after I started on the police beat in May 1981, I walked into the Juvenile Bureau and saw hand-made wanted posters on the wall:

Wanted
.38-caliber Service Revolver
Like New, Hardly Used

Juvenile Officer John Keene had been on special duty at a Huntington National Bank on North High Street. Police had received a tip that the bank was going to be robbed, and so the bank paid for a special duty officer. Keene was reading a newspaper when two robbers slipped in, took his revolver from him, and then robbed the bank.

He was consequently subjected to an inordinate amount of grief from his fellow juvenile officers.

Sheriff Harry

Franklin County Sheriff Harry Berkemer lived on Chestershire Road, just a short drive from my home on the west side. If I saw Harry outside, I would always stop and chat. I tried to call or personally visit the law officers I covered at times when I wasn't looking for a story. This helped establish a relationship so that the next time they were up to their ass in alligators and I showed up, it was not such a major issue with them.

Plus, I liked the Berkemers—Harry and his wife Grace. Harry was soft-spoken and pretty easygoing. Grace, however, was an absolute pistol—loud and proud. She liked me, too, though she never cut me an inch of slack for being a newspaper reporter. Every time she saw me coming she would groan, "Oh God, everyone be quiet, here comes that newspaper reporter again." Then she'd offer me an iced tea. She made great iced tea.

Harry was a Republican and had been elected sheriff without the nomination of the party. This made him less beholden to his political allies and it made Mrs. Berkemer particularly defensive of her husband's accomplishments, particularly when he was considering retirement and the other sheriff wannabes were lining up for his job, one of whom was the future sheriff, Earl Smith. I was talking to Harry about his possible successor in the living room of his home when Mrs. Berkemer overheard the conversation from another room and yelled, "You tell that goddamn Earl Smith that he can kiss my ass."

Harry looked at me and quietly said, "Don't tell him that."

"I won't."

I also sat in the same living room with Sheriff Berkemer after the death of one of his officers—Lt. Sharon Moore.

Sharon had been the first female in the sheriff's department promoted to the rank of lieutenant and had been the first-shift supervisor at the county jail. From a reporter's perspective, she had been great to work with. She was pleasant and always returned my phone calls.

Sharon died twenty-four days after being shot in the head by her former husband.

On the morning of April 11, 1983, Sharon and her husband, Joseph, a Franklin County sheriff's deputy, began driving to work from their Licking County home. No one was sure where the chase began, but at some point, Sharon's former husband, William J. Bryant, began chasing the Moores and firing at them with a .45-caliber handgun.

Injured by the gunfire, Joseph pulled into a parking lot in eastern Franklin County, and a gun battle ensued. Joseph was shot and killed. Sharon was hit in the head and paralyzed from the neck down. Bryant then shot and killed himself.

For more than three weeks, Sharon remained conscious, alert and able to speak. There was, however, no will to live. Harry spoke about his lieutenant with a combination of sorrow and relief. "I believe she simply willed herself to die," he said. "In her mind, I'm sure she wanted something to happen. She was not the type of person who would want to live like that."

Hogtied

"Want to see something funny?" the narcotics officer asked.

"Always."

"Okay," he said, "but you can't write about it."

I agreed and we walked into the alley behind the police station. He opened up the back of the unmarked police van. On the floor was a drug dealer they had just arrested. He was rocking on his belly, both feet and both hands hogtied behind his back with plastic ties. He had a gag in his mouth, held in place by duct tape that had been wrapped completely around his head. He was trying to scream through the gag.

"What's he saying?" I asked.

"Beats me," the officer said. "I can't understand a word he's saying with that gag stuffed in his mouth."

"Am I to assume that this gentleman was being somewhat less than cooperative about being arrested?"

The narc nodded. "You know, some guys just don't want to get with the program." He shut the door to the van. "That asshole tried to spit on me. So, we tied him up and I duct-taped his hair and moustache, then on the drive down, we hit every pothole we could find, locked up the brakes a couple of times, swerved all over the place. He was like a pinball back there."

I could still hear the man's muffled attempts to yell. "It doesn't seem to have changed his attitude any."

The narc smiled. "No, not yet. But I'm betting that ripping that duct tape off his moustache settles his ass down."

Heisman Trophy

The guys in the police Identification Bureau liked to pull out a photo of a former Ohio State football star, beaten purple and black and nearly beyond recognition, and play "Name the Heisman Trophy winner in this photo."

It was the police mug shot of a former Buckeye who had gotten pulled over for drunken driving. Apparently, he mistakenly equated the Heisman Trophy with a Get-out-of-Jail-Free card. Without the protection of a helmet, shoulder pads, or offensive line, he confronted the cops, who carried nightsticks and Mace and who were not overly impressed with his postseason collegiate awards.

Randy Walker

Despite the fact that he will spend the rest of his life in a wheelchair, Randy Walker has a wonderfully positive outlook on life. I am sure that in the nearly thirty years of his confinement he has had his dark moments—he was, after all, cheated out of a lot—but you would never know it from talking to him.

Walker is at the top of my most-admired list. He wore the badge known at the Columbus Division of Police as the "Four Aces"—No. 1111—which is given to the rare police recruit who is the academy class president and orator, and is first in the class in academics and shooting. Anyone who knew Randy Walker as a cadet or as a young officer would have told you that he was destined to someday be the Columbus chief of police.

That was until July 23, 1975.

He had been on the department just over a year when he and his partner, Phillip Turner, spotted two men arguing outside a carryout. One of the men was Ronald Bennett. The other was Nelson Lewis Jr., who had recently been paroled from a 1960 murder conviction

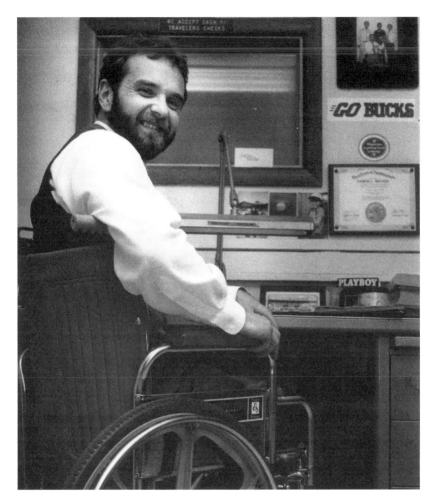

Randy Walker is a hell of a man. Paralyzed during a police shootout, he trained to be a polygraph expert. Randy maintains an incredibly positive attitude and asks for no pity. (Courtesy of the *Columbus Dispatch*)

in Cleveland. As Walker and Turner pulled up in the car, Lewis shot Bennett. A gun battle ensued between Lewis and the officers. One of Lewis's shots hit Walker under the armpit, slipping through a slit in his bulletproof vest, which protected his back and chest.

The bullet dropped him to the pavement and left him paralyzed from the chest down.

He described getting shot and the aftermath for a story I did for the *Dispatch*'s Sunday magazine, *Capitol:* "It felt like a log was rolling down my body, ironing the feeling right out. I couldn't move. I felt real helpless, and I knew the fight was over. The doctor told everyone the night I got shot that I would walk again, but with braces. Well, my idea of walking and his idea of walking are two different things. I took those braces head-on. I worked for hours and hours with those things. If there was any way possible I could have walked, I would have. I'm no quitter, but I'm a realist. When you're lying in a hospital bed with your eyes closed and eight doctors are standing around jabbing you with needles and you're supposed to tell them where they're jabbing you and you can't feel anything . . ."

His voice trailed off and he shrugged.

Although Walker could not continue as a police officer, the City of Columbus sent him to the Backster School of Lie Detection in San Diego. Since being forced to give up his badge, Walker has been the Division of Police's foremost polygraphist. Although he is a civilian employee, everyone looks at Randy Walker as a cop. He has solved countless crimes with his interrogation skills.

The crown jewel of his work was solving the Staci Weinstein murder. Walker took a case that every other investigator believed could not be solved and sent a Florida man to life in prison for the rape and murder of the ten-year-old Dade County girl.

Staci Weinstein had been murdered in October 1982. She was an honor student who had stayed home from school for the day because she was sick. She was found in her blood-soaked bed, pistol-whipped and shot in the head and chest.

One of the men Dade County authorities believed to be a witness in the case was Eddie Wasko, a handsome, clean-cut man and a former high school football star who had grown up in Youngstown, Ohio. He had been working for a carpet-cleaning company in Dade County at the time of Staci's murder.

After Staci's murder, Wasko left Dade County and moved to Columbus, where he continued to work for the carpet-cleaning company. Detectives from Florida flew to Columbus to interview Wasko in connection with the case. Wasko was not considered a suspect in the murder. In fact, he had reportedly passed a polygraph exam in Florida. Police wanted Wasko as a potential witness against co-worker John Pierson, who they believed was responsible for the murder. They were prepared to offer Wasko full immunity in exchange for his testimony against Pierson.

When they got to Columbus, the Florida detectives asked Walker to run a polygraph exam on Wasko, who had agreed to take another test. They simply wanted to verify his story for the Florida prosecutor, who would use it to charge Pierson.

Shortly after he began questioning him, Walker suspected that Wasko might have been involved. Wasko, Walker thought, simply knew too much about the girl's murder. "Originally, all he said he knew was that Pierson came back to the truck looking disheveled," Walker said. "But, when he described to me what that little girl was wearing, I knew that he knew more than he was saying. Eddie told me, 'the lady at the mailbox was wearing pink shorts and a sky blue top.' He was referring to the ten-year-old as a grown woman, which is typical pedophile behavior. Then, he told me that he did have a gun—and I knew it was the same kind used to kill the little girl—and that it was in his gym bag in the truck. Now, things were starting to fall into place."

Walker also read the results of the polygraph that Wasko had taken in Dade County and believed the Florida polygraphist had misread the test results. "This guy's lying. He knows more than he's telling you," Walker told Dade County detective Jim Ratcliff.

Ratcliff said he was skeptical of Walker's theory. "We thought Randy was really off base."

Part of Walker's investigative technique is to question suspects first without the polygraph machine. He is such a good interrogator and acute listener that he can often extract information from suspects without the machine. He began questioning Wasko on a Friday afternoon. After twelve hours, he said in a disgusted tone, "Eddie, you're not telling me the truth. Why don't you get up and get out of here."

By this time, Wasko had apparently begun to feel that he and the affable Walker were friends. When Walker told him to get out, Wasko replied, "No, I want to stay and talk to you about this. Can I come back tomorrow? I'm really sorry I lied to you today. I lied about everything. I want to come back and straighten this out."

Walker agreed and Wasko returned about noon the following day. Nine hours later, an exhausted Walker worked false tears down his face and pleaded with Wasko. "Eddie, Eddie, I really feel sorry for you. Let me help."

Wasko began to cry and the next words out of his mouth, in Walker's words, "about knocked me out of my wheelchair."

"I knew this night was going to come. She was beaten bad, Rand. She was beaten really bad. I saw her gasping. Then she took her last breath and died. I hit her so hard; I had to shoot her."

It was, Walker said, "the first time I ever saw the devil."

"It's hard to describe to someone, but you look in their eyes and you actually see the devil. If you talk to people who do a lot of interrogations, they'll tell you about 'seeing the devil.' This was the first time it ever happened to me. It's a different look; once it happens, you're never looking at the same person again. There's a transformation in how they appear. They know you've figured them out and, that quick, their entire appearance changes. It's mind-boggling.

"What got Eddie in the jackpot was the fact that he was such a narcissist. He was so narcissistic that he agreed to take the polygraph because he thought he could convince us, once and for all, that he wasn't involved."

The assistant state attorney in Florida who prosecuted the case, David Waksman, said, "Randy Walker's the greatest thing since sliced bread. Believe me, our detectives are good, but they were ready to give up. They had questioned Wasko for two days, and all they got out of him was, 'I don't know nothin'.' Randy brought fake tears to his eyes and showed Wasko he was concerned. He's some cop."

Walker has a framed photograph of himself and Wasko posing with an empty pizza box. He had the photo taken so defense attorneys could never say that Wasko's confession was taken under duress.

"I said, 'Eddie, we've spent all this time together, let's get a photo of us all together'. Now, here's what a narcissist he was. Before he got his picture taken, he turned and looked into the two-way mirror and primped his hair. Here's a guy who two hours later is going to be on an airplane and he'll never see anything outside of a prison for the rest of his life, and he's worried about how he looks."

Wasko was convicted and given the death sentence. The sentence was later reduced to life in prison.

Walker once allowed me to watch one of his interrogations through a two-way mirror. He was questioning a taxi driver who claimed to have been robbed of hundreds of dollars. The robbery wasn't in question. The insurance company, however, was questioning the amount of money that the cabbie claimed he had lost. Walker has a disarming manner. He offered the cabbie a stick of chewing gum and calmly explained how the polygraph operates. He is more than a polygraphist. At heart, he is still a cop. The polygraph is simply a tool. Walker is still working the cases, and in many instances he solicits a confession before he ever hooks up the polygraph.

"Do you think people confess because they feel sorry for you?" I asked.

He shrugged. "Hey, if they want to confess because I'm in a wheelchair, that's fine with me."

After giving the polygraph exam to the cabbie, Randy looked at the paper output of the polygraph and asked, "Do you really think you had that much money when you got robbed?"

The cabbie said, "It was just an estimate. I didn't know for sure."

"Do you think it might have been closer to $60?"

"Maybe." He shrugged. "Probably."

Walker is still with the Columbus Division of Police. He conducts polygraphs and still talks to recruits about the dedication required to become a police officer. To do so, he relates this story:

On the night he was shot, Walker and his partner were credited with saving the life of Ronald Bennett. For his efforts, Walker received the Columbus Division of Police Medal of Valor. Exactly one month after he was shot, one of Walker's nurses turned on the television in his hospital room. Through the haze of his pain medication, Walker saw his image on the news. He turned his attention to the story, which was about Ronald Bennett. Earlier that day, Bennett had been fleeing sheriff's deputies with a car full of stolen goods when he crashed and died.

"Isn't that bizarre?" he says. "I tell the recruits, you have to protect them all. You can't pick out the ones you want to protect. I end up paralyzed trying to save this guy's life and he gets himself killed before I can get out of the hospital. It's comical. If that isn't the summation of law enforcement, I don't know what is. And the message is, 'If you take it personally, you'll never be successful.' "

EIGHT
❑

The Dead and Missing . . . or Not

The Late Mrs. Wilburn . . . or Not

THE ONLY WAY ROBERTA G. WILBURN FIGURED SHE COULD escape an investigation for insurance fraud was by death. So, she died. At least, according to the paid obituary in the June 17, 1983, *Dispatch,* which stated tersely that Wilburn died June 12 in Sarasota, Florida.

I became familiar with the sixty-one-year-old Wilburn in March 1984 after she was indicted on twenty counts of theft and forgery. The phony obituary, one insurance investigator said, was a lame attempt to throw insurance investigators off the trail.

"I think she knew there was an investigation going on and she thought maybe this would cool it off." Keeping things in the family, Wilburn's two daughters also were indicted for theft and forgery. The indictments against all four women stated that they "faked injuries or illnesses and then made compensation claims for lost work."

"She's prolific at staging insurance frauds. This is the way she makes her living," said an investigator. "I've got a folder on her a

Roberta G. Wilburn died. Or, maybe she didn't. Wilburn took out a phony obituary in the *Columbus Dispatch* in an attempt to get insurance fraud investigators off her trail. (Courtesy of the *Columbus Dispatch*)

foot thick." Over the years, the county prosecutor said, Wilburn had tried numerous approaches to this racket: she claimed she had found a cockroach in her food and become ill; she got sick while eating meatloaf; she staged a fake fall while viewing a home for sale; she cut her hand in a restroom and sued for lost work; and she claimed she had burned her mouth on mints.

Other Scams

On several occasions while on the police beat, I went to cover house fires and found the home engulfed by flames. As I interviewed neighbors, they told me that the homeowners were either on vacation or out of town. How horrible, I thought, that they would return to find their homes gone. In reality, I later learned, most of the homes were torched by their "vacationing" owners. An insurance investigator said most home arsons are set by owners who have gotten in over their heads financially and torched the homes for the insurance money. Generally, he said, they would find clues of the arson and discover the homeowners could not prove that they were actually vacationing in Myrtle Beach. Also, the burned home would always be devoid of photographs, trophies and other personal treasures. Personal items are one of the first things an arson investigator looks for.

This same arson investigator said that if I ever wanted to burn down my house without getting caught, do this: "Have a party. Invite a lot of people. Have a lot of alcohol. After everyone has left, dump some ashtrays in the trash. Put the trashcan near something flammable, like paneling or in the pantry. Set the trash on fire until you set one of the walls on fire. Go back to your bedroom and wait until the fire really gets going. Then bust out a window and climb out. By the time you get to the neighbors to call the fire department, it'll be too late to save the house. No one will question you because you were in the house when the fire started. Oh, and don't go back to your bedroom and fall asleep."

"That would be bad," I said.

"That would be very bad."

"You've given this a lot of thought."

He shrugged. "It's what I do."

Along these same lines, in the early eighties I got duped into doing a story by a man in a Columbus suburb who claimed to have seen Bigfoot on his wooded property. I had been doing stories about Bigfoot sightings throughout central Ohio. He took me out back through the weeds and showed me an area where the weeds had been stomped down. The landowner theorized it was where the beast had been sleeping.

I wrote the story and the next day received a phone call from a banker who informed me that the man who claimed to have spotted the elusive Bigfoot was about to lose his home in a bank repossession. He was trying to stave off would-be buyers by claiming that Bigfoot was living on the property.

I got duped, and I got a colossal case of poison ivy, to boot.

After writing the series of stories about reported Bigfoot sightings in central Ohio, I became the *Dispatch*'s resident expert. The other reporters were grateful for this, because it meant I became a clearinghouse for anyone calling about Bigfoot, Martians, the Loch Ness monster, ghosts, or any other unexplainable phenomena. Actually, I enjoyed these stories simply because they were fun. The downside, however, was that there existed a loosely aligned, international network of Bigfoot hunters who swapped newspaper stories. (This was before the advent of the Internet.) Suddenly, my name was in the Rolodex of every Bigfoot fanatic in North America, all of whom felt duty bound to call and tell me about their personal contact with Bigfoot.

There were two basic theories about the central Ohio Bigfoot sightings. One was that Bigfoot—possibly a pack of Bigfeet—were migrating through central Ohio on their way to the denser forests of West Virginia or Virginia. The second theory was that Bigfoot was an extraterrestrial. (The humorous part to the competing theories was that each side thought the other side was completely daft. "Oh, right, Bigfoot is an extraterrestrial. That's the most ridiculous thing I've ever heard," a migration theorist would say. And the UFO proponent would counter, "Do they really believe it's a creature from earth? That's just so sad.")

One man in Columbus, who subscribed to the migration theory and who had spent years tracking Bigfoot, said he would shoot and kill Bigfoot at the first sighting, as it seemed that was the only way to prove the creature existed.

After the story about the hunter ran, I was deluged with telephone calls from angry defenders of Bigfoot, who did not want the creature killed. "He's a peaceful creature. How could anyone shoot him?" one woman said. "This man has to be stopped."

I wanted to engage her in a discussion about how he could shoot an imaginary creature, but I learned early on that there is no reasoning with Bigfoot believers.

One Saturday I received a 5 A.M. telephone call from the *Dispatch* operator. He had a man on the line who said he desperately needed to talk to me about Bigfoot. "I'm sorry to call at this hour, but he says it's an emergency," the operator said. I gave the operator permission to give the caller my home phone number.

Big mistake.

The phone rang a minute later. The caller was a UFO buff, and a Bigfoot-as-ET theorist, who wanted me to come to a 7 A.M. breakfast meeting of his UFO research group.

"Why would I want to come to this meeting?" I asked.

"Well, you've been writing the Bigfoot stories."

"Yeah. So?"

"Bigfoot's an alien, you know?"

This was my introduction to the theory. "Afraid I didn't know that. So, what you're saying is, Chewbacca from Star Wars wasn't really a Wookie, he was a Bigfoot."

I laughed at my own humor. Frankly, I thought it was a quick and funny line for just having been awakened at 5 A.M. on Saturday. He failed to see the humor.

"Now you're just talking nonsense," he admonished me.

Right. *I'm talking nonsense.*

"Okay, if Bigfoot's an alien, what's he doing wandering around Columbus?"

"Conducting research, we suspect. We're going to discuss all this at the meeting. We'd love to have you attend. It might be of great interest to your readers."

"I'm not coming to a UFO meeting at 7 A.M. on Saturday. Call me next week."

"There are going to be a lot of people at this meeting—lawyers, teachers. It's going to be very interesting."

"I'm sure it will be. Take good notes and call me at work."

Kidnapped . . . or Not

On May 17, 1982, police put out an all-points bulletin for a fifteen-year-old girl who had disappeared while jogging just a few hours earlier. This was highly unusual. I walked up to the juvenile squad and asked why the fuss. Unless there was direct evidence—like a witness—that she had been abducted, a missing teen did not usually warrant this kind of attention. I was informed that the father of the girl was a friend of Mayor Tom Moody. The father had called the mayor's office, which had called the chief, who had called the juvenile squad and ordered the bulletin and the search.

It occurred too late to get anything in that afternoon's paper. And, from the roll-of-the-eyes look I was getting from detectives, I could tell they were not overly concerned. However, it soon became a feeding frenzy for radio and television news, which gave the story top play.

When I arrived at work the next morning, our overnight reporter, Mike Norman, was furiously working at his computer. "They found the missing girl," he said.

"Outstanding," I said. "What happened?"

"She was kidnapped. Wild story. These two guys kidnapped her, had her gagged and blindfolded most of the day, threatened to kill her, made her sell drugs."

"How'd the cops find her?"

Mike stopped typing and turned toward me. "They didn't. She escaped."

"No kidding? How?"

"The guys who kidnapped her fell asleep in the car up along Route 23 in Worthington. After they were asleep, she got out of the car and ran to a friend's house."

"So, you're telling me that these guys decide to kidnap a fifteen-year-old girl, do it in broad daylight and no one sees it happen. They keep her blindfolded and gagged all day, make her sell drugs, threaten to kill her, then, with their kidnap victim in the car, they pull off the side of one of the busiest roads in Ohio to take a nap? And, amazingly enough, they decide to take their nap within walking distance of her friend's house? Bullshit. She's making that up. She was out with her boyfriend all day and when she saw that her name was being plastered all over the radio and television, she panicked and made up that story. Think about it. It even sounds like something a panicky fifteen-year-old would come up with."

Mike did not want to believe it. He was sitting on a front-page story and I was trying to piss all over it. It was not Mike's fault. He had dogged the story all night, which included getting an interview with the girl and her parents. When a reporter is tracking a big story, the adrenaline starts pumping, and the intense focus on getting the interview and writing the story makes it difficult to stand back and look at the big picture, even if the girl's story sounded like something she had seen on a made-for-television movie.

She claimed that two masked men—in daylight—ran up to her, grabbed her and threw her in the backseat of the car. The girl said, "I struggled, but they gagged me and blindfolded me so I couldn't scream." They threatened several times to kill her, she claimed, putting a handgun to her head. She added, "I think they wanted me to deal drugs. The one time they told me to get out of the car and start walking and that I would see a man in green to make a delivery. . . . The guy never came."

Of her purported 5 A.M. escape, she said, "The one guy was high on drugs and I was in the front seat. We were parked off the side of the road, so I just opened the door and the light went on, but I ran across Route 23 and hid."

I argued against giving the story big play, which did not ingratiate me with Mike. We played it at the top of the front page, along with a joyous reunion photo of the girl, her mom, and their dog.

One police source told me that the girl had an older boyfriend of whom her parents did not approve. The source said the girl was so vague in her answers that detectives did not have enough information to conduct an investigation. I followed up on the story later that day, interviewing Detective David C. Foote, who was heading the investigation. Foote said she had described her abductors as being one black male and one white male, but she was unable to give detailed descriptions, despite spending nearly twenty-four hours with them. Foote said they were going to ask the girl to take a polygraph test. I called the girl's father, who said he had no objection to that.

She was scheduled to take the test at 1 P.M. the next afternoon. Of course, she did not show up. When I went to the house for an explanation, the door was shut in my face, which caused me to smile because it confirmed my suspicions. I went back to the office and called the house and was told not to call again.

The Amazing Disappearing Spiderwoman

The Spiderwoman had disappeared. Her web was empty.

I received a call on a Sunday afternoon from a frantic man who said his wife had disappeared and he believed she had met with foul play.

The missing woman, he said, had secured a job portraying the Spiderwoman at the Ohio State Fair. Although I did not personally witness this feat of modern science, I understand that it works something like this: You give the nice woman in the booth a couple of bucks and she lets you inside the Spiderwoman's tent. The Spiderwoman appears in all her beautiful human splendor. Then, lights flash, smoke poofs, and this lovely woman transforms into a terrifying giant arachnid.

Somehow, the Spiderwoman had slipped her web. I interviewed her husband on the front porch of his home, which was within walking distance of the fairgrounds. The husband said he had a premonition that she was dead and lying under a pile of hay or straw at the fairgrounds.

"Are you sure she couldn't have just left for one reason or another?"

He was sure. She would never leave him. Never. Impossible. She loved him and only him. It was not possible.

Grudgingly, the police took a missing person report.

The Spiderwoman was located a few days later, spinning an evil web with her new boyfriend in Washington Court House, Ohio.

NINE

❑

On the Road; in the Road

Call a Cab

THE ROLE OF THE REPORTER IS THAT OF OBJECTIVE OBSERVER. There are times, however, when objectivity is impossible. You look at a situation and try to put a cheery spin on the story, all the while realizing there is a potential train wreck in the future.

Thus was the case with Margaret Chichka.

I had gotten a tip to call Margaret, a recently widowed seventy-three-year-old who had just obtained her first driver's license after failing the driving test the first four times she took it. It was to be a story of a woman's persistence to get her license, a story of a woman's will to move on after her husband's death and in the face of considerable odds.

I did the initial interview over the phone. Margaret was pleasant and giddy over the excitement of having a driver's license. She had spent more than four hundred dollars for private driving lessons. Margaret said she flunked her first driving test because she had a hard time turning right and she kept going left of center. She flunked test number two for speeding. She bombed test number three for making left turns too sharp and again going left of center. She flunked test number four right out of the blocks, failing to yield the right-of-way. After failing four times, state law required Margaret to take the written test again. She passed it, then passed the driving and parking tests on the fifth try.

Photographer Amy Sancetta and I went to Margaret's south-side home to get a photo. There, it became obvious to me why she had had such a difficult time getting her license. She was looking at the world through the thickest pair of Coke-bottle glasses I'd ever seen. Her left eye was magnified through the lenses to about twice its normal size. She posed for the photo in front of her car—a sedan so large that it would leave little room for driving errors. This was the aforementioned train wreck. Margaret was a nice lady, but she had absolutely no business behind the wheel of a car.

I felt like going door-to-door in the neighborhood and warning all the parents to keep their kids off the street.

Speaking of Not Being Able to See

In March 1985, eighty-eight-year-old Marie Quaintance found some letters lying in her front yard. Marie suffered from glaucoma, had had cataracts removed from both eyes, and wore glasses similar to those of the aforementioned Margaret. Marie decided to walk across Frebis Avenue to have a neighbor read the names on the letters because her eyes were not good enough to read the small print.

Unfortunately, they were not good enough to see the eastbound car on Frebis Avenue, either.

Fortunately, the driver saw Marie and hit the brakes. The car slid sideways and hit Marie, knocking her to the pavement. She was taken to the hospital and given a few stitches and was treated for a fractured shoulder and four broken ribs. She was pretty fortunate, I thought, for an eighty-eight-year-old who had just been hit by a car.

The kicker, however, was that while she was lying on the examining table at the Mercy Hospital emergency room, a Columbus police officer came in and gave her a ten-dollar ticket for jaywalking.

"I ain't going to pay it," she said.

Good for you, Marie.

Drunken Biking

Charles O'Brien was surely not happy with the way I handled the interview. I did not mean to be unprofessional, but could not stop laughing.

O'Brien had called the newsroom to complain to a reporter that police had impounded his bicycle because he had been driving (pedaling?) in a reckless manner. It was a slow afternoon and it seemed as if it might be a fun story.

When I got to his Nashoba Avenue home, O'Brien showed me the ticket he had received for reckless operation of a bicycle. A police officer had stopped O'Brien the previous day. His ticket stated that at 11:45 P.M., O'Brien, "while intoxicated, was zigzagging in the road, riding without holding the handlebars and riding without a light."

He went on, telling how the cops had stopped him and asked, "Where's your light?" When O'Brien explained that he had no light, they invited him to have a seat in the back of the cruiser. "I knew where I was going then."

The police called for a wrecker, loaded up the bicycle, and sent it to the impound lot. Meanwhile, the cruiser took O'Brien to jail.

I examined the ticket and said, "You didn't tell me you were drunk."

"I had a few beers, but not enough to get drunk."

"Oh."

After sitting in the jail until 4:30 A.M., O'Brien was released with his ticket. Police said they would have given him a ticket for drunken driving while operating a bicycle, but after spending a few hours researching the issue, they realized there was no such charge. The fine was still going to be $150, plus court costs.

And he could not even get the bicycle out of the impound lot because it was not his. He had borrowed it from a buddy, who O'Brien said was not pleased that his bike was in police custody.

Hot Rod Harry

In June 1981, Harry Johnson led police on a wild chase through the "Bottoms," a mostly residential area just west of downtown. Johnson, it was reported to me, was a former stock car driver. It showed. Before he was captured, a small armada of cop cars chased him for about seven minutes—an eternity for a high-speed chase through the narrow streets of a residential area.

The chase began in the parking lot of the Spaghetti Warehouse. Police had been called to the lot to investigate a report that someone had sideswiped a car and left the scene. As an officer was taking a report, Johnson drove back through the lot and was identified as the driver of the hit-skip car.

The chase was on.

Johnson hit six parked cars and, when it looked like police had him pinned inside a fenced-in area, he rammed a police cruiser. Police finally caught him after he hit an embankment at the corner of Town Street and Dakota Avenue. He was taken to Mt. Carmel Hospital to be treated for a cut on the forehead, which he no doubt received when police dragged him out of the car and slammed him over the hood.

A couple of the neighbors were yelling at me to report the rough treatment Johnson was receiving from the police. I did not. Considering the damage he had caused, and that a four-year-old boy was on his way to the hospital after a chunk of flying debris from John-son's car had hit him just below the left eye, I thought he was get-ting off easy.

Johnson set a new county record for most moving violations from a single incident—twenty-five. (The old record was twenty-one.) He was charged with eight counts of leaving the scene of an accident, drunken driving (big surprise), four counts of failure to control, five counts of driving the wrong-way on a one-way street, two counts of reckless operation, fleeing police, failure to yield, im-proper right turn, driving while under revocation, and driving with-out a license.

The next morning, when deputies went to fetch him for his court appearance, Johnson told them that he had an active case of tuberculosis. Franklin County Municipal Judge George Smith had to move his court to the first floor of the jail for the hearing because deputies refused to get near Johnson. After a conference with his public defender, who also kept his distance from his client, John-son agreed to plead guilty to eight counts of leaving the scene of an accident.

Tickets

Dick Radick stuck his head in at the door of the pressroom in December 1981 and said, "You need to go over to the traffic bureau and take a look at the Sad Sack over there. They caught him with hundreds of dollars in unpaid parking tickets and he and his dad are trying to get his car out of hock."

Richard A. Basham looked like Edgar Allan Poe, but with longer hair. He was thin, twenty-nine, unemployed, and living at the downtown YMCA. He and his father were in the middle of an hours-long ordeal to get the younger Basham's car—it actually was registered to the father—out of the police impound lot. He had racked up fifty-six unpaid parking tickets totaling $560.

It was Basham's second go-round with the Traffic Bureau in 1981. Basham had accumulated twenty unpaid parking tickets—totaling $375—when the police had impounded his car in February. After spending a night in jail, Basham promised to pay $100 every three months until the fine was paid off. Over the next eleven months, Basham paid just $70, while accumulating an additional $560 in fines; his car had been towed again. To get the car out of the impound lot, a form had to be filled out in triplicate for each of the fifty-six violations.

While Bashman explained all this to me, his father was doing a slow burn in the corner. It struck me that this probably was not the first time dad had bailed junior out. "We'll never get out of here if you don't quit talking and get to work," his dad growled.

Bashman regularly parked his car in one-hour parking spots near the YMCA, but did not pump the meter, explaining, "The most they can give you is one ticket. But, then I just forget to pay them."

His dad lit a cigarette and shook his head. "He's a slow learner, isn't he?"

A Lost Baby

One of my most memorable traffic accidents occurred on a Sunday night at the intersection of two country roads north of the city. A woman making a run to the grocery store ran a stop sign and got T-boned on the driver's side. Medics cut her out of the car and she was taken by LifeFlight to Grant Hospital. She was busted up, but she would make it.

I was talking to the police and medics while they cleaned up the intersection and waited for the tow trucks to arrive. That was when the woman's sister pulled up in a car, frantic.

"Relax. She took a pretty good jolt, but she's going to make it," one of the medics assured the sister.

"What about the baby?"

"What baby?"

"The baby. Her baby. The baby was in the car, too."

In the rush to free the unconscious woman, who was the only one in the front seat and the only human visible in the car, no one had looked for a backseat passenger. They assumed she had been alone. In the compressed backseat, the medics now saw the twisted piece of a child safety seat. As they ran for the saw and Jaws of Life, there was a sickening silence among the firefighters. These were tough, hardened men. But it is one thing to cut an adult from a car. It is totally different to root around for the remains of an infant. No one wanted to start back in; no one wanted to be the one to find a baby.

Blessedly, there was not one to be found.

Unbeknownst to her sister, the infant's mother had dropped off the child with a relative while she ran her errand. Only the carseat remained.

Most of the firefighters walked away in silence. One leaned against the wreckage and said, "Thank you, Jesus."

Cheryl Little

I watched Cheryl Little's birthday balloons disappear into the February sky.

Little was killed on her eighteenth birthday—February 25, 1982. A few hours before her death, they threw a little party for her at Heritage Temple Christian School, where she was a few months from graduation. Her mother, Elizabeth, had attended the party; a clown had presented the birthday girl with the balloons and a stuffed dog.

Her death occurred between the school party and a surprise slumber party that she never knew about.

After you had monitored the police scanner for a while, you could usually tell the seriousness of an accident by the tone of the dispatcher's voice. When I heard the call for the emergency squad, I knew the accident at the intersection of Reeb Avenue and Fourth Street was a bad one. Before I could get to the scene, they were calling for officers from the Accident Investigation Squad, a sign that someone was dead or close to it.

Little had been driving west on Reeb when she ran the stop sign at Fourth and was hit broadside by another car. She was killed when she was ejected from the car.

When I arrived, the stuffed dog was still in the car; the helium balloons had worked their way free and were sailing away.

Motorcycle Accidents

If the police beat did nothing else, it cured me of ever wanting to own a motorcycle.

The first motorcycle fatality I covered was that of Bruce Messer, a twenty-five-year-old man who was on his way home the evening before his fifth wedding anniversary. Messer had a three-year-old son and a wife who was eight months pregnant with their second child.

Messer had been following a large panel truck down a two-lane country road. When the truck slowed to make a right turn, Messer pulled out into the other lane to pass. The driver of the car that was stopped at the intersection, his vision blocked by the truck, pulled out in front of Messer. He hit the car and was launched into a field; he died a few hours later at 12:30 A.M. on his anniversary.

On the east side, a motorcyclist was going southbound and misjudged the speed of the southbound tractor-trailer in front of him.

He never touched his brakes; he wasn't wearing a helmet. Police estimated that he was traveling over 100 mph when he hit the back of the tractor-trailer, which was traveling about 30 mph. Pieces of brain were splattered up the back of the trailer much the way the contents of a stepped-on ketchup packet sprays over the asphalt. Accident investigators speculated that it may not have been an accident, but a very unconventional method of committing suicide.

One motorcyclist tried driving with a blood-alcohol level of .45, which is four and a half times what is considered legally drunk, and was killed when he plowed into an oncoming car. Another man, who had never in his life owned or driven a motorcycle, decided to take his inaugural spin after drinking a vast amount of alcohol. He, too, crashed and killed himself.

The police beat also cured me of ever considering jumping out of a perfectly good airplane. I made this decision after interviewing skydiver Carl Turpin, who jumped out of an airplane at 2,700 feet and a section of his parachute failed to open. He lived to talk to me about it.

Spiraling toward earth at what he estimated was at least 50 mph, Turpin said he fiddled with the chute until he was too close to the ground to cut away his main chute and deploy his reserve.

He said he landed on the top of a B&O railroad boxcar. "Landed," I thought, seemed like a gentle term for what had occurred. Although he survived, he cut his thigh to the bone and shattered the bones in his right ankle. He was unconscious for about twenty minutes. When he awoke, he said, "Everything was real fuzzy."

"Really. Things were fuzzy after falling 2,700 feet onto a boxcar. Imagine that, huh? Now, let me guess. As soon as your leg heals, you're going skydiving again?"

"I can't wait to get back up."

When Things Go Bad

In the aftermath of some heavy storms in central Ohio during the summer of 1983, the drainage ditches around the interstate highways swelled and flooded the surrounding ground. Beatrice Kindrix and her four children were driving in her Chevrolet Vega when they were run off a slick I-70 and into one of these large puddles. The water was so deep that it flooded the interior. As Kindrix and her children climbed out of the car and waited for the police to arrive, another accident occurred nearby and a truck spilled two fifty-five-gallon drums of red dye into the water, turning the puddle in which Kindrix's car was resting, and the once light-colored interior, a bright red. Kindrix had owned the car only ten days and it was not insured.

TEN
❏

Hercules and the Hippo

Heeerrrre, Hercules

I REPORTED TO WORK ONE AFTERNOON AND CITY EDITOR BERNIE Karsko handed me a scrap of paper on which was typed the address: 4460 Trabue Road. "Hurry and run out there. They're looking for a lion that escaped from its cage."

"A lion? A real lion?" I asked. "What's a lion doing on the west side of Columbus?"

"Beats me," Karsko said.

"So, what is it, a cub?"

Karsko shrugged. "I don't know Yocum. Go find out. They're talking about it on the scanner. They're out looking for it in a farm field, or something."

Kenny Chamberlain had drawn the assignment and was heading toward the city desk, his camera bag slung over a shoulder.

"Well, let me ask you this: What's someone doing with a real lion? That can't possibly be legal, can it?"

"I don't know, Yocum. You're the reporter. Why don't you get out there and ask someone that question."

"Is it tame, like a pet?"

"Yocum!" he yelled.

"Fine. I'll go, but I'm not getting out of the car."

Karsko looked up from his electric IBM typewriter. "That'll make it a little tough to get the story, won't it?"

"Maybe. But I don't need to run into a burning building to write a story about a house fire."

"You're wasting time, Yocum."

"Bernie, I don't even like house cats, and I'm afraid of dogs."

Kenny was laughing.

I'm not an animal person. Never have been. I'm not mean to them; I just don't like to be round them. They sense my fear. I don't like getting dog hair on me and I don't like animal slobber. I hate getting sniffed and licked. And I'd really hate to get eaten. My angst was obvious.

"Oh, the big, bad police reporter has met his match," chimed in our medical reporter, who was more noted for delivering excuses than stories. He was enjoying my hesitation.

"Hey, Johnny Bravo, how 'bout I stay here and finish your story on angioplasty or whatever disease-of-the-day story you're writing, and *you* go out stomping through the cornfield looking for a lion?"

He went back to pretending he was busy.

As a reporter on the state desk, I had done a story on the animal breeding program at Kings Island amusement park near Cincinnati. While I was there, they let me play with three lion cubs, which I thought would be a blast. They always look so cute on television. My play session with them lasted about twenty seconds. They tore my arms to pieces. I could only imagine what an adult lion could do.

When we got to the address, which is bordered on the west by I-270, the Columbus outerbelt, police officers, Columbus zoo employees, and the lion's owners, Bob and Anna Griggs, were walking through the surrounding bean fields. As we got out of the car I could hear someone yelling, "Heeerrrre, Hercules."

"Fabulous. It's named Hercules."

"It's a lion, Robin. What did you expect they'd call it? Fluffy?" Ken looked over at me, still laughing, and said, "Hey . . ." He tapped the side of his camera bag, a reminder to me that he was carrying his .22-caliber pistol in the bag.

"I appreciate that, Ken. I really do. But remember this: it's a goddamn LION! I'd feel better if you had something a little bigger than a twenty-two. You hit him with that it'll probably just piss him off."

"You worry too much."

"Yeah, you're probably right. After all, it's only the fiercest predator on the face of the earth. I'm probably just needlessly fretting, huh?"

"Hey, you were a ballplayer. Just outrun him." Ken laughed.

"Oh, that's funny. Hilarious, in fact. Glad you're enjoying this so much. Just remember this, old man, I don't need to outrun Hercules. I just need to outrun you. So, just keep that heavy camera bag on your shoulder."

Kenny just kept smiling.

We had been at the address for several minutes when someone yelled, "There he is."

For the record, I *did not,* despite rumors that may have been circulated around the newsroom by my photographer, jump back in the car. I made a move toward it. I may have even touched the door handle. But, I stopped short of jumping back in.

Hercules, it turned out, was little more than a cub—about seventy-five pounds. He had been hiding in the bean fields and came home when he got hungry. According to Mr. Griggs, Hercules had been playing in the backyard with the family dog earlier in the afternoon when he jumped the fence and went for a stroll in the bean field.

Mr. Griggs had purchased the animal from a private citizen and donated it to the Columbus Zoo. The zoo, having all the lions it needed, gave Hercules to a professional animal trainer in Akron, who in turn sold it to a Dayton manufacturer to use in television commercials. Mr. Griggs had bought Hercules back two weeks before the current search after finding the animal undernourished and being kept in a dark barn. He had been declawed and his front teeth filed down. They were in the process of looking for another home for Hercules, which was just fine with me.

As we walked back to the car, Kenny said, "See, you did all the fretting over that little guy."

"Little guy? It was still seventy-five pounds of lion, Kenny."

"He couldn't hurt you."

"Uh-huh. Let me ask you this. If you got up tomorrow morning and found a seventy-five-pound raccoon sitting on your back porch, would you go out there? No, you wouldn't, because you'd be thinking, 'That's a hell of a big raccoon.' Well, lions are fiercer than raccoons, aren't they?"

Kenny smiled, shook his head, and said, "Get in the car, Tarzan."

Animal Stories

I hated doing animal stories.

As I said, I'm not an animal person, but that isn't why I hated doing them. I hated them for this reason: I once worked on a story after a pit bull and a rottweiler mauled two-year-old Shannon Tucker to death. Shannon went out to play behind her condominium when the pit bull and rottweiler got out of their yard and attacked her. She died of blood loss and a broken neck. A witness to the mauling said: "She only screamed short and quick. They tossed her around like a rag doll. It was like they were eating lunch."

It made me sick.

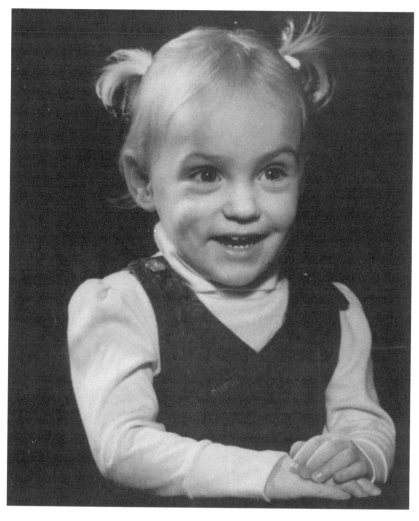

Shannon Tucker was just two when she was mauled to death by two dogs. It infuriated me when animal lovers would call in wanting to know what they could do to save the dogs. (Courtesy of the *Columbus Dispatch*)

Ultimately, we reported that the dogs would be killed.

I received no fewer than ten calls from people who wanted to know what they could do to save the dogs. (I do not know how many calls other reporters received.) The most common comment was: "It wasn't the dogs' fault. They were just being dogs."

"No, they weren't!" I countered. I could feel the enamel grinding. "Dogs are supposed to wag their tails and lick kids' faces; they aren't supposed to maul them to death."

"Well, they can't help it. They're just dumb animals."

I received zero calls from people who were concerned about the little girl and her family. In fact, I received more calls from people wanting to save those dogs than I did from people concerned about the kidnapping of Kelly Prosser, an eight-year-old who disappeared on her way home from school in September 1982, and that was after the police made a public plea for neighborhood search parties to organize.

This lopsided sense of priorities made me crazy.

Occasionally, the police would bust a dogfighting ring. In one case, they captured twenty-five pit bulls, which the county pound said had to be destroyed. They were bred to be fighters and killing them was the only humane thing to do. Still, the phones rang.

Now, the *Dispatch* did not help matters. We would do stories on the dogs and take sad-eyed photos of them on the floor of their pen at the pound, looking pitiful. In one case, one of our reporters wrote about the "butter-colored paws" of a pit bull that had already received a death sentence.

The phone started ringing.

I have always figured that if I ever get hit by a car, it will probably be while crossing an intersection at the same time as a cocker spaniel, and one of these people will be first to the scene. I'll be crumpled on the asphalt bleeding to death while they race to the veterinarian with Fido.

A Hippopotamus in the Scioto River . . . or Not

It was a Sunday afternoon in April 1982 when the call came over the police scanner. "A gentleman on West North Broadway reports seeing a hippopotamus in the Scioto River."

I was the only reporter on duty and I headed out the door. I called for Kenny Chamberlain on the two-way radio from the press car.

"Yocum to Chamberlain . . ."

"I'm already headed in that direction," he responded.

By the time I arrived, the man who had called police, and who had a home with a rear deck that overlooked the river, was standing on the deck and pointing police officers and firefighters to the spot where he reportedly had seen the hippo. (I'm not sure why the fire department responded, unless it was for the amusement value of the call.) A police helicopter circled overhead. "You're sure it was a hippo?" one officer asked.

"Yeah, I'm sure."

"A hippopotamus?"

"Yeah. It might have been one of those pygmy hippos. But it was a hippo. It was huge."

It was plausible. Located several miles upstream is the Columbus Zoo. Maybe, the cops surmised, one of the zoo's hippos had escaped and was making its way back to Africa via the Scioto River.

One of the firefighters at the scene suggested that it was an otter.

"It was no otter," the man replied. "If it was, it was a world-record otter."

"There aren't any otters in the Scioto River, are there?" I asked the firefighter.

"Probably not," he muttered, flashing me a wry smile. "But I'm bettin' that we don't have any hippos, either."

Jack Hanna, then-director of the zoo and known for his appearances on the Late Show, left a family barbeque to check out the report. Hanna was a favorite of Columbus reporters because he was eminently quotable. And tonight was no different. Hanna waded into the water and scoured the river behind the man's home. All he could come up with was one large muskrat. He called the zoo to find all hippos present and accounted for.

"I can see how you could mistake a muskrat for a hippopotamus; I've had nights like that, too," Hanna quipped.

When the story ran the next day, the man who had reported the hippo sighting, who was also a local businessman, called the paper and threatened never to advertise in the *Dispatch* for making him look, ah, not smart.

ELEVEN
❑

The Competition

Protecting the Story

IF NECESSARY, I WOULD DISTRACT MY COMPETITION TO PROTECT a story, a fact that probably makes some journalism professors bristle.

Many guileless journalism professors like to talk about the brotherhood and sisterhood of the journalism profession and would cast scorn on such duplicitous behavior. What they do not teach is the reality of the newsroom, which is, "Produce, or go sell washing machines at Sears."

Today, the Internet and increasingly electronic media are blurring the line between print and television. Most cities have only one major paper and a chain of suburban weeklies. This was not the case when I was covering police for the *Dispatch*. I fought daily with the three network stations and my primary competition, the morning *Citizen-Journal*. The community was better served with competing newspapers, and I loved the rivalries.

I loathe losing. Always have. I can still remember my first defeat as an eight-year-old in the Brilliant, Ohio, Little League. I cried all the way to my dad's pickup truck. Accepting defeat never got any easier, though I eventually learned to control the tears. The victories in my life have never been as sweet as the defeats have been bitter. I can lose with grace, but I do not dislike it any less, and I make no apologies for that fact.

This on-field attitude carried over into my job as a reporter. From my perspective, it was a competition, and a fierce one. My team was the *Columbus Dispatch*. I did not consider reporters from the *Citizen-Journal* or the television stations to be brothers or sisters in the pursuit of journalism. To me, they were simply the competition and someone to be beaten.

It is critical to be accurate. It is even more critical to be accurate and first. The newspaper business is about selling newspapers. If you get beaten every day, which paper is the guy on the street going to buy? And you get beaten only so many times before you find yourself trying to sell someone an extended warranty on a Kenmore. The *Citizen-Journal* had a guy covering the police beat in the early eighties that I really liked. Great guy; fun to be around. I beat him so many times that they fired him. And he had a family to feed, too. I was determined that was not going to be me.

The play-nice-in-the-sandbox theories of journalism schools do not hold up on the police beat, which is a free-for-all and the journalistic equivalent of a combat zone. If you are the city hall reporter, you go to the council meetings and report on what passed or did not pass. Sometimes, the mayor will call a press conference, and everyone sits in the room and gets spoon-fed information. But when you're covering a triple homicide, you don't sit in a police briefing room where they tell you everything you want to know. You have to go find the news. Get to the scene. Identify the dead. What is their sex? Age? Home address? Please spell the names. How did they die? Who killed them? When? Why? Is the suspect in custody? If so, what is his age and home address? What's his connection to the victims? Any previous convictions? Can I get a mug shot? What do we know about the victims' personal lives? How can we get photos of the victims?

You're fighting with the cops and other reporters, trying to interview scared witnesses and grieving relatives, many of whom the police have asked not to talk to the press. Now, the next day, find a follow-up story that no one else has. Do it again the day after that. Then again. And again. And again.

Now, imagine doing all this while sharing an office the size of a one-car garage with your primary competitor, who is eavesdropping on every telephone conversation you have. If I forgot to turn off my computer, do you think the *C-J* reporter wasn't looking at it? Of course he was. When I wasn't around, he was going through my desk and my trash, and if I left something of value where he could find it, shame on me.

As the night police reporter, I was always at a disadvantage since the *Citizen-Journal* printed in the morning. If I had a story, I had to protect it from the *C-J*. Conversely, the *C-J* reporters could tell me what they had and laugh, because there was no way I could beat them on it. Thus, if I had an exclusive story, it was naïve to think that I wasn't going to protect it. I wanted to be the reporter to break the big story—not most of the time, but all the time.

Dick Radick, my buddy in the Accident Investigation Squad, was usually a willing accomplice in my deceptions. He thought they were funny, too. So, when I had a good story that I needed to protect from the *C-J*, I would tell Radick, "Hey, Dick, I've got a hot one. Can you throw him off the trail?"

This always brought a smile to his face. "Sure. Do you want it wildly unbelievable, or just moderately unbelievable?"

"I don't care. Just try to keep it within the realm of possibility," I'd say.

The following are Radick's three most memorable whoppers, which he "leaked" to the *C-J* reporter:

- The chief of police and his deputy chiefs were moving from the fourth floor of police headquarters to a luxury suite at the LeVeque Tower, one of Columbus's nicest office buildings. There were underground tunnels connecting the buildings and that's how they planned to stay in contact with the police station. The vacated fourth floor of the police department would be converted to a fitness center and sleeping area for third-shift officers who needed to catch a nap before going to court to testify.
- The police department was going to change the 10-code. The 10-code was the numerical code used by the police when dispatching information. Such as, we've got a 10-17 at such-and-such an address. (A 10-17 was a domestic violence call.) Radick told the *C-J* reporter that so many people in Columbus owned scanners and knew the 10-code that it was causing the police problems, so they were being forced to change the numbers.
- At least twenty-four Columbus police vice and narcotics officers were under investigation by the Franklin County Prosecutor's Office for a variety of offenses ranging from theft to having sex on duty to drug abuse. Apparently, the prosecutor's office had infiltrated the ranks of the vice and narcotics squads with a Franklin County deputy sheriff. Radick warned the reporter, "Don't ask anyone in narcotics about it because I don't think they know."

In each case, the *C-J* reporter spent hours trying to track down the bogus leads and each time the story I was trying to preserve was protected.

The *C-J* went through a series of police reporters during my tenure. When I first started on the police beat, they had a reporter who had been covering it for years. He looked and acted like a cop.

He had cultivated many sources and occasionally a cop would show up at the door, look at me, then wave him out into the hall.

Fortunately for me, he was a mercurial sort and wound tighter than any human I have ever known. He had a hatred for the *Citizen-Journal's* management and a self-destructive nature. He would get on the phone with his wife, verbally degrade her intolerably, then say, "love you," and hang up. Then he'd pick up the receiver and pound it on the desk or kick his trashcan or slam a drawer, his facing burning crimson.

"Problems?" I asked on one such occasion.

"She stopped for gas and drove off without the fuckin' gas cap," he raged. "And she laughed about it, like it was some big joke." (Another time he had a similar blowup because she had hit a railroad crossing too fast and flattened a tire.)

"You're going to have a stroke over a $2.95 gas cap?"

"It's always something with her."

"I'm going to come in here one of these days and all that's going to be left of you is a pair of smoking shoes on the floor and a big, red splotch on the ceiling where the rest of you ended up. Relax."

He would sit there, every muscle in his jaw straining, grinding his teeth.

When he told me that he had an offer of a job at another paper, I wholeheartedly urged him on. I told him it would be great for his career, when in reality the only career I was concerned about was my own. I would much rather compete with a less experienced reporter. He accepted the offer and I congratulated him. Been great workin' with ya; see ya around; don't be a stranger; have a nice life.

Suddenly, I was the senior reporter at the police station.

The best reporter the *C-J* ever put on the police beat was Jim Dillon. I liked Dillon, which was good because we shared such a small space. We got to know each other's habits. I could always tell when he was working on a big story because he hunched his shoulders forward as he typed, as if trying to block my view.

"Whatta ya workin' on there, J.D.?" I'd ask, smiling.

He would look at me and grin, not because he was trying to be smart, but because he couldn't keep a straight face. "Nothing," was the standard response.

"I think you're fibbin' to me. I think I need to make some more rounds."

Conversely, if I was working on a big story, he sensed it. As I would leave the pressroom toward the end of my shift, Dillon would ask, "You got something big, don't you?"

I'd nod.

"What is it? You can tell me," Dillon would say, looking at his watch. "It's eleven-thirty. I don't have time to track it down."

The *C-J*'s final deadline was 1 A.M. He had plenty of time. I'd say, "I can't chance that, Jim, but I'll tell you this. It's national." That meant that it was such a big story that the Associated Press would want to pick it up for national distribution. That was not always the case, but it was always enough to ruin his evening.

(Dillon was a big guy, a college rugby player and amateur boxer. Still, he had a soft, baby face. We were making rounds together one day when Jim Cottrill, the Juvenile Bureau sergeant called him "Baby Schnooks." Dillon, in front of about seven juvenile officers, said, "I wish you wouldn't call me that. I don't like that." Instantly, he became "Schnooks" for the rest of his tenure at the Cop Shop.)

Bomber Harris

Shortly after a statue of former Ohio Gov. James A. Rhodes was dedicated on the northeast corner of the statehouse lawn in December 1982, '60s radical William "Bomber" Harris drove his car into the statue. It was, I assume, a lame protest of the 1970 shootings at Kent State.

Harris was an air force lieutenant stationed at Lockbourne Air Force Base in August 1970 when he planted bombs at two east-side department stores—a JCPenney and a Zayre's—injuring thirteen people. He was captured as he fled the Zayre's store. He then led police to three other bombs, which were defused. One of the bombs contained sixteen, half-pound sticks of dynamite and was disarmed just seconds before it was set to explode. After his arrest, police found a diary at Harris's apartment that stated he was setting the bombs as a diversion for a robbery. He was going to use the robbery money to "set up an autocratic, feudal system of states in Central Europe."

Harris was sentenced to twelve to sixty-five years in the State Reformatory at Mansfield. When he made his grand reappearance in Columbus in January 1983 behind the wheel of a 1980 Pontiac Grand Prix that was planted at the base of the Rhodes statue, it was big news. He was charged with drunken driving and grand theft. The car he had been driving had been reported stolen from the Eastland Mall parking lot. The crash did only minor damage to the base of the statue.

About the same time, a television reporter from Channel 10, Drew Hadwal, started making daily visits to the pressroom. He was showing up when I was at lunch and I suspected that he was foraging for stories in my desk. I placed Scotch tape on the underside of my desk drawer one day and went to lunch. When I returned and checked under my desk, the tape had been pulled away from the drawer.

The following day, just before I left for lunch, I took the back of an incident report and wrote: Bomber Harris, Tulsa, second-degree murder, 1976 or maybe '77, technicality? I set the report on my desk and left.

About three that afternoon, the police public information officer, Mary Helen Van Dyke, came down to my office with an exasperated look on her face. "Robin, have you heard anything about Bomber Harris being convicted or charged with second-degree murder in Oklahoma sometime in the '70s?"

I certainly had not intended to draw Mary Helen into the fray. Mary Helen had the unenviable position of being the liaison between the media and the police. I relied on her for information on a regular basis, and I was sure she would not appreciate being dragged into the middle of one of my stunts. Instantly, I had to choose between saving my skin and confessing to Mary Helen.

Self-preservation is such a dominating instinct.

"You know, Mary Helen, I'd heard a few sketchy details, but nothing solid. Why?"

"Drew Hadwal's got me running all over the place trying to track this down. I can't find anything about it. No one in Oklahoma has heard anything about it."

"Maybe it's bogus information."

She shrugged. "He swears it's solid."

"How'd he hear about it?"

"He says he has a source. He won't tell me who."

It was one of the few times in my life when I was able to keep a straight face in the clutch, mostly because I knew that little Mary Helen would chew a hole in my forehead if she knew that I was the cause of her annoyance. "Well, if you find out it's true, let me know," I said. "That would be a great story."

Out of Order

Ned Stout taught me a little trick that worked wonders in the days before cell phones. Before covering an event that would undoubtedly cause reporters to scramble for the pay phones, I would tape a small "out of order" sign on one of the receivers. Then, while reporters lined up for one of two available phones, I would walk up and call the newsroom on the one that was "broken."

Not All in the Family

Robin Durrer was nineteen and mildly retarded. She was found murdered—beaten to death with a tree limb—in a heavily wooded area behind her house in southern Franklin County in September 1981. Since the body was found so far from the street, we had to wait near the family home for the detectives to come talk to us. In the meantime, I gave one of her high school classmates ten dollars to let me borrow his high school yearbook so I could be sure to have a photograph of the girl. When he delivered, Ron Johnson, a cameraman for WBNS-TV who went by R.J., hoisted his camera up on his shoulder and said in his gravelly voice, "Hey, man, point her out so I can get a shot for the eleven o'clock."

"You must be on drugs. Get your own yearbook."

He winced. "Man, open it up and show me which one she is. We work for the same people."

The reference was to the Wolfe family, who owned both the *Dispatch* and his television station. In my mind, however, this did not make us teammates.

"No, we don't, R.J. I work for (*Dispatch* Editor) Luke Feck. You work for (WBNS President) Gene D'Angelo. There's a big difference." For a minute, I toyed with the idea of opening the book and intentionally pointing to the wrong photo. But I realized that some kid's dad might be sitting in a bar watching television when his daughter's photo suddenly appeared on the television as being dead. I did not want to be responsible for that, so I tossed the yearbook into the trunk and slammed it closed.

"You're an asshole," he growled.

"I'm not an asshole, R.J., I'm a prick. There's a big difference. Assholes can't help themselves; pricks know exactly what they're doing. I'm a prick, and that's why you're not getting the picture."

I thought he was going to put the camera down and take a swing at me. He did not. He just walked away, muttering, which was the smart thing to do, since he considered us teammates and all.

The Disadvantage

Cops love female television reporters.

Female television reporters are acutely aware of this fact, and they use the resources available to them to get cops to talk.

I once covered a story at a trucking company on Frank Road where a tanker was leaking a fluid thought to be hazardous material. I walked up to the yellow crime scene tape and the township cop who was guarding the entrance to the lot and asked, "What's going on?"

"I don't know anything, and I'm not permitted to speak to reporters. You'll have to talk to my supervisor." He stood erect, hands locked behind his back, looking straight ahead, as if he were guarding the front door of the White House.

"Is your supervisor here?"

"No."

"Do you know when he'll be here?"

"No."

"Uh-huh. Okay, so do we even know what's leaking? Is it water; is it dangerous; are they going to start evacuating people?"

"Sir, you're going to have to talk to my supervisor. As I clearly stated, I am not authorized to release any information to the media."

So, I backed up a few steps. Not two minutes later, Allison Ash, an attractive reporter with WCMH Channel 4 in Columbus, walked up and asked me what I knew. "Nothing. I asked Sergeant Rock over there for the basics, but he just gave me the silent treatment."

Allison walked up to the cop, lightly touched one of his arms, giggled, and all of a sudden Mr. I'm-not-authorized became a blathering idiot. He couldn't tell her enough about the semi and its dripping contents.

I never blamed Allison. If I could have used such devices for stories, I would have. But that tactic never works on women. It only works on men because as a species we're not smart enough to realize that not every woman in the world wants to sleep with us. Allison smiled and flirted, and all of a sudden that cop was thinking, "Hey, I've got a shot."

Of course, he had no shot, whatsoever. As soon as she got her information, she was ready to leave.

Moron.

TWELVE

❏

Death by Fire

Left Alone

AN EIGHTY-ONE-YEAR-OLD WOMAN WHO HAD BEEN CONFINED TO a wheelchair for nine years died on a Tuesday night in March 1982 when a fire swept through her south-side home. She was found on the floor by the back door, apparently trying to get out of the house. The fire, arson investigators said, had been ignited by a cigarette that was smoldering in a couch.

I arrived at the scene a few minutes after the fire department had the blaze under control. Wispy gray smoke was still seeping from the blackened door jambs and window frames. The body of the victim was still inside the house and neighbors were crowding around the tiny home.

The battalion chief told me that the dead woman's husband, seventy-nine, had not been home at the time of the fire.

"Where was he?" I asked.

"Well, there seems to a little confusion there," the chief said. "A couple of neighbors think he's down the street at a bar. They went looking for him. One neighbor said smoke was coming out of the house when they saw him leave."

"He left his wife in a burning house!"

"We don't know, for sure. He might not have realized that his wife had been unable to escape."

"She was in a wheelchair, for God's sake. How could he not know?" I asked.

"Apparently he's not all together upstairs," the chief said, tapping his helmet.

When the husband returned, escorted by the neighbors, he appeared confused by the fuss. I'm not sure he understood that his home had been destroyed. I wasn't sure if it was the result of alcohol or senility, or a sad combination of the two.

The dead woman's son—the husband's stepson—was among those in the crowd. Several neighbors were keeping him away from the husband, whom the son was blaming for his mother's death.

"Where's the missus?" the old man asked his neighbors, seemingly not understanding what had occurred.

She died in the fire, they told him.

"Died! Oh, no." And he began to cry. Then he took a breath and said, "Well, she was about dead, anyway."

It took several additional neighbors to keep the son from attacking the old man.

Thelma Tack and John Smith

In most fires, people die of smoke inhalation before they are burned. During my time on the police beat, there were two cases in which that was not the case. One was Thelma Tack, a thirty-eight-year-old north-side woman who accidentally set herself on fire in February 1982.

Tack had been depressed and was on heavy medication; she was smoking when she apparently set her couch on fire. The fire caught her clothes on fire and she was burning alive when her twelve-year-old daughter walked into the room. The daughter ran to a neighbor for help. When the neighbor arrived, Tack was crying, "Help me." He wrapped her in a blanket, but she was already burned over most of her body and was dead by the time they got her to the hospital. The fire did only about $350 damage to the house. The autopsy showed Tack had toxic levels of diazepam, the generic name for Valium, in her blood.

The other victim was John Smith, a fifty-six-year-old multiple sclerosis victim who dropped a cigarette that ignited his clothing. He was unable to grasp the burning butt and when his wife found him, he was sitting in his wheelchair, burning alive. He died a week later.

The Christmas Tree

The call was coming over the scanner as I was preparing to head to the police station to make my morning rounds. There was a bad house fire on the far west side of the county; kids were trapped inside. I grabbed a press car and headed out. I was working the day shift and was under pressure to get the story in before deadline.

It was December 19, 1983, and it was bitter cold. By the time I arrived, four siblings, all under the age of thirteen, were dead. The house must have burned like paper. The only structures left standing were two chimneys. A twelve-year-old brother of the dead children was in the hospital being treated for smoke inhalation and minor burns. The father was being treated for two broken ankles that he received when he jumped from the second-floor window. Firefighters were soaking down the embers, trying to clear the debris to find the bodies.

This was before the widespread use of cell phones and I was carrying a two-way radio that kept me in touch with the city desk. Usually, I would get information for a story, then find a pay phone and call it in. We didn't like to use the two-ways for passing story information because the *Citizen-Journal* and the television stations monitored our frequency. However, we were running up against deadline and I was communicating to the newsroom via the two-way, dictating information as fast as I could track it down.

"What was the cause of the fire?" the assistant city editor asked.

"They don't know the cause. They're still investigating."

"Could it have been a spark from the Christmas tree?"

"The chief said he doesn't know. They're still investigating."

"Get me that," he said. "Ask him if it could have been started by a spark from the lights on the Christmas tree."

I went back to the chief and asked about that possibility. We had just had the same conversation two minutes earlier. "Robin, nothing has changed in the past two minutes. We don't know what caused the fire."

I radioed back the information.

"Ask him again," the editor persisted. "Ask him if there's any possibility that it could have been a spark from the tree."

I knew what he was after, and it was an opportunity to write a sensational headline and lead, tying together a human tragedy with their family Christmas tree.

"Look, they don't know. They just got the fire out. They're trying to figure it out now," I said.

"Ask!" he countered.

I trudged back to the chief, who saw me coming and must have seen the look on my face. "We still don't know."

"But, could it have been the tree?"

"You know, Rob, it could have been a hundred things. A kerosene heater. A cigarette in the couch. Faulty wiring. Spontaneous combustion. Something on the stove. A spark from the Christmas tree. We don't know."

I repeated the chief's message to the assistant city editor, who said, "Terrific." I went to Doctor's Hospital West in an attempt to get an interview with the surviving relatives, then went back to the paper. The final makeover attributed the possible cause as a spark from faulty wiring on a Christmas tree.

The next morning, Pleasant Township Fire Chief Harry Jahn called me on the phone, highly upset. Of course, every media outlet in the city was calling him for an interview to follow up on my story, which wasn't totally inaccurate, but certainly not an example of responsible journalism.

It was personally embarrassing and one of the reasons the media, deservedly, gets criticized. And, it was as much my fault as it was my editor's. I knew what he was trying to do and I allowed it to happen. Also, it damaged my credibility with the chief. The editor's name didn't go on the story; mine did. It would be the last time I would ever let an editor beat me into submission like that.

Crossing the Line

In the days before cell phones, the two-way radio was a crucial tool in reporting. The two-way was linked back to the newsroom and the photo department. It enabled the reporters and photographers to keep in touch, call for backup or, as was mostly the case, get direction—good and bad—from the city desk. Still, there were times when a reporter needed to turn off the two-way and use his own good judgment.

I was covering a murder on the far south side of the county and the sheriff's department had yellow crime scene tape stretched around the driveway, which was an eighth of a mile from the murder scene. Night City Editor Bernie Karsko was on the two-way with me and was irate that the cops wouldn't let us any closer to the crime scene. "They've got no right to keep you that far back," he said. "Cross the tape."

The deputy guarding the scene was only three feet away and heard the conversation. He looked at me like he couldn't believe what he'd just heard. I asked him, "What happens if I cross the tape?"

"I'm going to arrest you."

I went back to the two-way. "Bern, the deputy guarding the scene says if I cross the tape he's going to arrest me."

Bernie was now yelling. "Yocum, get back there. He's not going to arrest you."

I looked back at the deputy. "You will, won't you?"

"Oh, count on it."

"Uh-huh. Let me ask you this. You're just going to arrest me, right? I mean, no rough stuff. I'll just step across the tape and you can cuff me and put me in the cruiser, real easy like, okay? You're not thinking of throwing me down and hitting me with the Mace, are you?"

"How about you save us both a lot of aggravation and just stay over there where you belong."

"Yocum!" Bernie yelled.

And I turned off the two-way. Bernie would be gone by the time I got back to the newsroom. Maybe, I hoped, he would cool off by the next afternoon. And, even if he was still mad, I was certain that *he* couldn't arrest me.

He never brought it up again.

THIRTEEN

❑

The Governors and the Mayor

Richard F. Celeste

THE POLICE DEPARTMENT DAILY PROVIDED COPIES OF ALL INCI-
dent reports to the media. They were photocopied and placed in the
"Pressroom" mailbox in the Records Bureau on the second floor.
This was usually a stack of paper several inches high, which might
generate one or two stories a month. Generally, they were a waste of
good trees. The reports were at least twenty-four hours old by the
time I read them, and the offenses were usually too insignificant to
be of interest, ranging from burglaries to complaints because a
neighbor was playing his stereo too loud.

One set of reports was provided for all reporters to share. So, in
theory, if I picked up the reports, I would read them and then place
them on the desk of the *Citizen-Journal* reporter for his inspection.
In reality, if there was a report of interest, it never made its way to
the *C-J* desk. If the *C-J* reporter picked up the reports first, he was
happy to return the favor. If the reports were picked up while we
were both in the pressroom, we would often view them together,
neither of us trusting the other.

On a Sunday afternoon in the summer of 1982, I was in the pressroom flipping through the reports when I found one for petit theft. Ordinarily, I would not have given it a second glance. However, the report listed the name of the suspected thief, and the name practically jumped off the paper—Richard F. Celeste.

At the time, Celeste was making his first run for Ohio governor as the Democratic nominee. According to the report, the attendant at the BP station on Neil Avenue said the driver of a van pulled into the station, pumped $20 worth of gasoline, then left without paying. The alert attendant was able to get the license plate number; the plates came back registered to Celeste.

The *C-J* reporter was out making rounds, so I slipped the report into my pocket and went back to the *Dispatch* newsroom to make some calls. I frequently did this when I did not want the competition to hear my conversations.

I certainly did not think Celeste would intentionally dash off without paying for his gas, but the story was still worth pursuing, even if he just forgot to pay. I was the only reporter in the newsroom that night. I called Duane St. Clair, one of our political writers, who helped me track down Celeste, who was at a Cleveland hotel for a fundraiser. I was able to get in touch with Celeste's press secretary, Paul Costello, who promptly began busting my chops.

"Who are you?" he asked.

"I'm Robin Yocum. I'm a reporter with the *Columbus Dispatch* and I need to talk to Mr. Celeste."

"Well, he's very busy. He can't talk to you."

"He can't talk to me for two minutes?"

"No way. He's too busy. And, who are you, anyway? Why are you calling?" he asked, a condescending tone to his voice. "Where's Gene Jordan? (Gene was our chief political writer.)"

"Gene doesn't work Sunday nights."

"Well, we'll contact Gene tomorrow."

"Tomorrow's going to be too late, and Gene doesn't know anything about this."

"What's it about?"

"I don't really want to share that with anyone but Mr. Celeste. Are you sure he can't spare two minutes?"

"Didn't you hear what I said? No!"

I'd had my belly full of this guy. There are times when, as a reporter, you know that by the end of the conversation you are going to have them by the shorts. I was ready to show my hand.

"Okay, look, if Mr. Celeste isn't available, that's fine. But you can tell him this: I'm writing a story that's going to run in tomorrow's *Columbus Dispatch*, and I don't know exactly what the headline's going to be, but let me read you my lead:

Democratic gubernatorial candidate Richard F. Celeste stole $20 worth of gasoline from a Columbus BP station Saturday, according to a Columbus police report. The gas station attendant said he watched as Celeste pumped the gas, then jumped into his van and sped away, heading south on Neil Avenue.

"And I've got the police report right here in front of me to back it up. So, you tell that to Mr. Celeste, and if he thinks he can carve a couple of minutes out of his busy schedule to give me a call, I'll give you my number." This was followed by an expected silence as my words sunk in. "You still there?"

"What's your number?" he asked.

I swear, I wanted to jump up on the desk and do a victory dance. Why are you calling, indeed.

Within five minutes, the phone rang.

"City desk, Robin Yocum."

"Rob, Dick Celeste, how are you?" He greeted me like we were old war buddies. Funny how things work out, I thought. A few minutes earlier I was catching a rash of grief from his press secretary, who had deemed me unfit to speak to the candidate. And now, the future governor and I were suddenly amigos.

I read the report to him. He said he had been in Columbus that Saturday for his wife's graduation from Capital University and that he had, in fact, bought gasoline at that BP station. However, he said, "Rob, I paid for it. I gave the guy a twenty-dollar bill."

"Thanks for calling me back," I said. "I'm going to write the story. Obviously, the decision on whether it runs or not is going to be made much higher up the *Dispatch* totem pole than where I'm standing."

"Understood," he said.

He was pleasant on the phone, but I assumed that my call was causing a red-rage panic in the Democratic camp. And I was right.

Within a half-hour after I hung up with Celeste, the phone rang again. It was John Tilley, a lieutenant in the Columbus Police Narcotics Bureau who worked as a part-time private investigator and polygraphist for BP, mostly doing background checks. "Jesus Christ, Yocum, what the hell are you doing?" he asked, laughing. "You've got the entire Ohio Democratic Party in an uproar. In the last twenty minutes I've talked to the head of the Democratic Party and the president of BP for North America."

I explained everything to Tilley, who couldn't quit laughing. I got a comment from him for my story and he promised to keep me apprised of his investigation.

I wrote the story, but it didn't run the next day. It appeared a week later as a brief in a political roundup section. That was the prudent decision. Tilley investigated the case and found that the sadsack attendant had decided to steal twenty dollars from the till. To justify the shortfall to his boss, he had decided to say it was a pump-and-dash, and he blamed it on the driver of the first vehicle he saw with out-of-county license plates. Unfortunately for him, the van with the Cuyahoga County plates belonged to the future governor of the state of Ohio.

He was fired.

Celeste won.

Governor Rhodes and the Tornado

In the summer of 1980, the state was hit with huge windstorms and tornados. Gov. James A. Rhodes decided to take an airborne tour of the state to survey the damage. The statehouse press corps was invited to go along. None of the *Dispatch*'s statehouse reporters were available, so they asked me to pinch hit.

I had been up all night reporting on the storm, but I was excited to go along. Governor Rhodes loved an audience and once we were airborne he had a captive one in the statehouse reporters. In fact, surveying the storm damage seemed secondary to the governor, who did a two-hour monologue.

"It was only two in the morning and he wanted to leave, said his wife was going to be mad, and I said, 'What's the hurry, Bob, the fight can't start until you get home.'" The press corps would laugh, and the governor would glance out the window and say, "Boy, that's terrible. Look at all that crop damage." Then it was right back to the storytelling. "So, then I said to the lieutenant governor . . ."

After a swing over eastern and southeastern Ohio, the governor asked if we were hungry. This was a ridiculous question. Of course we were. Reporters are notorious lunch whores and rarely turn down a free meal. So, the governor frowned and said, "Let me go talk to the pilot and see if we can't find a place to set down and eat." He strolled up to the cockpit and was back in two minutes. "We're going to put her down somewhere and see if we can't find someplace to eat."

The plane landed at a small airport and an armada of state

patrol and state-owned cars were lining the runway to take us to lunch. We had landed in Lebanon, Ohio, and he took us to the Golden Lamb for lunch. The Golden Lamb is Ohio's oldest inn and was one of the governor's favorite restaurants. We walked in; it couldn't have been more than forty minutes after he first asked if we were hungry, and there was a huge table all ready. A reporter from the local weekly was there to do a story on the governor and his press entourage taking lunch at the Golden Lamb.

Of course, he had planned the lunch long before the plane ever took off, but made it look like a spur of the moment idea.

Dana "Buck" Rinehart

Dana "Buck" Rinehart was the mayor of Columbus from 1984 to 1992. I was not one of his favorite reporters. (I was not, however, his least favorite; Bob Ruth was everyone's least favorite.) When Rinehart received word that America West had selected Port Columbus International Airport as a site for a regional hub, his office called the newsroom and asked that a reporter come over for an exclusive interview with the mayor. The city hall reporter wasn't available, so I was asked to fill in. When I walked into his office, the disappointment on his face was palpable.

"Hey, mayor, guess who's writing the big story for tomorrow?"

He shook his head. "Robin, this is an important story for the city of Columbus—a real positive. Do you ever write any positive stories?"

I helped myself to a chair. "Occasionally, but don't spread that around, okay, mayor? I've got a reputation to uphold."

I still had a sour taste in my mouth over the way he had treated my father-in-law, replacing him as head of the municipal garage with his brother, Skip. But that was not the only problem between the mayor and me.

A month or so before the America West story, I walked into the pressroom at the police station to find the mayor furiously pounding out a message on an old manual typewriter. "What are you doing in here?" I asked, sweet as you please.

"I'm writing you a note. You're never in your office."

"They pay me to track down stories, mayor, not sit in here. What do you want, anyway?"

"I want you to clean up this pressroom. It's a pigsty."

I scanned the room and nodded. "Can't argue with you there, mayor." It was a trash heap. There were newspapers and copies of incident reports stacked four feet high across the entire back wall of the room. The wastebaskets were overflowing with the night shift reporter's Burger King bags. The pressroom's deplorable condition was a result of the fact that the custodial staff at the police department came into the pressroom only to hide from their supervisor and sneak cigarettes. "You know, mayor, if we could ever get one of those highly skilled city employees to empty a trash can once in a while, it wouldn't be so bad."

"Hey, the city gives you this room to use free of charge. *You* clean it up."

"I think John F. Wolfe would take issue with that, Buck." (Wolfe was publisher of the *Dispatch*.) "He pays me to write stories for his newspaper, not empty your trash cans."

This apparently wasn't the response the mayor was expecting as his face turned an immediate crimson. "I want it cleaned and I want it cleaned today," he said, storming out of the room.

Most of the time, the perfect response comes to mind fifteen minutes after an argument has ended. Occasionally, it comes right on cue. As the door closed, I responded, "Why don't you have your brother come over and clean it up? He doesn't do anything."

The door was closed for a fraction of a second before he came charging back in, a tad on the angry side. We were nearly nose-to-nose across my desk. "My brother is a very busy man."

"Hey, mayor, remember who you're talking to, here."

Those were the last words spoken. He left. The pressroom remained a mess.

I did, however, write a glowing story about the America West regional hub.

FOURTEEN
❏

The Fighters

Dale Wolford

Dale Wolford had eyes like cracked crystals of blue ice; they seared through you from behind a pair of wire-rim glasses. There was no emotion in the eyes, no life, no humor. I wondered if they were as lifeless before his daughter was strangled. Or, if suffering through the ordeal of Jean's murder had simply drained the life from them. He never smiled. His jaw was square and set, stern under his gray flattop.

"I was on my way to Columbus to kill him," Dale Wolford told me as we sat in his office in Mansfield, Ohio. "I had my gun, I knew where I could find him, and I was going to kill him. It certainly wouldn't have bothered me. A friend of mine was my attorney and he said, 'Wolford, I know what you're thinking and I know what you're planning to do. Don't. Let us handle it.'"

The words rang hollow for a man whose daughter had been murdered. Wolford slipped the revolver under the seat of his car and left his home near Ashland, Ohio, eighty miles north of Columbus. Within minutes of leaving his house, he was driving south on I-71, with designs of killing his former son-in-law, John Shrader. He had played it through in his head a hundred times. Not only would it be easy, but he was actually looking forward to pulling the trigger.

As he passed the Lexington-Bellville exit, near the home of another daughter, Wolford began thinking of the rest of his family and how they would be affected with him in prison. He knew the cops would come looking for him. He did not plan to run after he killed him. Prison, he said, was a virtual certainty. At the Route 36 exit, he pulled off and pointed the car back north.

As he finished talking about the aborted trip to Columbus, he leaned forward on his desk and said, "Put your pen down. I don't want to see this in the paper."

I put pen and pad on the edge of his desk. "Okay."

"I turned around and came back that day. But I'll tell you this: If I ever get cancer and I know I'm going to die, I will kill him. And, I don't mean maybe. I'll kill him and I'll look that gutless son-of-a-bitch right in the eye when I do it, which is more than the coward could do when he killed my daughter. I believe in a just God and I don't believe God wanted Jeannie dead. I've got to believe God will forgive me. John Shrader better get things right with the Lord and hope to God in Heaven that I drop dead of a heart attack. Otherwise, he's going before me."

The murder of Jean Shrader was the first really big story I covered on the police beat. In the late evening of October 4, 1981, a Columbus attorney needed to fetch an umbrella from his wife's car, which was parked on the sixth floor of the parking garage just a half-block behind the *Dispatch* building. As the lawyer exited the elevator on the sixth-floor landing, he looked down the ramp to see a man dragging the body of a woman into the stairwell. He jumped back into the elevator, went down to the first floor, and called the police.

Jean Shrader's October 1981 murder remains unsolved. Her husband John was considered a suspect, but never charged. (Courtesy of the *Columbus Dispatch*)

The woman police found strangled in the stairwell was Jean Shrader, a beautiful, twenty-five-year-old rising star at the Columbus accounting firm of Deloitte Haskins & Sells. According to her husband, she had come home to their north-side apartment, then went back downtown to finish up some work at the office.

In the days after his wife's death, John Shrader left town and stayed with his in-laws. He returned to Columbus after the funeral. When he returned, I interviewed him at the apartment he had shared with his wife.

A team of *Dispatch* reporters had been working on the story and we already had quite a bit of information on the couple. John was married and had two sons when he met Jean Wolford at Hillsdale High School in Ashland County. She was a student, an accomplished musician, and he taught music and was director of the marching band. When she graduated in 1975 and went to Mt. Union College in Alliance, Ohio, he quit his job at Hillsdale and followed her, taking a teaching position in Alliance. They were married in 1977. He ultimately quit teaching and tried to start a business waxing airplanes, which is what he was doing at the time Jean was murdered. Meanwhile, she was on the fast track at the accounting firm and the marriage was reportedly in trouble.

I started the interview slowly, making sure not to alienate him. I said I was sorry that he had lost his wife, and he muttered, "Thanks, Rob, that means a lot."

He spoke of Jean in loving terms, and I had to ask few questions. At one point during the interview he put his head in his hands and sobbed. But when he looked up, there were no tears.

As he warmed up to me, we covered a variety of topics, including his theory on the reason for his wife's murder. Shrader said that he believed his wife had been murdered by members of organized crime.

"The Mafia killed her?" I asked. "Why?"

Shrader related a story to me of using the pay phone at the airport where he waxed planes and overhearing another telephone conversation between Columbus podiatrist Donald Plotnick—who had reported mob ties—and his organized crime superiors. Plotnick had been indicted (and later convicted) of aggravated arson and extortion after he doused an east-side drug dealer with alcohol and set him on fire in an effort to collect $200,000 for an associate. Plotnick had been in the paper repeatedly for his alleged misdeeds.

"How do you know that Plotnick was talking to someone in the Mafia?" I asked.

"I heard him talking about the 'Rainbow Fund.'"

"Rainbow Fund? What's that mean?"

"I don't know. He told them to put the money in the Rainbow Fund. At one point, Plotnick looked over at me and gave me a dirty look. He knew I had overheard that conversation. They killed Jean as a message to me to stay quiet."

"Well, if they were so worried about you talking, why didn't they just kill you and be done with it? Why would they murder your wife?" I asked. "She didn't overhear the conversation."

"I don't know, but I'm sure it was a message. They were telling me, 'Be quiet or you're next.'"

It was an absurd theory, but entertaining. At one point during the interview I asked Shrader, "John, did you murder your wife?"

He got this hurt look on his face and said, "Oh, Rob, I can't believe you'd ask me such a question. That's so hurtful."

"Yeah, well, it's sort of my job, John. And, that doesn't answer my question. Did you kill her?"

"Of course I didn't kill her. I loved her."

The question ended the interview. He said he had another commitment and asked me to leave.

A source in the homicide squad had privately told me that Shrader was a suspect in the murder. After a few weeks, he told me that Shrader was the only suspect. Shrader said his wife had left their apartment to go back and finish up some work at the office. Police theorized that she was strangled and made the trip downtown in the trunk of a car. However, Shrader was never charged in his wife's murder. Police said they lacked the evidence needed to charge him with a crime. And, eventually, the case was relegated to the unsolved file.

Dale Wolford, however, was not content to allow John Shrader to walk away, and he began his own investigation. He talked to neighbors and potential witnesses. He made the trip from the apartment to the parking garage, timing it to prove that John could have made it downtown and back to the apartment before he received the call from police that night. "It consumed every second of my spare time," Wolford said. "It wasn't a job, it was a quest. I would go to bed at night and make lists in my mind of things I had to do the next day."

Wolford filed suit in Franklin County Common Pleas Court to prevent his former son-in-law from receiving the quarter-million dollars in life insurance benefits. He challenged Shrader's right to collect the benefits because he was responsible for Jean's death. It became known as the "civil murder trial of John Shrader." In preparation, Wolford spent 80 hours building a scale model of the parking garage where his daughter was murdered.

After the civil trial began, one of Shrader's attorneys called me to his east-side office, promising me information for a story. It was a bait-and-switch. No doubt they had tape recorders operating in the office. The attorney said, "John said that you have information that Jean's death was a mob hit."

I looked at the attorney. "I thought you had a story for me?"

"We'll get to that. So, is it true, do you have information that Jean was murdered by the mob?"

"John Shrader told you that *I* said that?"

"That's right. Is it true?"

I thought for a moment, wanting to choose my words carefully. "Yes, I have been told that Jean's death was a mob hit."

The lawyer's eyes widened. "Who told you that?"

"John."

"John Shrader?"

"Yeah. John Shrader. He told me that bullshit story the first time I ever interviewed him. I didn't believe it then, either. He told me Jean was murdered to silence him. He said Donald Plotnick had Jean killed because he'd overheard a supposedly secret telephone

conversation. So, counselor, would you like me to come in and testify to that?"

Of course, he didn't. They didn't have a story for me, either.

The next day I was driving to work, heading north on Front
Street, listening to WTVN radio, which was giving extensive coverage to the trial. They aired a soundbite of Shrader on the witness
stand. He told Wolford's attorney that he believed his wife had been
the victim of a mob hit, implicating Plotnick. I started laughing.
"Johnny, Johnny—again with the mob conspiracy."

"Really," Wolford's attorney said. "How do you know that?"

"Robin Yocum, a *Dispatch* reporter, told me."

I about drove into the side of the Lazarus building. Not only was
it a blatant lie, but it was a lie about a guy who had already been indicted for making a human torch out of a drug dealer.

It's probably something of an understatement to say that I was
not happy with Mr. Shrader. Afterward, he ducked me every time I
tried to get an interview. Once, I drove down the street and walked
back to his apartment, staying close to the walls. He was sitting on
the couch in his living room, seated very close to a woman. I rapped
hard on the door and they both reacted as if they had just sat on
tacks. He answered the door and refused to talk.

The civil murder trial was a debacle for Shrader. His attempt to
hold on to the insurance money went south when one of his alibi
witnesses recanted his testimony, saying Shrader had offered to pay
for the testimony. Apparently, the promise to pay didn't materialize,
and the jilted witness turned the tables. Wolford received the
$250,000 in insurance money; Shrader received a six-year prison
term for perjury.

The night Jean was murdered, the attorney who had witnessed
Jean's body being dragged into the stairwell fled when reporters tried
to talk to him. His car was parked in a surface lot near the garage. I
scribbled down his license plate number as he was driving away—

going the wrong way on a one-way street. He was very scared for his family and left town for three days following that night. I gave the license plate number to my city editor, Bernie Karsko, who had a source in the Ohio Bureau of Motor Vehicles run the plate, so I had the attorney's name by the time he got back. I went to the parking lot every day until I saw the car parked there again. I staked it out and waited for him to return that evening. At first he denied that he was the witness.

"I was standing right beside you that night when you walked out of the parking garage. Of course, it was you," I said. "Look, I don't want to use your name. I just want an interview. Just tell me what you saw that night."

Eventually, he agreed. I think he was afraid that I would print his name if he didn't cooperate. I wouldn't have done that, but it got me the interview. Later that night, I spent an hour at his home. He refused to let me take notes while we spoke; he said it made him nervous. I memorized everything I could, then scribbled like crazy when I got back to the car. The story earned the Freedom of Information Award from the Central Ohio Chapter of the Society for Professional Journalists, my first journalism award.

A police source later told me that one reason Shrader was never indicted was because the attorney could not positively identify Shrader as the man he saw dragging the body out of the car.

The murder of Jean Shrader remains unsolved.

I have not spoken to John Shrader in years. I do not know where he went after his release from prison.

It was Shrader's good fortune that on Monday, August 14, 1989, Dale Wolford dropped dead of a massive coronary. He was sixty-one, but aged beyond his years.

Ron, Barb, and Jeanette

I was with Ron Nichols in the hours before he died. He was lying in a bed at Mt. Carmel Hospital, eaten up with cancer and, I think, barely aware that I was there. Barb said, loudly, "Ron, Robin's here to see you."

He forced open his heavy lids and reached for my hand. After a minute, Barb and I helped him out of bed to stand and urinate. He was very thin and weak.

I sat with Barb while her husband slept. His time on earth was being measured in minutes. Barb, too, was tired. Ron's last months had taken a toll on her. But then, the entire nine-year marriage had never been easy. She had helped him overcome a battle with alcohol. That had been the easy part. The difficult part had been sharing the relationship with the ghost of Ron's first wife.

I met Ron and Barb Nichols after I started working the police beat. She was the mother and he the stepfather of a girl who played volleyball at Columbus Beechcroft High School, where my wife was the head coach. I had known Ron for several months before he told me that he had been the husband of Jeanette Nichols. Of course, I knew of Jeanette Nichols. She had been murdered when I was a senior in high school, but anyone who covered the police beat knew of Jeanette. All the old reporters and cops talked of her murder as one of the most gruesome, savage tortures and homicides they had ever seen.

On May 9, 1974, Jeanette was abducted as she reported to work at St. Anthony Hospital, where she was a nurse. Her body was found two days later. She had been tortured, raped, and shot to death. Ron told me that he was certain that Jeanette was praying for death when they finally killed her. Five men were sentenced to prison in connection with her death. Two of the men were sentenced to die, but escaped the electric chair when Ohio's death penalty law was ruled unconstitutional.

I began writing stories about the case after two of the men, Baxter Martin and Eric Maurice, had been paroled. Ron called and asked for my help in getting publicity for his efforts to toughen Ohio's parole laws. His efforts began after he learned of Maurice's release by reading about it in the paper. "It was a mockery of the legal system," he said. "I didn't think any of them would get out. Ever!" He began working with state Representative E. J. Thomas on the parole legislation.

Over the years, I wrote stories about Ron and his battle. We kept in touch and occasionally went to lunch.

I felt sorry for Barb. She was such a sweetheart and she had helped Ron get on with his life. But Ron was never able to put Jeanette's death completely behind him. When he learned he had terminal cancer in January 1987, he made Barb promise to continue the fight to keep the other three men—John W. Harris Jr., James J. Royster, and Clarence Edward Smith—in prison. Of course, she agreed.

Thus, as Ron lay dying, Barb had to promise to continue fighting a battle for a woman she had never known, but one that had been with them throughout their marriage. "He should have given it up when he got so sick, but he couldn't let go," she said.

On the very day that Barb went home from the hospital after Ron died, she found a letter addressed to him from the parole board. Smith was up for parole.

Barb was good to her word. She attended the parole meetings on Ron's behalf. "He wanted to know who was going to take care of it," she said months after Ron's death. "He was afraid that after he was gone people would forget. He didn't want them to ever get out of prison. There isn't a day that goes by that I don't deal with it."

Ron Nichols battled to keep the killers of his first wife in prison. His second wife, Barb, continued the battle after Ron died of cancer. (Courtesy of the *Columbus Dispatch*)

Martin was the first of the five to be paroled. After his release, he was murdered in Columbus. Maurice was paroled to New Orleans, where he, too, was murdered.

Harris, Royster, and Smith remain in prison. All three are due for parole hearings in 2004.

Shoeman Schulman and his Trusty .38

Charlie Schulman was seventy-one and though he didn't say so, I got the distinct impression that he was quite proud of himself. He had just shot a would-be robber who was fifty-three years his junior and who had believed—quite mistakenly—that Charlie was an easy mark.

When a man fifty-three years his junior tried to rob Charles Schulman, he did not realize that Schulman kept a .38-caliber revolver in his smock. Schulman shot the would-be robber. (Courtesy of the *Columbus Dispatch*)

In 1948, Schulman had been mugged by two men who clubbed him over the head and robbed him. He vowed it would never happen again and bought himself a handgun.

Schulman, a soft-spoken man who had operated Graceland Shoe Repair Shop on North High Street for thirty years, was behind the counter of his shop in November 1982 when eighteen-year-old

Mark R. Murphy pulled a knife and tried to relieve him of his wallet. It was a bad move, because Murphy had unknowingly brought a knife to a gunfight.

While Murphy was reaching for Schulman's wallet, Schulman was reaching for the .38-caliber revolver he kept hidden in his work smock.

When I went to his east-side home to interview him, Schulman greeted me at the door in a bathrobe and asked me to join him in a glass of sherry. Charlie was all smiles as he recreated the incident for me in his living room. He made a gun out of his index finger and thumb and demonstrated how he had pulled out the revolver and shoved it into Murphy's gut. "I held the gun to his stomach and said, 'You know what this is?'"

Apparently not, because he kept grabbing for Schulman's wallet.

"He didn't back off or say, 'Let's call it quits' or 'Let's be friends,' or anything. So, I shot him."

Murphy ended up in surgery at Riverside Hospital and charged with aggravated robbery.

And, Schulman said, he had no intention of permanently holstering the revolver. "Thirty years ago, I could handle myself pretty well. But if I didn't have the gun, I might be the one in the hospital."

FIFTEEN

❑

The Truly Unusual

Michael-Michelle Neff

No matter how dignified reporters want to make you think they are, there is a little tabloid journalist in all of them. It's not that we want to be sensational, it's just our attraction to the unusual. Thus my interest in the story of Michael Bruce Neff, a buff, handsome Westerville firefighter and father of three, who had announced to his chief that he was having a sex change operation and would soon be reporting to work as Michelle Panabecker Neff.

Photographer Kenny Chamberlain, who also was the photographer for the Mifflin Township Fire Department, had first heard of Neff's decision through some of his firefighter buddies. At the time, Neff was on a thirty-day medical leave from the department, during which he was learning to live, dress, and act like a woman. Fire Chief Richard Morrison had suggested the leave after Neff said he had been dressing as a woman when off duty.

I called the name in the phone book and Michael answered. It was Valentine's Day, 1983. I danced around the reason for my call, making some baloney introduction about the struggle of being a firefighter and a woman. After a few minutes of listening to me stammer, Neff said, "It sounds like you want to interview me about my sex change operation."

"Ah, actually, yes."

"Come on up," he said.

Neff was living in an apartment off Schrock Road near Westerville, a suburb north of Columbus. It took me a little over a half-hour to make the trip. I knocked on the door of the second-floor apartment where Neff was living. I knocked twice. There was no answer and I assumed that Neff had gotten cold feet after agreeing to the interview. I tried to peek into the window; the apartment appeared to be empty. In fact, the entire complex appeared empty except for a woman throwing trash in the Dumpster. "Crap," I muttered, pulling my two-way radio from its holster. "Yocum to city desk."

"Go," Karsko said.

"Bernie, he bailed on me. No one's home."

"Why don't you wait around in the press car. See if he comes back."

"Okay."

I was ready to walk down the steps when the woman who had been at the Dumpster reached the second-floor landing.

It was, in fact, a very ruggedly built woman. A woman with a bad wig and in bad need of a shave. Her blouse strained at the buttons, pulling over a thick chest; a pair of massive calves were sticking out from a skirt; her biceps were bigger than mine. In a deep voice, he said, "You must be Mr. Yocum."

"I am. You must be Michael."

"No," he said, matter-of-factly. "Michael's gone. I'm Michelle. Come on in."

I'd be lying if I said I wasn't a little uncomfortable in these situations. Michael-Michelle had the body of a guy who had lifted a lot of weights. Prior to deciding he was going to have a sex change, Michael-Michelle had been a body builder. He had a side business as an electrician. He rode dirt bikes. Take away the dress, wig, and makeup, and he looked like a guy's guy. And, he was sitting before me with a five-o'clock shadow, lipstick, and stuffed into a very poofy, curly wig and an ill-fitting skirt and blouse. The visual was hilarious. But, again, I was forced to conceal an overwhelming urge to laugh. The same principle held true for Michael-Michelle that applied to Monique, the six-foot-eight, transvestite-prostitute that I wrote about earlier. That principle is this: I did not laugh because I did not want to get my ass kicked by a guy in a dress.

"Now, before we get started, you are going to show me the article before it runs, right?" Michael-Michelle asked.

"No, I'm afraid I can't do that, Michelle. The paper's policy is very strict: no prior review of stories."

"Then, I'm not going to be interviewed."

"Well, it's more of a guideline than a policy. It's certainly not set in stone."

"Good. Because I don't want you writing something that's going to make me look ridiculous."

I was biting through the insides of my cheeks. "If I bring the story back up, you've got to promise that you won't tell anyone I did it."

"I just want to make sure that it's fair." He sat down in a rocking chair, adjusted his skirt and said, "What do you want to know?"

Michael-Michelle had been a Westerville firefighter for nine years. In fact, he had been one of the city's first full-time firefighters. He had been married—though now separated—for eight years and was the father of three sons. At the time of our interview, he had already started taking hormone injections through the Central Ohio

Gender Dysphoria Program. A receding hairline was starting to thicken, his hands were softening, and he was beginning to develop breasts. Ultimately, he said, he would have the operation to change his equipment.

"I've known I've had the problem since I was about ten," he said. "I just didn't know what to do with it. When I was younger, it wasn't much of a problem because I looked like a girl. I didn't start to man-out until my early twenties. When I looked at *Playboy*, all I'd say was, 'God, I'm never going to look that way.' I was very afraid to tell anyone when I was younger. I accepted the fact that I wasn't female, so I tried to become a good-looking male. I went the European Health Spa route and built up a chest and biceps. Someone like my-self is not a homosexual who wants to make things right with an op-eration. I've never had a relationship with a man."

He said he wasn't interested in a relationship with a man until he could "properly take care of him." I assumed this was a reference to the actual sex change operation, but I elected not to explore that particular area, so to speak. (There were, after all, still limitations to what I could get into the paper.) He told of watching his wife breast feed his sons and wishing that he could do it. "She saw me staring at her and said, 'You're sitting there wishing this was you, and it can never be, Michael.'" He looked at me and shrugged.

When I had finished the interview, I told Michael-Michelle that I was going back to the newsroom, write the story, then hustle it back up for him to read. Several times during the interview he had apologized for his appearance. The hormone injections had yet to cause his beard to disappear and his five o'clock shadow made him look, in his words, "frightful."

I wasn't sure how to respond. I didn't want to be insulting, but I certainly wasn't going to say, "No, Michelle, really, you look great."

I stammered around until he said, "I'm going to shave and

change into something different. I'll look much nicer when you get back."

"Really, don't go to any trouble," I insisted.

"Oh, it's no trouble. No trouble at all."

"Well, if you're going to dress up, is it okay to bring a photographer when I come back up?"

"Sure. Go ahead."

As I was walking down the stairs to the press car, I remember thinking, if only I had worked a little harder on hitting a curve ball, maybe I'd be playing second base for the Pittsburgh Pirates instead of worrying that a body-building firefighter was going to shave and put on a nicer dress for my return visit.

I wrote the story and when I returned, true to his word, Michael-Michelle had shaved and changed into another skirt and a silky blouse. I gave him a copy of the story, which he read, smiled, and said, "fine." My photographer snapped a few shots of Michael-Michelle and we headed for the door.

As we were leaving, he said, "I'll probably win the most-changed award at my fifteenth class reunion."

"Michelle, I feel pretty confident that you have a total lock on that award," I said, making a mental note to include the comment in the story when I got back to the newsroom.

The next morning, Michael Bruce Neff, wearing a plaid skirt and white blouse, appeared before Franklin County Probate Court Judge Richard Metcalf in an effort to have his name legally changed to Michelle Panabecker Neff. His attorney said that Neff was in the process of changing sexes and the name change was part of the process. His wife testified that the change would be detrimental to their sons, who also lived in Westerville. The judge denied the request, at which point Michael-Michelle dropped his head on the table, sobbed, and pounded the table with this fist, crying, "How long? How long do I have to wait?"

Following a year-long separation, the Neffs were divorced in November 1983. By this time, Michael-Michelle had been fired from the Westerville Fire Department. The judged awarded Mrs. Neff custody of the three boys, their home, and the car. Michael-Michelle was ordered to pay $90 a week in child support and $300 a month in alimony. Michael-Michelle attended the day-and-a-half divorce proceedings dressed as a woman.

I called Michael-Michelle once after the original story. He did not want to talk to me anymore and told me not to call back. I got the impression that the publicity had been a little overwhelming. Twice afterward, I saw Michael-Michelle, in his wig, driving up the interstate in his electric company truck. The original story was interesting, though it troubled me to think of the verbal abuse his sons would receive. Any updates on his plight, I thought, would amount to little more than voyeurism. I'm sure some people thought that of the first story. Like so many subjects of police beat stories, he became nothing more than a page in my clip file.

And Clean the Windshield, Too

I was covering a homicide at a gas station on the south side in which a robber had shot and killed the attendant. Detectives had taped off the entire lot as a crime scene. Police had to threaten to arrest a woman who became irate because police would not let her inside the crime-scene tape to put air in her tires.

Christian Nurse Assistant Institute

During an investigation of illegal colleges operating in Ohio, I had found an advertisement in the supermarket tabloid *The Globe* for the Christian Nurse Assistant Institute at 2368 South Fifth

Street in Columbus. The address was on the far south side, virtually in the shadows of the Buckeye Steel mill.

I drove up and down the block several times, unable to locate anything that looked like a school. Only a few of the houses had a street address attached. My best guess for 2368 was a duplex with vinyl siding and a yard adorned with plastic flowers and pink flamingos. There were moans emanating from the house. I knocked on the door; a woman yelled from the upstairs window, "Who is it?" I backed off the porch and looked up at a woman in a nurse's dress in the upstairs window. "Whatta ya want?"

"Sorry to bother you. I think I have the wrong address. I'm looking for the Christian Nurse Assistant Institute."

She smiled. "Oh, this is it. I'll be right down."

The woman's name was Mary Ann McEnroe and she introduced herself as the owner and director of the "college."

First of all, it should be noted that you do not need a degree to be a nurse assistant. As one hospital official later told me, "Basically, if you can drive to work, you qualify." However, McEnroe had worked as a nurse assistant and said she believed people could learn from her correspondence course, for which they would pay $240.

The students received a poorly written text she had authored. It was loaded with grammatical errors and littered with misspellings, and included such critical questions as: You should wash your hands after going to the bathroom. True or False? The rest of the book consisted of illegally copied pages from other, legitimate textbooks.

Tests were taken independently and mailed back. She said anyone who paid the registration fee graduated. Each graduate received a plastic name pin and a diploma.

McEnroe allowed me to examine a copy of the Christian Nurse Assistant Institute diploma. In the lower right corner was the school seal, which was hand-inked and looked suspiciously like a USDA Grade A beef seal.

"This looks like a meat inspection seal," I said.

"It is," McEnroe said. "We got some steaks from a truck over at the JCPenney Outlet. It was what I was looking for so I darkened out the government wording and copied over it with the name of the school."

The institute was closed by the Ohio State Board of School and College Registration shortly after the story appeared.

The moaning coming from the upstairs window, by the way, was an elderly woman who was living upstairs in the "institute." Authorities also began investigating McEnroe for running an illegal nursing home.

As I was preparing to write the series of stories on bogus colleges, I received a call from Ed Mason, a former FBI agent who had been retired just a few years as vice president and head of security at the *Dispatch*. It seemed that Ed held two degrees from Columbia Pacific University, a nonaccredited school and one of the mail-order colleges that would grant a person credit for "life experience." In exchange for your life experience—you might also be required to write a paper—and a tidy sum, CPU would confer upon you a master's or doctoral degree. After I contacted the college about my story, CPU asked Ed to act as the school's spokesman. We met in a small conference room at the paper where he tried to explain why the degrees were legitimate. When I resisted his explanation, he grew visibly angry and said, "You just don't get it, do you?"

"Oh, I get it just fine, Ed. You bought yourself a couple of phony degrees and now you want to justify it."

Ed was a big man and not one accustomed to being talked to in such an insolent manner by a reporter. He looked as if he wanted to punch me. "I'm going to go talk to John F. Wolfe about this," he said.

"Be my guest. I assume you remember where his office is."

He stormed out of the room in search of our publisher, trying to get the story killed. It ran, along with Ed's old *Dispatch* file photo.

Years later, I was working on a story and had to interview the head of public relations for a local defense contractor. If you called this gentleman "Mister," he would correct you and say, "It's Doctor." (Our policy at the *Dispatch* was that you did not get called doctor unless you had blood or saliva on your hands.) I was sitting in his office and noticed that on the wall were his master's and doctoral degrees—both from Columbia Pacific University. On a hunch, I asked him about his undergraduate degree. He had none. He had dropped out of college, but later went back and bought his other degrees.

Yes, by all means, allow me to call you "Doctor."

Bill Golden

Bill Golden was the chief of police in Plain City, a village on the Union-Madison county line, west of Columbus. He was an easygoing, chain-smoking man who became a buddy of mine when I was on the *Dispatch* state desk, covering western and southwestern Ohio. We used to meet at the Golden Safe restaurant for coffee once a week. Bill had a son who was a state trooper and a son-in-law who was a sheriff's deputy, so Bill always knew what was going on.

I met Bill in early 1980 when I was doing a series of stories concerning some mischief created by Conrail work crews in western Ohio. In preparation for an inspection tour by company officials, local supervisors eager to collect incentive bonuses, ordered workers to dig giant holes and bury tons of perfectly good railroad materials, such as rails, tie plates, anchors, and spikes. Supposedly, burying the material would clean up the right-of-way and project the image of an operation that was ahead of schedule. One of the burial locations was rumored to be near Plain City.

I was brand new at the *Dispatch* and had no contacts in my territory, so the first place I stopped was the Plain City Police Station.

Bill was the only one on duty, and when I told him what I was working on, it must have piqued his interest, because he put me in the cruiser and drove me all over the area looking for someone who might give me a lead. When we found one, we drove about ten miles out of town looking for a burial site.

"Aren't you worried about being this far out of town?" I asked.

He flicked his cigarette ashes out the window and shook his head. "They'll track me down if they need me, which they won't. Not much happens in Plain City."

From that day forward, Bill and I became friends.

In January 1981, Bill called me with a gem of story.

Several *Dispatch* reporters had been working on stories about David Britt Jensen, a local seventeen-year-old who was under investigation for impersonating a physician and was wanted by police for having a stolen oscilloscope. Jensen was a high school dropout who had been described as a genius. By the time Bill called, Jensen had checked himself into the University Hospital's Upham Hall, a psychiatric ward.

It was just after noon on a Friday when Bill called. "Come on out. I've got something for you," he said.

"You want me to come to the police station."

"No. Meet me over at the Golden Safe."

The Golden Safe was a restaurant at the main intersection of Plain City. It was located in an old bank building. When I arrived, Bill was sitting alone at a table, a cigarette in his hand, and a cup of coffee and a manila folder on the table in front of him. "The good doctor has been a busy boy," he said, sliding the folder across the table.

Inside the envelope was an emergency squad report that had been taken in Plain City on July 21, 1980, following the death of seventy-three-year-old Carl B. Stewart, who suffered an allergic reaction to a bee sting and died before emergency squads could arrive.

"Read this line," he said, pointing to a line toward the bottom of the page.

Stewart was pronounced dead by Dr. Jensen from University Hospital.

"Whoa. Did he sign the death certificate?"

"I don't know. But his word that old Carl was dead certainly made it official."

Bill put me in touch with David Hay, the local fire chief who had been on the scene the day Stewart died. Hay said the paramedics were at the scene when Jensen pulled up in a sports car. He identified himself as Dr. Britt Jensen from University Hospital. He examined the body and officially pronounced Steward dead.

"He came walking up with a lab coat on with "Dr. Jensen" on the front, an Ohio State medical emblem and an Ohio State ID card hanging from it, and a stethoscope around his neck," Hay said. "He looked old enough to be a doctor and no one questioned him."

Hay said the previous fall, Jensen showed up at a three-car accident just north of Plain City. Said Hay, "There weren't any serious injuries and as we were about ready to leave, he came walking up and said, "I'm Dr. David Jensen. I live just down the road there; can I be of any help?"

Jensen was committed to the Ohio Youth Commission in March 1981 after being convicted of three delinquency counts of receiving stolen property when he was found in possession of computer and medical equipment valued at nearly $32,000. After his release from the Youth Commission in November 1981, Jensen continued to find trouble. He was again charged with receiving stolen property, writing a bad check for $1,750, and grand theft. He was sentenced to prison for three years in 1984 after being convicted of forgery in Franklin County, and later sentenced to eighteen months in prison after being convicted of theft in Cuyahoga County in 1991.

Unfreeze the Fuel Line

An east-side man burned himself after putting a pot of gasoline on the stove to heat. His plan was to pour the gasoline into his frozen fuel line to thaw it. Of course, it exploded on the stove, sending him to the hospital.

The Matador of the Garbage Truck

The lesson of July 25, 1983, was, I guess, don't mess with a soon-to-be former husband who has access to a garbage truck.

I was standing in an east-side alley with Homicide Sgt. Jerry Knoblauch and looking at him with slack-jawed disbelief. "I guess at least we need to give him style points," I said. Minutes earlier, police had put out an all-points bulletin for a garbage truck and its driver, the aforementioned husband, who had reportedly used the loading tong on the front of the truck to gore his estranged wife's boyfriend.

Knoblauch had just finished interviewing the gored man's girlfriend, who related this story:

Rick Osborne, nineteen, and his twenty-eight-year-old girlfriend, Cheryl Kirk, were in her car with her two sons, ages seven and eight, when they realized that Kirk's estranged husband, Richard Kirk, and a female companion were in a garbage truck behind them. Mrs. Kirk told police that she was separated from her husband and had started divorce proceedings against him.

At the intersection of St. Clair and East Fifth avenues, Mr. Kirk used the loading tongs to pick up the rear end of his wife's car and drop it. He then threatened everyone in the car.

Mrs. Kirk said she ran red lights and drove through the neighborhood at speeds reaching 80 mph trying to get away from the garbage truck. Unable to lose the truck, she drove into the alley and jumped out of the car. Osborne shoved his girlfriend and the boys over a fence, but was unable to get away from the loading tong, which pierced his stomach. The assailant used the tong to pick Osborne off the ground and shake him before dropping him on the pavement. Mr. Kirk then drove over Osborne's legs with the double-tandem wheels.

One of the paramedics said Osborne had been taken to St. Anthony Hospital with what appeared to be two broken legs and an abdominal injury.

Mr. Kirk, meanwhile, had made his escape in the garbage truck.

"That must be one haulin'-ass garbage truck," I said. "She says she was going 80 mph and running red lights, and he still caught up with them?" Knoblauch shrugged. "So why did she stop in the alley?"

"She said they were trying to get away from him."

"Couldn't escape him in a car, so she thought maybe she could outrun him, huh?"

Knoblauch smiled.

So many questions.

SIXTEEN
❑

The Truly Bizarre

If I Only Had a Brain

ROOM 100 AT THE OLD COLUMBUS DIVISION OF POLICE head-quarters served as a quasi information desk, and most people wandering in off the streets eventually found their way there. It also was the room where people involved in minor traffic accidents came to file their reports, and the room was lined with one-piece, school-type chair-desks. Officer Dan Canada manned the desk during the dayshift.

On October 26, 1983, at 8:30 A.M., the scanner crackled with the broadcast that a paramedic unit was being sent to the police station, Room 100. This was not unusual. Generally, it was a homeless person in need of either medical or psychiatric help. But, since it was only about five steps from the pressroom, I always checked out the runs, just in case it happened to be the chief of police having a heart attack.

On the far side of the room was a man in his early twenties sitting in one of the chair-desks with his back to me. Two uniformed officers were standing next to him. "What's up?" I asked Canada.

He rolled his eyes toward the young man and said, "Go see for yourself."

Viewing the man from the back, nothing seemed amiss. I walked up for a closer look. Protruding from the middle of the man's forehead, just below the scalp line, was a six-inch piece of bailing wire. Blood was smeared on his forehead and there was a nasty cut on his right temple, from which a line of dried blood snaked down the side of his face. He seemed oblivious to the pain the wire had to have been causing, and he spoke in a clear, calm voice. At first, I thought someone had stabbed him in the head with the wire—until I heard him speak.

"I don't think I have a brain," said the twenty-two-year-old, who was dressed in jeans and a white T-shirt stained with dots of dried blood. "So I was trying to find it. I drilled a hole in my head and was putting in the wire to try to find it. But I couldn't. I don't think it's there."

The two cops looked at me. Even by the standards of things seen by a street cop, this was bizarre. They put a pair of handcuffs on him in hopes of preventing him from causing further damage to himself.

"Where do you think your brain went?" I asked.

"The aliens took it. I'm sure it's not in there because I couldn't find it."

I could see a ridge of protruding skin where the bailing wire was running along the inside of his scalp and around the left side of his head. He had apparently drilled through the skin and then tried to insert the wire. Fortunately, he wasn't able to penetrate his skull.

"How did you drill through your head?"

"My dad's three-eighths-inch power drill. "He put his two cuffed hands in the air in front of his head as if holding an imaginary drill. "I tried to drill in through the side," he said, pointing to the cut on his right temple, "but I couldn't get inside there, so I went in from the front."

Everyone else in the room cringed in unison.

"Didn't that hurt?" I asked.

He shook his head no.

"Hurts me," one of the cops said.

By this time, the paramedics were coming through the door. Canada was standing next to me as the paramedics tried to figure out how to protect the forehead.

"He came walking in and said he wanted an X-ray," Canada said. "I said, 'You mean a medical X-ray?' He said he wanted to check if his brain was still there. He said, 'I don't think I have one. Look.' Then he started pulling a wire out of his head. He pulled it out two or three inches. Blood was going all over place. Those guys were here and they got him cuffed and sat him down."

The paramedics looked at the man, then at everyone in the room. One of them asked, "What'd you do to yourself, partner?"

And, again, the man calmly explained his concern and solution.

The paramedics poked a hole in the bottom of a Styrofoam coffee cup and placed it over the wire, then secured it by wrapping a spongy pre-wrap around the cup and his head. He walked out and they took him to Grant Hospital, where he was admitted to the psychiatric unit.

We ran the story without the man's name, which seemed proper. When I returned to the newsroom later that day, Ned Stout greeted me by whistling a few bars of, "If I Only Had a Brain," from the *Wizard of Oz*. Cops and newspaper people were alike in this respect: They never missed an opportunity to exchange a little sick humor.

Cavewoman

Sara Wilburn became known as the Columbus Cavewoman after police found her, two of her five children, and her fourteen-year-old boyfriend living in a dugout, cave-like area in the landfill near the Central Ohio Transit Authority bus barn.

Juvenile Officer Ruth Wilcox rapped on my door the morning of Monday, April 26, 1982, and said, "Follow me out to the west side. You're not going to believe this one."

By the time we arrived, the thirty-five-year-old Wilburn had been arrested after she told police that she and the three juveniles had spent the weekend in the cave. Her two children had already been taken away by caseworkers for Franklin County Children Services. One of the patrol officers at the scene said the soot from the fires they had started in the cave had blackened Wilburn's children. "You'd have thought they fell in a coal bin," the officer said.

Wilburn had been living in a west-side apartment, but accepted $100 from her landlord to move out the previous Friday. On Monday, the family's possessions were heaped in the backyard of the apartment; a meager amount of clothing and crossword puzzles littered the ground near the cave.

Wilburn had $77 remaining in her pocket when she was arrested and taken to the Women's Workhouse, charged with endangering her children and interfering with custody for her relationship with the 14-year-old, who had been reported missing by his parents the previous Thursday.

The following day, after Wilburn had been released from the workhouse, reporter Julia Keller tracked her down. Wilburn gave Keller and a photographer a tour of her landfill cave. Wilburn said of her weekend home, "It's paradise," and that her weekend in the cave was "a ball."

Keller also tracked down Wilburn's estranged husband, who further ingratiated himself with Children Services with this quote:

"I've got a shotgun, and the next time Children Services interferes with me and my family, I'm taking some of them along with me."

The Big Bribe

A woman from Jamaica was living as an illegal immigrant on the northeast side when Immigration and Naturalization officials showed up to take her into custody for deportation. It became a hostage situation when she barricaded herself in the bathroom with a knife and several children.

I was standing outside the house with an Immigration officer who was watching the house while police hostage negotiators tried to talk the woman out of the bathroom. A neighbor of the woman—a man in his late sixties or early seventies—walked up to where we were talking. "What's going on?" the neighbor asked.

The Immigration officer explained that they were deporting the woman. "She's an illegal alien," he said. "She has to go back."

"No, don't do that. I like her," the neighbor said.

"Sorry. There's nothing I can do about it," the officer said.

The old man looked around, then pulled his hand out of his pocket with a ten-dollar bill folded between his fingers. "You think maybe this could make the problem go away?"

The Immigration officer looked down at the money, then at me and winced. "You better put that way and get back home before you get yourself in trouble. You're trying to bribe a government official right in front of a newspaper reporter. That could get you in a lot of trouble."

The old man shoved the money back in his pocket and went quietly home.

"You handled that well," I said.

"Story of my life," the agent said. "The first time in my career that someone tries to bribe me and it's for ten bucks."

The woman released the children unharmed; she was deported.

Suicide by Police

Wayne Godsey committed suicide by police.

This is a phenomenon whereby a person has decided to end his or her life, but lacks the courage to complete the act. In Godsey's case, he put himself in a position where police officers had no choice but to shoot him.

Godsey was a forty-seven-year-old mechanic. Co-workers said he lost job after job because of his alcoholic binges. One former employer said that Godsey would tear apart a carburetor, announce that he was going out to get a sandwich, and would not return for two months. About midnight on Saturday, May 23, 1981, Godsey discharged a gun several times in the lot of a service station on Lockbourne Road, where his house trailer was parked. Police arrived and he ran back into the trailer. With police surrounding the trailer, Godsey remained inside for about four hours, screaming that he wanted to die; he wanted to go to heaven; he wanted to meet Jesus.

At about 3:40 A.M. on Sunday, Columbus police SWAT officers accommodated him.

Godsey set his trailer on fire and came out the door, walking toward police officers with a revolver pointed at them, yelling that he wanted to die. Two officers shot and killed Godsey before he could shoot. He was dead at the scene.

All Points Lookout

I reported to work one morning to find that the Ohio State Highway Patrol, which has jurisdiction over all state buildings, had put out the following all-points bulletin:

We have an all-points lookout for a 7-foot, 280-pound black female, 30 years old. She has a yellow thread in one ear and a blue thread in the other. She's wearing a pale red shower curtain, a diaper and tennis shoes and has a Findlay-based credit card up her anus. Traveling with her is a black male, 5-10, who claims to be blind. They both escaped from the Tiffin Mental Health Center.

We didn't write about the escape. However, it was debated in the newsroom. Several editors thought it was a gag. I reasoned that it was legitimate because I had never in my life met a cop with that much imagination.

I kept the bulletin for its absurdity. I assume the pair was found and returned, but I always wondered whose job it had been to look for the credit card. Probably the new guy.

SEVENTEEN

❏

The Art of the Interview

Putting Away the Notebook and Other Tricks

THERE ARE MANY TECHNIQUES FOR GETTING PEOPLE TO OPEN UP during an interview. For me, the most effective was the simple act of putting away my notebook and pen. I discovered this method on February 7, 1982, after narcotics officer Charles Sealy was shot in the back of the head during a botched raid.

The mayhem began on a Sunday afternoon. I was in the newsroom with a couple of copy editors when the first call came over the scanner. There was so much screaming on the police radio that I could not discern what was going on. I called the police dispatcher, got an address for the chaos, and left.

Sealy and two other narcotics officers—Thomasina E. Jacobs and Bertha M. Johnson—had planned a buy-bust with Earl F. Jeter at his home. This is a simple arrest that occurs immediately after a suspect sells an officer drugs. The plan was for Sealy to go to the door, make the purchase, and give a signal to the two officers in the car, who would join him and assist in the arrest. Somehow, things got fouled up in the translation. After making the purchase, Sealy identified himself as a police officer and tried to make the bust without a badge or warrant. Jeter thought he was being ripped off by another drug dealer, and the shooting began. Sealy caught a .22-caliber slug in the back of his head, sending him sprawling in the front yard.

The two officers in the car responded to their fallen comrade by diving under the dashboard and screaming incoherently into the police radio. They would not take their fingers off the "talk" button. No one could discern what was going on; uniformed officers could not immediately secure the scene; paramedics could not get to the scene. Meanwhile, Sealy continued to lie and bleed in the front yard until a uniformed officer ran up, returned fire, and dragged him to safety.

It was a mess.

That night, I was at the Narcotics Bureau with Lt. John Tilley while they tried to sort out the events of the afternoon. I was given the standard police line, which I had expected. They did not want to go into detail on whether the two officers who had stayed in the car had acted appropriately. As I got ready to go back to the newsroom to write the story, I put my notebook and pen into my hip pocket.

Immediately, the narcotics officers began telling the real story of the afternoon's events. It was as if by putting the notebook away, I had turned invisible. I sat back in my chair, laughed when the cops laughed and frowned when they frowned, but no one paid any attention to me. (One of the things they were laughing about was the fact that Sealy had taken a bullet to the back of the head and was seemingly no worse for the experience.)

Obviously, I did not need my notebook and pen to gather information. Reporters are like sponges for information. If they can see it or hear it, they will absorb it. I used the technique numerous times in the years I was on the police beat. They did not seem to understand that a reporter did not need a pen and paper to collect information. Every time I used the technique, I had a follow-up conversation that went something like:

"Hey, Yocum, what's the deal? You used information that wasn't part of the interview."

"What do you mean, it 'wasn't part of the interview'?"

"It was off the record."

"Why was it off the record?"

"You put your pen and pad away."

"So what?"

Then, they would start to realize the sponge theory.

I liked Tilley and most of the narcotics officers, and I did not want to burn them. Rather, the next day I went to the narcotics captain, who had not been part of the previous night's conversation, and said, "A source gave me some information on the shooting and I want to run it by you."

He said, "That's accurate. You've got a pretty good source."

Miraculously, Sealy was released from the hospital five days after the shooting. The bullet penetrated the scalp, then traveled along the outside of the skull until coming to rest near the temple. It never penetrated his skull.

Police investigated the incident, including the behavior of the two officers who failed to come to Sealy's assistance. They were never charged in the case.

The man who shot Sealy, Earl F. Jeter, was acquitted of attempted murder charges after it was determined that Sealy attempted to charge into the house with gun drawn and without a badge or warrant. The jury ruled that Jeter was acting in self-defense.

Other Methods

Putting the notebook away was my favorite trick for getting sources to let their guard down and talk. There were, however, other tactics. One of the best is the "silent treatment." Ask a question, listen intently to the answer, and when the source is done answering, don't ask another question. Just sit and stare. The silence is so uncomfortable that the source will continue talking just to fill the void. One of my former editors, Jim Breiner, was an expert at this technique.

Another tactic was to simply play to the ego of your source. I once went over to East Liverpool, Ohio, to do a story on an oil slick rolling down the Ohio River from Pittsburgh. I called the mayor and asked if I could stop over for an interview. He moaned that he had been spending too much time talking to reporters. "You can come on over," he said, "but I've got a full-time job that I have to get to. I can't give you any more than five minutes."

His wife let me into the house; she said the mayor was showering and getting ready for work. She asked me to wait in the living room, which had one entire wall filled with leather-bound, gold-embossed reproductions of classic novels. I pulled one off the shelf and opened it. The spine snapped like a dry piece of wood. So did the next one, and the next and the next. None of them had ever been opened.

When the mayor came back down the steps, I had just cracked the spine of *A Tale of Two Cities*. He smiled and said, "Oh, admiring my collection of classics, huh? As you can see, I'm quite a reader."

"Reader," I thought, might be a bit of an exaggeration. "Yes, this is quite an impressive collection. You should be quite proud of it."

"Oh, I am. I am."

"It must have taken a while to accumulate such a collection."

"Years. They're quite expensive, you know."

We chatted for a few minutes and he finally said, "Oh, I can be a little bit late for work."

And off we went.

In another instance, I had to go to Canton to interview the head of a railroad workers union. During my initial interview on the phone, the union man mentioned to me, at every opportunity, that he had graduated from Harvard. Now, this gentleman's grammar was as atrocious as any I had ever heard and I thought, "Harvard?" And, the obvious question, "What is a Harvard graduate doing working for a railroad union in Canton, Ohio?"

When I arrived at his office, he was seated behind his desk, prominently sporting a huge Harvard class ring. On the far wall was his ornately framed Harvard diploma. With apologies to Bowling Green State University, I thought, "Yocum, you really sold yourself short." During the interview he continued to mutilate the English language. When he took a restroom break, I strolled across the room to take a closer look at the diploma.

So, technically, he did graduate from Harvard. However, it was a two-week business leadership seminar!

Harvard graduate, indeed. He even bought a class ring to authenticate his accomplishment.

But this had no bearing on my story. And he became a welcome resource because from that point on I gushed about his Harvard diploma and that beautiful ring. I got all the cooperation I needed.

Another tactic was to get a police officer to let me use information attributed to "sources said." Most of the time, the cops did not care if I put the information they gave me in the paper, they just did not want it attributed to them. Go ahead and use it, but say, "sources said."

I disliked using unidentified sources, but sometimes it was the only way to get cops to talk. While homicide detectives did not want to be seen talking to me, I could still get an occasional story out of them if I did not identify them as my sources.

One memorable instance occurred after Roy Howard Sage was charged with the shooting death of eighteen-year-old Ohio University student Catherine Wanner in February 1982. Sage, forty-seven, had told detectives that Wanner, a freshman accounting major, had shot herself as part of a mutual suicide pact the two had. Both Sage and Wanner had chest and head wounds. Sage's wounds, however, were minor and police suspected that was simply a bogus story to attempt to cover the homicide.

Police said they found a suicide note, purportedly written by Wanner to her parents, in Sage's apartment. However, a source in the detective bureau also told me that another woman, Christine M. Lindsey, had contacted police and said Sage had made her write a suicide note before he would sell her drugs. He kept the note to use against her, Lindsey told investigators.

Meanwhile, Sgt. Bill Steckman had imposed another virtual news blackout. In a written statement, he said: "Because a police investigation is continuing and witnesses still have to be interviewed, information cannot be released on the probable cause for the warrant, the scope or direction of the investigation, or Mr. Sage's reaction to his arrest."

In other words, go screw yourself.

Desperate for a follow-up story and armed with a snippet of information that Suzanne had given me, I caught a detective in the downstairs hall and said, "Let me run something by you. Sage says Wanner committed suicide. So, she was shot in the left side of her head. But the trace-metal test came back positive on her right hand." I reached across my chest with my right hand as if holding an imaginary gun, demonstrating that it would have been impossible to hold a revolver and shoot herself as Sage claimed. "So, he had to have pulled the trigger. It would have been impossible for her to put the gun to her head and still pull the trigger."

He frowned and said, "How'd you know that?"

"I didn't. I was guessing. You just confirmed it."

He shoved me out of the main hall and into the stairwell. "You can't use my name with that. They've got orders that no one is to talk to you," he said. "They'll kick my ass out of the detective bureau."

"Sources said?" I offered.

His eyes widened. "Yeah. Sources said. Great. Go for it, but protect me."

I agreed.

(Several reporters covered the Sage-Wanner case. Bob Ruth wanted to get an interview with Sage, who had been admitted to Riverside Hospital following the shooting and was under police guard. Mike Harden had just been hired by the *Dispatch* as a columnist and had received a congratulatory bouquet, which was on his desk. Ruth walked by and said, "Hey, you don't want these, do you?"

Harden wasn't sure how to respond, but said, "No, I guess not."

"Good, because I need them."

Ruth took the flowers to the hospital and posed as a relative going to visit Sage. He actually got into the room and got a few brief quotes from Sage.)

Sage was convicted of aggravated murder and sentenced to life in prison in 1982. In 1985, he won a retrial on appeal, but was convicted again. He remains in prison.

Jeffrey Scott Took an Ax . . .

At 8 A.M. on Monday, February 28, 1983, the bodies of Raymond and Nellie Tennihill were found in their Linden-area home. There were signs of a struggle and broken glass and blood covered their one-story home. The bodies of the couple were found after Nellie's sister-in-law, Janet McDonald, feared something had gone wrong at the Tennihills' and contacted police. A patrol officer found the body of the sixty-nine-year-old Raymond in a hallway; his fifty-three-year-old wife was in a bedroom. They had been beaten and hacked to death with an ax.

The following day, eighteen-year-old Jeffrey A. Scott, Janet McDonald's son, was charged with the murders. Scott, who had a long history of mental problems, was questioned after the bodies were found; he was jailed on an outstanding warrant for driving without a license. This enabled police to hold him while they conducted their investigation.

Police searched Scott's apartment, which was within walking distance of the Tennihill home, and found a blood-splattered, short-handled ax. After he was charged, the cops began referring to Scott by the macabre nickname, "Lizzy," after the famous ax murderer, Lizzy Borden.

On Tuesday afternoon, I drove up to interview the parents of the accused killer. As I walked up to the door, I passed the two *Citizen-Journal* reporters who had been in conducting the same interview that I was now seeking. They smirked, satisfied that they would beat me to the story the next morning.

The interview took place in the kitchen of the small home on the north side of Columbus with Janet and Frank McDonald, Scott's mother and stepfather. The dynamics of the household and the connection to the murdered couple were as odd and intermingled as any I had ever dealt with. Frank and Janet McDonald were divorced. They explained that they had filed for divorce the previous year. By the time the divorce became final, however, they had reconciled. (Either they had decided not to remarry, or they had yet to get around to it. I was never quite clear on that point.) Nevertheless, they were living together as husband and wife, though technically divorced.

Jeffrey Allen Scott took an ax and butchered his aunt and uncle. His mother told me she wanted her son to be executed if he was found guilty of the murders. (Courtesy of the *Columbus Dispatch*)

Mr. McDonald was the brother of the slain woman—Nellie Tennihill. Janet McDonald and Mrs. Tennihill were best friends. "I couldn't get closer to my sister than I was with Nell," Janet said. "We were tighter than sisters. Anytime she needed something, I was the only one she'd ever call."

In fact, the McDonalds and the Tennihills had been married eleven years earlier in a double-ring ceremony on Jeffrey's seventh birthday.

Mrs. MacDonald explained that Jeffrey, her son from a previous marriage, had spent most of the previous ten years in juvenile detention centers and mental institutions. "Jeffrey has a lot of problems," Mrs. McDonald conceded.

Frank McDonald had a strained relationship with his stepson to begin with, and now the boy was charged with butchering Frank's sister. By the time I walked in the door, just a day after the bodies were found, Frank was already talking about "her son," and "my sister."

There are times when the best interview is no interview at all. Sometimes, if you are fortunate, you meld into the scenery and become like a piece of furniture. You are simply an observer and no one seems to notice you. At times of great tragedy, people can become so consumed by grief and their own concerns that they converse and act as though you do not exist.

Frank McDonald's face was drawn and tired; he looked as if he had not slept or shaved in a couple of days. He offered me a can of Hamm's Beer. I accepted and he apologized because it was warm. He poured it into a plastic cup and set it on the kitchen table in front of me. My pen and pad were in my hip pocket. I made no attempt to take notes. To pull out the notebook might remind them of just who was sitting at their table.

Janet wanted to defend her son. She wanted desperately to believe that he was not capable of such a crime. She said her son was quite close to the Tennihills and would visit them up to six times a day. "They were real close," she said of Raymond Tennihill and her son. "He and Jeff would sometimes go to a bar together and then stay up talking 'til four in the morning. That's why I can't understand this." (Taking someone with a history of mental illness out drinking until the wee hours didn't seem like a good idea to me, but I didn't bring it up.)

Frank, meanwhile, had already made up his mind about his stepson's guilt. After spending years in institutions, Jeffrey had moved back in with the McDonalds about eighteen months earlier. Frank said the boy was a problem from the minute he walked in their door and was largely responsible for their divorce. He related a story of the time Jeffrey had taken Frank's machine gun (again, I was curious as to why Frank had a machine gun, but I didn't want to disrupt the flow of the interview) and used it on the family bathtub, shooting out one end. Frank said that was only one of Jeffrey's many bizarre stunts, noting that the boy was fascinated with guns and knives.

The police had taken Frank through the ransacked Tennihill home. Their safe was open and empty. There were bloody hand marks all along the baseboard where, Frank theorized, Raymond had made a desperate attempt to crawl to his wife's aid. "I told the cops right then and there that Jeffrey killed 'em," Frank said.

After the bodies had been found, Frank recalled, "I asked Jeff when was the last time he stopped over at Ray and Nell's. He said Friday, and I said, 'You're lying.' He got white. I mean real white, and started shaking. He put his head on his mom's shoulder and started crying. I'm going to kill him. That was my sister. If he don't get the electric chair, I'll get in jail and kill him. If I've got to beat up a cop to get there, I will kill him."

The comments brought a hateful stare from Janet. "Yeah, you talk big," she said, sneering at Frank from across the table.

"I could get him killed," Frank said. "I've got connections in the prisons. I could get it done. I'd get a hold of one of my connections and they'd put out the word and . . ." He snapped his fingers. "He's a dead man."

"Frank, you don't know that he did it. He's only been charged, not convicted," Janet said, her voice climbing.

"I know. I know plenty."

"How do you know?"

"The law told me."

She leaned across the kitchen table, her jaw tightening, and she said, "The law told you SQUAT! Why in hell would they tell you anything?"

"Woman, I'm telling you, they told me he did it. When I was over at the house with 'em, they told me they knew Jeff did it. They know it for a fact. He took that ax and hacked Raymond and Nellie to pieces."

"Well, I'm hurtin', too, Frank. She was my best friend." Janet pulled out a chair and sat down. For the first time since I had entered the kitchen, she made eye contact with me. "As God is my judge, if that boy did wrong, I want him to burn," Janet said. "If he truly did it, yes, he should get the chair. He's my son and I love him. I brought him into this world, but I'd be willing to take him out."

The lead for my story had just exited her mouth.

Now I worried that she would consider the gravity of her comments and ask me not to print them. I would have denied the request, which would have brought the interview to an abrupt close. I continued to maintain my silence, nodding as though I understood and sympathized. During Frank's tirade, I had slowly taken the notebook out of my pocket and had it in my lap. Between sips of warm Hamm's Beer, I was jotting notes, trying to write while keeping my eyes focused on the McDonalds.

She swiped tears from eyes that were already red from a day-and-a-half of crying. "In my mind I know Jeff did it, but in my heart I know he didn't," Janet said. "I want to see proof. Proof is what convicts people . . ." She turned her gaze from me to Frank and finished, ". . . not talk."

The story ran across the top of the front page under the headline:

MOTHER WANTS SON TO DIE IF HE'S GUILTY

The greatest satisfaction, however, was comparing my story to the lame article that appeared in the *C-J* under the headline:

SUSPECT'S TROUBLED LIFE RECOUNTED

One of the *C-J* reporters saw me the evening after the story ran and asked, "Did she say that during your interview yesterday?"
"She did."

He didn't ask any further questions, but I assumed that some *C-J* editors had screamed when they compared the two stories, and they had first dibs. I shared a warm beer with Frank and was able to slide into the background. I would like to tell you that getting the story was the result of superior interviewing skills, but frankly, it was simply knowing when to keep my mouth shut.

After numerous delays in his trial, Scott was convicted of aggravated murder and aggravated robbery in 1986 and sentenced to life in prison. His first parole hearing is scheduled for March 2013.

Faux Heart Attack

Sometimes, you couldn't help but laugh at the tragic. The cops always said it was a defense mechanism to keep you from going crazy while dealing with one tragedy after another. To a degree, they were probably right. But, other times the circumstances surrounding a death are so bizarre that you can't help but see the humor through the tragedy.

In July 1981, I covered a story of a woman who had been killed by the tire of a cement truck. The lug nuts on the rear wheel of the cement truck broke, causing the 300-pound tire to break away. Free of the axle, the tire began bouncing down the berm and hit the sixty-two-year-old woman as she was pedaling her bicycle home from the fitness center. She was sixty-two and worked out every day. According to her husband, she never missed a workout and was in incredible shape. He said she would have lived to be a hundred.

And she gets killed by a runaway cement truck tire on her way home from the gym.

The evening after she was killed, I went to her west-side home to interview her husband. He was a friendly little man and grateful for the company. He had been sitting in the house alone. They had been married forty-three years, but had no children or relatives in Columbus. A few hours earlier, the police had shown up to tell him his wife had been killed. "I went down to the hospital as quick as I could, but she was already dead," he said. "They told me on the phone she was in bad shape."

After he got home, I was the next person to the door. We talked for a long time. He told me about his wife, her likes and dislikes, and their life together.

"I don't know what I'm going to do now," he said. "Just when we were getting to where we could enjoy life. We have no children, that's what is really bad. She was the perfect wife. We used to take long bike rides in the evening all over the west side, but not any more."

I felt terrible for him and I stayed after I had finished my inter-view. He showed me his collection of autographed photos of coun-try singers and we talked. Mostly, I just listened. That is, until my mind began to wander. I hadn't made a round of calls in a couple of hours and I needed to get back to the newsroom and start writing, but I felt bad that he was alone.

Suddenly, in midsentence, the man gasped, pitched forward in his chair, clutched his chest with both hands, and fell forward onto the floor.

I bolted out of my chair and started looking around the room for a phone. This was not good. I immediately envisioned the teaser for the 11 o'clock news. *Dispatch* reporter badgers grieving man to death . . . film at eleven.

However, a few seconds later he lifted himself back into his chair, brushed at the dust on his knees, and continued with his story. He had been telling me about a heart attack he had suffered at a country music concert in Oklahoma. I had not been paying attention and thought he was having a real heart attack.

It was a lesson learned. From that day on, once I had my story, I left.

Get Out

There had been a shooting in the Columbus suburb of Urbancrest, a largely African American community southwest of the city. A seventy-seven-year-old man shot one of three women who were breaking into his house about 5 P.M. I went down to cover the story and found the man standing outside his house with a group of about two dozen neighbors. I began interviewing the man, who was having trouble following my questions. In fact, he seemed totally out of touch. After a few minutes, his son, a large, no-nonsense type, walked up and said, "You know, I don't think you need to interview my dad," he said. "He's been through a lot, he's confused, and I don't want anything getting in the paper that's going to cause him problems."

I said, "Okay, just a minute. I only have a few more questions."

The son said, "Uh-huh, let me put it to you this way: I want you to get your pasty white ass out of here."

I said, "That, I understand. See ya."

The story ran just seven paragraphs, sans quotes.

Stun-Gunned

My lead, I thought, said it all.

It was a pretty courageous move for a man who as a senior in high school had to be tricked into going to the dentist.

Columbus police Chief Dwight Joseph was considering issuing stun guns to his officers. A stun gun is about the size of a cell phone and is powered by a 9-volt battery. When the user compresses a button on the gun, a blue arc jumps between two steel diodes on the business end of the device. When the gun is pressed against a victim, the arc disperses between 20,000 and 150,000 volts through the body. The jolt knocks the victim to the ground and temporarily immobilizes him. It's a great device for using against belligerent drunks and in close-quarter battles.

For whatever reason, rather than simply interview the experts on the power of a stun-gun, I decided to do a first-person story on what it is like to get zapped with one.

I went to the Davis Gun Shop in the Columbus suburb of Dublin for the test. Assisting me in the experiment was Dr. Steve Ditto, a Sigma Nu fraternity brother from Bowling Green who had just completed medical school at Ohio State University. I worried that Steve had been a little too eager when he volunteered to deliver the zap, but I allowed him to go along anyway.

Susan Davis, manager of the store, handed Steve the stun gun. He pressed the activation button and the blue electric arc jumped from diode to diode, making a crackling sound. Zzzzt. He smiled.

"Enjoying this, are you?" I asked.

He made the arc jump again. Zzzzt. "Don't worry, Robin. Remember, I'm a doctor." Zzzzt. He grinned an evil grin. Zzzzt.

"The only thing you might be concerned about is, if you get a good jolt, you might wet your drawers," Davis said.

"Excellent," Steve said.

"You didn't tell me that on the phone before I came up," I said.

"You didn't ask," Davis said.

Zzzzt. Zzzzt. "Let's get started." Zzzzt.

"Steve, let's remember that you're now a man of healing."

Zzzzt. Zzzzt. Zzzzt.

Steve reached out and gave me a jolt with the gun. He pulled back too quickly. Or maybe I jumped away too quickly. The jolt was weak, but strong enough to buckle my knees, though I was able to brace my fall. Davis said, "Try it again. This time press it right against his leg and turn it on."

Steve smiled again. "This will make for some great stories at parties." He did as Davis instructed. There was a loud crackle. This time I had no time, or ability, to brace my fall. I crumpled backwards, hit my rear and sprawled. It burned my thigh.

Steve looked at me and then disappointedly at the stun gun. "I thought it was going to knock you out."

"I'm sorry to disappoint you, pal!"

Davis added, "It only incapacitates someone if it is held against them a few seconds."

Zzzzt. "Want to do it again?" Steve asked.

I most certainly did not.

EIGHTEEN

❏

Deadly Wagers

Deadly Drinks

My little boy said he wishes he would get hit with a train so he could go visit his dad.

Deanna Wagner

Money was tight for the Wagners. Steve Wagner, who had been in the navy since graduating from high school, had left his job as a recruiter in 1981, hoping to start a new career in the private sector. However, work had been sporadic at best. So, in March 1982, he re-enlisted. With money so tight, re-enlisting looked like the most secure move he could make in order to provide for his young family. He was awaiting a permanent assignment to a recruiting position in Columbus.

On April 1, 1982, a man at the Rainbow Bowling Lanes bet Wagner, who was known to his friends as Waggs, that he couldn't drink ten shots of whiskey one after the other.

The wager was $120.

He won the bet, then went out and drove his car into the side of a Norfolk and Western coal train at the Williams Road crossing.

He was dead at the scene.

The $120 was still in his coat pocket.

It had been more than a month after the death when Accident Investigator Dick Radick tipped me to the story. Investigators had known Wagner had been drunk when he wrecked his car into the train. Then, someone from the bowling alley had called and told investigators about the source of the alcohol. Radick speculated that Wagner had consumed the alcohol so fast that it had yet to fully affect his system when he left the bowling alley. He probably believed he was sober enough to drive. As he was driving, however, the whiskey took over.

He left behind a beautiful wife, Deanna, and two equally beautiful children—an eight-year-old daughter and a three-year-old son.

I had assumed that the police had already spoken to his wife about the bet. They had not. She found out about it when I told her.

I never liked delivering the bad news. For one thing, I did not think it was my job. It should come from a more official source than a newspaper reporter. And I wanted to be the conduit by which they could tell the world about their loved one. If I delivered the bad news, they could indirectly blame me for the tragedy and refuse to talk. It happened several times when I covered the cops. Sometimes, when you're on deadline, you don't have any choice.

I sat with Deanna in the living room of her home on the far south side of the county. She knew her husband had been drinking, but she had been unaware of the whiskey-drinking bet. I delivered the news, and I might as well have punched her in the stomach.

"I know the only reason he did it was for the money. He didn't have any money. I wish whoever made that bet with him would come out and tell his kids why," she said.

When I called the bowling alley, an employee said they did not know the man who made the wager with Wagner. The employee also said Wagner left the bowling alley with a friend who was supposed to drive him home. "Everyone here is just sick about it," the employee said. "The guy he was supposed to ride with was at the bar with him. We didn't know he drove himself until we heard about it the next day."

Police said Wagner's blood-alcohol level was nearly two-and-a-half times the legal limit.

Another Bad Bet

John Martz made a similar bet and it met with the same fatal results.

In April 1985, Martz had been drinking for several hours with some buddies at a private home when he was bet $5 that he could not chug a fifth of gin and a fifth of vodka, one right after the other. He downed the two bottles of alcohol, collected his winnings, but gave the money back before passing out on the floor of the basement party room.

His buddies continued to drink, not realizing that not only had Martz passed out, but that he was dying from alcohol poisoning. It was an hour after he passed out before an emergency squad was called.

An autopsy revealed a blood-alcohol count of .48, nearly five times the level at which an individual is considered to be intoxicated.

NINETEEN

❏

The Kids

Brad Porter

I<small>T WAS A FRIGID</small> J<small>ANUARY AFTERNOON IN</small> 1984 <small>WHEN</small> I <small>ARRIVED</small> at the old Ohio Penitentiary on Spring Street, just outside downtown Columbus, to interview Brad Porter. A guard walked me to a visitation room near the front of the prison and said, smirking, "We'll have young Prince Charming here for you in a minute."

A few minutes later, through the large picture window in the room, I saw a guard escorting Brad Porter to his interview. He was wearing a gray, hooded sweatshirt and a black baseball cap. He was carrying two sheets of notebook paper. On one he had a list of questions he had prepared in advance. On the other were his responses. "Here," he said, handing me the sheet with the questions. "I want you to ask me these questions."

Obviously, Brad did not understand the concept of an interview, but I humored him. Dutifully, I asked him the questions and allowed him to give me his answers. Each time I finished a question, he would look down at the corresponding answer, then try to recite as much as he could remember. I'm sure he had rehearsed them a dozen times before our meeting. The one question that sticks in my mind was:

If you could say one thing to your mom and dad, what would it be?

He smiled, waved, and said, "Hi, Mom. Hi, Dad."

It was pathetically sad. He was just a kid.

Brad Porter was seventeen years old and the youngest inmate in the Ohio prison system. It was such a waste of life, yet it was certainly hard to have much sympathy for Porter. He had murdered his mother and father. Carolyn Porter had been an English teacher at Hilliard Middle School; James Porter had been a science teacher and wrestling coach at the same school.

On December 28, 1982, after he had argued with his parents and been grounded, Brad took a .22-caliber rifle and shot his mother in the back of the head while she fixed dinner. He then dragged her body to the garage and hid in the utility room for his dad to come home. He fired a bullet through his eye.

After showing the bodies to a friend, Brad got into the family's 1980 Ford Fairmont station-wagon and started driving south. He was eventually arrested in Jacksonville, Florida. He pleaded guilty to two counts of aggravated murder and was sentenced to fifteen-years to life.

Porter was a good-looking kid and he talked about the day he would get out of prison. He talked about wishing he could be on the wrestling team in high school. Instead, he had been put in protective custody to prevent him from getting raped. He was living in a twelve-by-seven cell with a bunk and a porcelain toilet. His prison job was loading and unloading laundry, for which he was paid eighteen dollars a month.

I had no intention of using the answers to the questions he had prepared. But I listened intently. Sometimes it was necessary to humor the subjects of interviews. When he had finished his prepared text and I had finished pretending to be interested in what he was saying, I asked him why he had killed his parents.

Brad Porter shot and killed his mother and father. He was 17 and Ohio's youngest inmate when I interviewed him. He said he missed being on the high school wrestling team. (Courtesy of the *Columbus Dispatch*)

"You know, I am not a criminal," he said.

"Well, Brad, actually, you are. That's why you're in prison."

"No," he said, shaking his head and lifting his hands so his palms were toward me. "You see, I've committed a criminal act, but I'm not a criminal. There's a difference."

"Okay, why don't you explain it to me."

"I've done a bad thing, a very bad thing. I'd give a million dollars to bring them back, but I can't."

I was trying to understand the rationale, but ultimately it came down to the fact that he was a seventeen-year-old kid. As I stated earlier, Brad could never give me a reason why he felt it was necessary to kill his parents. He didn't know. There were rumors that he was fed up with their strict Mormon faith and this was part of the rebellion. Drugs may have played a role. It didn't matter.

He had a pair of dark brown, depthless eyes. They showed no emotion, a sign, I thought, that despite his youth he knew that his life had ended the moment he squeezed the trigger.

Scared Me Straight

I've heard that Scared Straight programs don't work. These are the prison programs in which young offenders are taken to adult prisons for face-to-face meetings with inmates. The goal of the programs is to introduce the realities of prison life to teenagers while they have a chance to change their ways. Critics of the programs say those who attend might straighten up for while, but they ultimately return to their criminal behavior.

The Ohio Department of Rehabilitation and Correction allowed me to attend a session at the Ohio Penitentiary. This session might not have worked on the juvenile delinquents they were trying to reach, but it worked on me.

Let me say that I understand my limitations. I have been in nightclubs and bars with a dozen other men and I am always the one the drunk wants to pick a fight with. There is just something about me that makes strangers want to punch my face. (A girlfriend once said this was because I had the look of having had a privileged, Catholic upbringing, which is odd, because my upbringing was neither privileged nor Catholic.) It took only minutes inside the walls for me to realize how this problem would be magnified in prison.

And having someone pick a fight would no doubt be the least of the problems.

I attended the session to watch Brad Porter. The stars of the show, however, were much bigger, hairier, and meaner. One of the visiting teenagers, a kid with long, kinky, red hair, made the mistake of smirking during the presentation. In an instant, one of the convicts charged over three rows of metal chairs to get to him. "You think that's funny, Red. Keep laughing. I can't wait for you to get in here, because I'd love to fuck you."

Redheads three miles away quit smirking.

They brought Brad out last. He was paraded out as the example of where these kids were heading. In fact, there were kids in the audience who were older than Brad, a point that he made sure they understood.

"It'll be a long, long time before I get out of here," he said, calmly standing before the group, delivering his talk in matter-of-fact terms. "It's no fun. If you've been in juvenile prison and you think it's like this, you're wrong. You're really wrong."

I talked to Brad after the session. It disturbed him greatly to see the group of young men leave, while he stayed. "If you can stop one out of a hundred from coming in here, it's worth it," he said. "I'm not doing it as [leverage for] parole. I'm not using anything for parole. I'm just doing the best I can."

He will next be eligible for parole in July 2007.

Bubbie and Nathaniel

A trail of blood, barely visible in the dark, could be spotted in the flashlight beam of the patrol officer who was following the specks on the sidewalk from the back door toward Highland Street, where the blood formed a small pool, mixing with the dirt in the gutter.

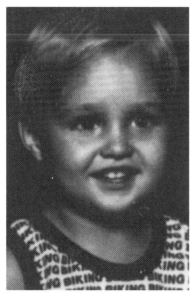 

Raymond "Bubbie" Kuntz was stabbed to death by his mother's boyfriend, Clarence Walker. Once I had kids of my own, these stories became much more difficult to cover. (Courtesy of the *Columbus Dispatch*)

That is where the three-year-old fell and died.

His name was Raymond Kuntz. His family called him Bubbie.

On the night of June 22, 1983, he was stabbed by his mother's boyfriend, an odious, sleazy ex-convict named Clarence R. Walker Jr. For reasons that remain baffling, at best, Walker took a hunting knife, yanked the sleeping boy out of his bed, and repeatedly stabbed him. Walker stabbed Bubbie after attacking the boy's pregnant mother, Billie C. Kuntz, who also ran bleeding from the house.

Bubbie tried to run. He made it out the back door and staggered to the street. That's where Walker caught up to him and stabbed him again, and again, and again. Bubbie collapsed in the gutter. The emergency squad scooped him up and rushed him to nearby Doctor's Hospital North.

Homicide Sgt. John Cherubini came over and talked to me about 11:30 P.M. I asked him if he had gotten a condition report on Bubbie. He said, "There isn't any."

Bubbie was pronounced dead at 11:12 P.M. The declaration was just a formality. He had died in the street; he had been stabbed twelve times.

In the four years that I covered the police beat, I can't remember becoming more enraged when covering a story. Domestic disputes were common. Adults fight and kill each other all the time. But why would anyone stab a three-year-old boy?

Mike Norman, the overnight police reporter, met me at the scene. He went to the hospital to try to get an interview with the family. I went back to the *Dispatch* to start writing. I was working on the story when Mike came back from the hospital an hour later. He had a photo of the boy—a color shot that looked like the ones taken at Kmart. He slid it between the top two rows of my keyboard. Bubbie had been a cute kid—blond hair neatly combed and a baby-teeth smile. It just broke my heart. I was consumed by a combination of rage—wishing I could get my hands around Walker's throat—and incredible grief. In all my years in the newspaper business, it was the only story I could not finish.

I stood up and said, "Okay. I'm done. You finish it up."

Nothing bothered me like the death of a child. And after I had children of my own, it got considerably more difficult to cover stories involving kids. My son Ryan was almost two when Bubbie was killed. I could see Ryan's face in Bubbie's photograph. It always made me wonder why some kids were born into nice families and had wonderful childhoods, while others ended up in a gutter bleeding to death from knife wounds.

Walker, a forty-year-old with long, greasy hair, had run after killing Bubbie. He lived in an abandoned car for four days before turning himself in. He called police from a phone booth in front of the Mister Donut on Cleveland Avenue.

Walker was convicted of aggravated murder and sentenced to life in prison. He was denied parole in July 2003. His next parole hearing is scheduled for June 2008.

I covered the deaths of many children. Another child homicide that kept me awake at night was the shooting death of eight-year-old Nathaniel Smith. Nathaniel and his stepmother were murdered in October 1984 by a punk named Wesley B. Compton.

The murder stuck with me because Nathaniel had begged for his life before Compton killed him.

On October 17, Compton, eighteen, stole a pickup truck and $250 from Terrance and Melody Smith. (Compton and Mr. Smith were cousins. Prior to taking the truck and money, Compton had been living with the Smiths.) When he returned to the Smith home on October 23, Mrs. Smith called her husband at work. During a brief telephone conversation, Mr. Smith told Compton, "Wait there until I get home."

When Mr. Smith got to the house he found his wife and son from a previous marriage dead in the basement. Police arrested Compton the next day after a chase that reached speeds of 115 mph on the Columbus outerbelt. Under questioning, Compton calmly confessed to killing Melody and Nathaniel.

Melody was loading clothes into a dryer when Compton shot her in the head, legs, and torso. Nathaniel was crying and screaming as he watched his stepmother die. According to detectives, Compton said Nathaniel cried and pleaded, "Please don't shoot me. I won't tell."

Compton reloaded and shot the boy five times in the head.

Investigators said Compton was cool and unremorseful as he

confessed. He said he killed Melody and Nathaniel because he was going to be kicked out of the house.

Compton was convicted of murder and aggravated murder and sentenced to life in prison. He will be eligible for parole in October 2017.

My Little Runaway

By the time he was ten years old, Stephen Rodgers had run away from home forty times. One time, he made it all the way to New York City. He had attempted another run to New York, but got intercepted in Cleveland. Things were getting so bad that his father was putting handcuffs on his legs at night to keep him from running away.

Stephen's father, Gerald, had called the *Dispatch* because he was hoping that a little publicity about his son would pressure Franklin County Children Services to take physical control of the boy.

Gerald had given up.

When I showed up to talk to Gerald, he was wearing a T-shirt on which was printed "Jogging for Jesus." He showed me two photos of Stephen at Manhattan police station, handcuffed to the wall for safekeeping. "They had to handcuff him to the wall so he wouldn't run away again. He goes down to the bus station and sits in the chairs. When he hears of a bus loading that he thinks he'd like to be on, he mingles with the people. When the bus driver turns his head, he sneaks on.

"He steals, lies, runs away from home. I've tried whipping him and I've tried talking to him . . . everybody has tried talking to him. Nothing works. We've got something here we can't control. If he doesn't change, he's going to end up in the penitentiary. He's been caught stealing I don't know how many times. He tried to set a fire behind a store. He's done so much now that I can't keep track of everything."

Gerald said there was little doubt that Stephen was going to run away again and he encouraged me to ask Stephen about his travel itinerary. Stephen was a cute, scrub-faced kid. He sat next to his dad while I conducted the interview, seemingly oblivious to our conversation.

"Stephen," I said, getting his attention. "Your dad thinks you're going to run away again. Is that so?"

"Yes," he said, matter-of-factly.

"Why?"

"I don't know. Something in my head just keeps saying, 'Run, run, run.'"

About five days after I interviewed the father and son, before I had written the story, Stephen was caught at the downtown bus station trying to sneak on another bus at 3 A.M. He had sneaked into his parents' bedroom and found the key to the handcuffs.

By the time my story ran, Franklin County Children Services had taken custody of Stephen.

Walter Mitchell

I walked the tightrope when I did an in-depth story on Walter Mitchell for *Capitol,* the *Dispatch*'s Sunday magazine. I had to write a story that defended Walter Mitchell, the accused killer of an eight-year-old girl, yet did not defend Walter Mitchell, the convicted child molester.

It was an important story to write, but not an easy one.

As a parent, I wanted to ignore Walter. He was a child molester. Let him rot in prison. Who cares?

But what happened to Walter could have happened to anyone without the money or power needed to fight public opinion.

And the media, the *Dispatch* and Robin Yocum included, helped create the problem.

On September 20, 1982, Kelly Prosser, a cute third-grader at Indianola Alternative School, disappeared on her way home from school. It was a fifteen-block walk from the school to her home on West Tompkins Avenue. Kelly was abducted, police believed, somewhere along High Street, the busiest north-south corridor in Columbus, between Sixteenth and Maynard avenues, near the Ohio State University campus.

Neighbors and police searched for the eight-year-old girl. The media gave the story extensive coverage. Two days after the abduction, Kelly's body was found in a Madison County cornfield, west of Columbus. She had been beaten, sexually molested, and strangled.

Before Kelly's body was found, investigators had identified Mitchell as a suspect.

Mitchell became a suspect the day after Kelly disappeared, when the mother of an eleven-year-old girl—a friend of Mitchell's granddaughter—had filed a police report accusing Mitchell of child molestation. Police said Mitchell had taken several children to the park and, while the other children went to play, molested the girl in his car. The sixty-four-year-old Mitchell, Prosser and the eleven-year-old girl all lived in the same part of Columbus.

Once Mitchell had been accused of molesting the eleven-year-old, it was a logical step for investigators to question him about Prosser. When police investigating Prosser's disappearance called Mitchell's house, he assumed they were investigating the molestation charge and fled to hide out with relatives in West Virginia.

Investigators, however, figured that he had fled because he was involved in Prosser's disappearance. After Kelly's body was found, police distributed mug shots of Mitchell, who had previously been arrested, but not convicted, of child molestation.

The media frenzy was in high gear.

When Mitchell learned that he was a suspect in the kidnapping and murder of Kelly Prosser, he returned from West Virginia. He was publicly called a suspect in the murder, and over the following days and weeks the police released information that implicated him in the case. However, he was never charged. Despite this fact, police continued to identify him as the primary suspect in Kelly's death, and he continued to be flogged in the media.

My story in the magazine was the result of an investigation that showed that police knew, without question, that Mitchell had not kidnapped and killed Kelly Prosser. However, without a viable suspect, they were content to let the public believe he was a murderer. This kept the heat off the police, who could shrug and say, "We know he did it, but we just don't have the evidence to convict him in court."

However, the alledged evidence linking him to the crime was nonexistent. For example:

- Police told the media that on the afternoon of Prosser's disappearance, a man matching Mitchell's description was spotted walking down High Street with a girl matching Kelly's description. However, when another man contacted police and said that it had been he and his granddaughter who had been walking along High Street, police never corrected the earlier information that implicated Mitchell.
- Police announced that a tracking dog followed Kelly's scent to Mitchell's porch. That was not true. Police had taken the dog to the residence, and it ran up on the porch. It had not followed the scent from High Street, which police had earlier stated. Also, police took the dog inside Mitchell's house and inside his car. The dog could not find Kelly's scent in either. Police never released that information.
- Telephone records show Mitchell made a telephone call from

Mineral Wells, West Virginia, the day Prosser disappeared. In the time between Kelly's abduction and when the call was made, it would have been impossible to cover the distance in a car. Police and the FBI had copies of the phone records but failed to release them.

- Tests were conducted on Mitchell's car, clothes, blood, urine, head, and pubic hairs. No connection with Kelly Prosser was ever found. Similar tests were conducted on Kelly's body, and no connection to Mitchell was found. However, police never released the results.

Mitchell was eventually charged with gross sexual imposition and convicted of molesting the eleven-year-old friend of his granddaughter. During deliberations, jurors openly discussed Mitchell's possible involvement in the death of Kelly Prosser. He was sentenced to three to ten years in prison and fined $5,000.

Mitchell was released from prison in August 1988. The last I spoke to him he was planning to move out of state.

Teenage Runaway

Hazel Johnson was interviewed in the living room of her home on Hamlet Street in the Short North section of Columbus. She sat on the couch; on the coffee table in front of her was a framed photograph of her daughter Mary Ann as a smiling, precious eleven-year-old. The photo had been taken seven years before the interview.

Between the time the photo had been taken and the evening when I sat down with Hazel, the cute little girl in the photo had been arrested for prostitution at least one hundred times. Juvenile arrest records were not public and the estimate of one hundred arrests came from vice cops who worked the Short North. Her mother sadly laughed and scoffed at the estimate. "It was every bit of that and probably more," Hazel said. "Every time that girl turned around she was getting arrested for prostitution."

Johnson admitted that she had no control over her daughter, who by the time my article appeared had turned eighteen and had already been arrested for prostitution as an adult. She was found guilty and fined $50.

Mary Ann began turning tricks on High Street, her mother believed, when she was fourteen years old. She began prostituting herself to support a drug habit. During the interview, Hazel said she had given up on her oldest daughter. Hazel said she had not seen her in several months and was simply waiting for the phone to ring to have a police officer inform her that Mary Ann was dead.

"I still love her, but I really expect to get a phone call someday and have someone tell me she's dead," Johnson said, tears welling in her eyes. "I keep the phone by my bed and wait. It's scary, but I know it's coming."

The Others

Mary Ann was just one of the dozens of young prostitutes—male and female—who were included in a series on teenage prostitution that I wrote just after leaving the police beat in the summer of 1985. I rode with vice cops and interviewed the kids after they were arrested.

One was a fourteen-year-old boy named David who had been born with a harelip—the surgery to repair it looked like it had been performed by a blacksmith—and had a flattened, deformed nose smeared over the left side of his face. His hair was matted down with dirt and he desperately needed a bath.

David had been arrested after offering to perform oral sex on an undercover vice cop for $25. He told police he needed money for drugs.

I sat down with David at a desk in the Columbus police juvenile squad. He was severely undereducated; he could barely read and had a difficult time conversing with a speech impediment. He had dropped out of school following the seventh grade. David said he sometimes stayed at the men's Open Shelter, although he preferred to stay with friends and acquaintances because after they were asleep he would steal their money and anything that could be easily sold. His meals came from anyplace that was giving away free food.

I gave him a Coke that one of the juvenile officers kept in a mini refrigerator. "The police officers say that you're supposed to be living at Franklin Village. Why aren't you there?" I asked.

He shrugged. "I ran away."

"Why'd they send you to the Village?"

"I kept fighting with my mom and the judge sent me there."

"Where are your parents?"

"My dad's dead. I don't really know where my mom is now. I haven't seen her in a long time."

"How long have you been working as a prostitute?"

"That was the first time I ever did anything like that."

Vice Officer Mike Martin, who was the would-be recipient of David's offer of oral sex, about choked on the Coke he was drinking. "Christ," he said. "It's amazing. Just about every kid I've ever arrested for prostitution is doing it for the very first time. I mean, what are the odds?" His sarcasm was not lost.

"I saw other kids do it, and it looked like a good way to make money," David explained. "The other kids told me to just stand on the corner and someone would pull up."

"They didn't tell you that it might be a cop that would pull up?" Martin asked.

A pair of uniformed officers came to pick up David and take him to the juvenile detention center. Martin, who had arrested hundreds of prostitutes over the years, shook his head as David was hauled away. "That is really sad. That kid doesn't have a chance in the world. I can't blame him for taking drugs. I'd be taking them, too, if I were him."

The youngest prostitute I found working the streets was a ten-year-old boy who would skip school and hustle the streets. His home-school counselor said the boy "didn't see anything wrong with what he was doing. To him it was simply a way to make some money." The boy's guardian was a grossly overweight former carnival worker who had been given the boy while working the carnival circuit in the South. The counselor said she suffered from elephantiasis so bad that she couldn't get out of bed much of the time to supervise the boy.

Most of the young prostitutes I interviewed were white, in their early teens, and the product of the poor, Appalachian population that dominated the area. Incest, one Franklin County Children Services counselor told me, was a huge factor in kids turning to the street. A common saying among the police who patrolled the Short North was, "The only virgins around here are the ones who can outrun their brothers and their stepdaddies."

The counselor said that was a sad fact. "Sometimes these kids have been abused for a long period of time by parents, stepparents, and live-in boyfriends. They have been coached and prodded into doing it for free. They figure, why not get paid for it?"

TWENTY

❑

Sex Trade

Jenny's Pleasure Arcade

DURING THE EARLY '80s, THE COLUMBUS POLICE VICE SQUAD
and the Franklin County Sheriff's Department were working together on a growing prostitution and illegal drug problem being
generated from the local strip clubs and peep show joints. (Of
course, they could work on prostitution and illegal drug problems
at strip clubs every day of the year.)

Over a two-month period, I went out with the task force about
a dozen times, working on a story for the *Dispatch*'s Sunday magazine. The cops all used aliases and decided that I, too, should have
an alias. Mike Powell, a deputy and undercover officer with the
Franklin County Sheriff's Department decided it should be
"Rowdy," after Rowdy Yates, Clint Eastwood's character in the
Rawhide television show.

I knew my limitations. I was wearing braces on my teeth and
looked a little too young and wholesome to be a "Rowdy."

"I don't know about Rowdy," I countered. "I think I'm more of
a 'Dutch.'"

Powell shook his head. "Nope. You're Rowdy."

"Okay. I'll try to frown a lot."

I had gotten to know Powell and Columbus Police vice squad officer Mike Martin a year earlier when the two were heading up an undercover drug operation in Washington Court House and Fayette County, southwest of Columbus. The local cops needed some experienced undercover officers who were not known in rural Fayette County. After working the area undercover for several months, Powell and Martin allowed photographer Tim Revell and me to tag along on the bust. On the night of the bust, the primary suspect—the man believed to be responsible for most of the county's drug traffic—thought that he, Powell, and Martin were leaving on a drug run to Florida. Powell had told him to meet them at a Washington Court House bar—sober and unarmed.

We met the task force outside town. Now that Powell and Martin had done all the undercover work, the local cops were allowed to don their bulletproof vests and break out the heavy artillery. The initial raid was on the bar, but there were enough cops and firearms there to invade a small country. Powell instructed Revell and me to wait until the bar was secure, then we could come in and take photographs. I agreed; Revell agreed.

The cops got out of cars and vans and sprinted into place, lining up tight against the exterior walls of the bar. When the word was given, they charged through the front and side doors. We were near the front door. Then, as the third task force member charged through the front door, I pushed Revell into the line and yelled, "Go, go, go." He hesitated for a second, then ran in with the troops. He got great photos and I got great details of the bust, including watching a cop allow a police German shepherd to get about two inches from the face of the prime suspect, who was having the side of his head ground into the felt of the pool table by a couple of heavily armed cops.

Hanging with Powell and Martin in Fayette County enabled me to slide into the mix when they began their Columbus investigation. I liked them both and they trusted me. They knew I was not going to print anything that would jeopardize future investigations. The first stop on my first night out with the task force was at a strip club on Agler Road. Powell and Martin had already been in the club several times. Powell introduced me to the woman at the front door, who had a beautiful face, but whose stripping days had ended about forty pounds earlier. She smiled, slipped her hand very seductively into mine and said, "Nice to meet you, Rowdy." She eyed me up for a moment and asked, "Are you a cop?"

Even though I wasn't, I could feel the heat creeping up my neck. I leaned forward and whispered, "Do I look like a cop, or do you ask everyone that?"

"No, you look like a cop."

"Really? Well, that's a little scary. No, I'm not a cop."

"You swear, Rowdy?"

"Darlin', I swear on a whole stack of Bibles."

It seemed to placate her. And, of course, it was true. There was a myth floating around at the time that undercover officers were not permitted to lie about their true identity. Of course, it was just a myth and a lot of prostitutes and drug dealers found out the hard way.

The Agler Road club, like the others we visited, was certainly not an upscale strip club. Most of the clubs were simply fronts for prostitution, and drug use was rampant. *Playboy* once published an article that stated that Columbus had the ugliest prostitutes in the country. The author must have been frequenting the same strip clubs that the undercover unit was investigating.

We sat down at a table directly in front of the stage. It was early and the crowds had yet to appear. A petulant young thing with long brown hair was walking around with a plastic cup collecting money for the jukebox. There was enough money in the cup to play the jukebox for a year, but she had the cup firmly wedged between her naked and ample breasts and guys couldn't stuff money in quick enough. Powell and Martin were cozying up to two women. One was in her mid- to late twenties, blond, and in a silver body suit. The second woman—if she was eighteen, she wasn't much older—was wearing a skimpy buckskin outfit adorned with beads and fringe. She was the most attractive woman in the place. "She hasn't gotten the mileage on her yet," Martin later said. "She stays at it for a couple of years, she'll start aging pretty quick."

They nicknamed her Pocahontas and would later use her as an informant in the operation. That was a common tactic. Jam someone up early on drug charges, then get them to flip on the others in exchange for reducing or dropping the charges.

"You can't change 99 percent of these girls, and that's not our job," Powell said. "But you hate to see someone that young get hooked in this business. If we jam her up when she's young, maybe she'll turn her life around. But usually not. They're here because they want to be. The money's easy; the drugs are available. After a couple of years, there's no turning back."

Powell and Martin had found the only two cute strippers in the place. (At least they appeared that way in the black lights.) Meanwhile, of course, an aging stripper with a cold sore on her lip the size of a dime and tassels hanging from her pasties, snuggled up next to me and offered to take me into the john and give me head for $20.

"No, thanks. I don't have that kind of dough."

"Ten bucks and a 'lude," she said. "Your buddy has 'ludes."

She was talking about Powell, who a few minutes earlier had downed a sugar pill that looked like a Quaalude. "Yeah, but he's into that. I'm not. I don't have any."

She quickly determined that I was a waste of time and moved to the other side of the room. I watched her take a seat at a table next to a portly man—fortyish and balding—with oversized eyeglasses. Martin and Powell had nicknamed the guy "Specs," for the prominent eyeglasses. Before long, he was slipping bills into her left hand, while she stroked his crotch with the right. After a few minutes of this, he went into the john and she followed a few seconds later.

"Specs," the cops noted, was a regular at the strip clubs. They said he was certainly part of the problem, but they were concentrating on the girls and the drug traffic. It seemed that we ran into "Specs" at one of the strip clubs nearly every night that I went out with the unit.

One of the unit's targets was Jenny's Pleasure Arcade on the far north side, which advertised a live sex show. I guess everyone needs to make a living, but the "talent" at the Pleasure Arcade was just sad.

Martin bought $5 worth of tokens, gave me a handful and pointed toward one of the booths. "Go get yourself a show," he said. I went into the booth and closed the curtain behind me. I was standing in a booth about three feet square. A roll of paper towels hung on one wall. In front of me was a Plexiglas window with a sliding door inside the window. A sign on the coin receptor stated that a twenty-five-cent token got you a fifteen-second peek. I slipped in a token and the door opened, revealing a flabby, naked redhead who was lying on her back and reading a paperback. She immediately tossed the book aside and began moaning and masturbating. She then leaned forward and licked the Plexiglas.

This all occurred in the span of about five seconds, so apparently she got a glimpse of me and thought I was *very* hot.

"Do you have anything you want to show me?" she asked.

"Not right now," I said.

She moaned some more. "Oh, come on. Take it out and show me." The door was starting to close. "Put more money in," she said, licking the Plexiglas with increased intensity. "Hurry."

Hmm, I thought. That certainly explains the need for the paper towels.

I left the booth. "See anything you liked?" Powell asked.

"I think I might want to shop around a bit."

There were sex shows going on in some of the booths. The evening "finale" involved all the "performers" participating in an orgy. This included some husband-wife teams and a bunch of people who looked like they should be putting on clothes, not taking them off. The manager offered the two Mikes $15 an hour—and a third of the cash spent by viewers—to perform sex acts in the booths with the redhead and her friends. "You gonna take 'em up on the offer?" I asked later. "Sounds awful tempting."

Martin just shook his head. "When you tell people you're a vice cop, they immediately think you're screwing the whores," he said. "You got a good look at those women. Do they look like something you'd want to bang?"

It didn't even need a response.

Martin continued. "You know how nasty I think they are?"

"No," I said. "How nasty?"

"They're so nasty, I wouldn't screw with Powell's dick."

Powell looked over, grinned, and flipped off his partner.

They raided the Pleasure Arcade on July 9, 1982, arresting the co-managers and five other participants and charging them with a variety of prostitution-related offenses.

(I went out with the unit during the summer and fall of 1982. The magazine story appeared on December 5, 1982. In 1991, I left the *Dispatch* and took a job as the media relations manager for Battelle, a large research and technology firm in Columbus. I had been working with one of the researchers on a project and couldn't shake the feeling that I knew him from somewhere in my *Dispatch* past. He insisted that we had never met. We had worked together for weeks before it finally dawned on me. It was "Specs.")

Amen

Following the drug arrests in Fayette County, the string of accused dealers and users were paraded through the court system for months. One of the judges presiding over the cases of accused drug dealers was known to be quite religious. A rumor apparently spread around the jail that she had a soft spot for convicts who had found God. One of the accused drug dealers showed up for his sentencing carrying a Bible.

She smiled and inquired, "Do you read your Bible."

"Oh, yes, ma'am," he said. "Every day."

"That's wonderful, just wonderful. Have you read it all?"

The accused smiled. "Well, no, ma'am, not all of it, yet, but I'm working on it."

"That's good, because you're going to have plenty of time to finish it in prison."

She sentenced him to seven years.

David Drake

During the summer of 1985, just as I was leaving the police beat for a post on the *Dispatch*'s investigative team, I began work on a series of stories on teenage prostitution in the Short North section of Columbus. This is the area of Columbus just north of the downtown area. At the time, it was a haven for runaways and teenage prostitutes. Consequently, it also was a favorite area for pedophiles.

As part of the story, the vice cops unanimously said I needed to interview David Drake. David was actually twenty, but he had been working the streets as a male prostitute—sometimes in drag—since his early teens. He was Columbus's most notorious male prostitute.

Using vice officer Mike Martin as an intermediary, David agreed to be interviewed and told Martin that he was staying at the 40

David Drake began working the streets as a prostitute in his early teens. He later died of AIDS. (Courtesy of the *Columbus Dispatch*)

Winks Motel on East Main Street. When photographer Jeff Hinckley and I arrived at the motel about 9 A.M., David was still sleeping from the previous night's work. The door was answered by an overweight stripper who was wearing a nightie that revealed way more than I wanted to see. She had a smattering of teeth, several homemade tattoos, and dirty blonde hair. She and her boyfriend were sharing the tiny room with David.

"David, there's a reporter from the *Dispatch* here to talk to you," she said.

"Oh, not today. Tell him to go away," he moaned. "I'm too tired. Tell him to come back tomorrow."

"No way, David, right now," I said. "You're too damn hard to track down."

"I can't. I'm too tired. Maybe this afternoon."

The stripper turned, took a few steps across the room, slapped him on his ass and said, "Come on, bitch, get out of bed and talk to the man."

"I can't. I just can't. Come back in an hour. I just need one more hour. I promise."

"No way. Right now, David," I said. "Officer Martin said either you do the interview now or he's going to bust you the next time he sees you on the street."

It was a lie, but it got him out of bed.

David staggered out to the steps of the motel and sat down, squinting into the morning sun, wearing an open bathrobe and boxer shorts. He had orange polish on his toe- and fingernails, blue glitter makeup under his eyes and a colostomy bag attached to his side.

"What's with the bag, David?" I inquired."

"I tried to commit suicide," he said. "And, I wasn't very good at it."

A few months earlier, David's boyfriend had broken off their relationship, which so devastated David that he decided to extract his revenge by committing suicide in front of the boyfriend. He did this by diving off the boyfriend's third-story balcony. However, he forgot that the boyfriend's apartment building was terraced. Thus, he first hit the railing of the second floor balcony, rolled off and fell to the first-floor balcony, hitting the railing and then falling to the ground. He wasn't able to kill himself, but he did manage to bust up his insides to the point that it had required an extended hospital stay and a colostomy.

"I hate this bag," he said. "It's really bad for business."

"No doubt," I agreed.

David gave me a spirited interview of his life on the streets. "I think I was thirteen when I turned my first trick," he said. "I remember it was about the same time that I dropped out of school. I only finished the seventh grade. I work as a waitress, too. But I like the streets. I can make $100 a night." He emphasized the point, as though I could not fathom someone making that much money.

"How many tricks do you have to turn to pull in a hundred bucks?"

"Sometimes, only one or two. I have some regular customers, my sugar daddies, who take good care of me."

By the time I had finished my series on teen prostitution, David was just a small part of the story. The series was scheduled to begin on Sunday, October 20, 1985. On the Thursday night before it was to begin, Mike Martin called me at home. "Hey, the cops have put out an APB for David Drake. The Health Department is trying to get him off the street. He's got AIDS."

David had become the first Columbus prostitute to be diagnosed as positive for HIV. While this wasn't a crime, the Columbus Health Department knew he was still working as a prostitute and they wanted him brought in for counseling. This was a huge event in 1985 as the AIDS epidemic was taking a firm hold.

And, I was sitting with an entire interview—David's life story— that had been deleted from the series. Early the next morning I began writing a story that would be page-one news that afternoon. It was packed with details of David's life and everyone in the newsroom thought it was a great story. Outside the newsroom, however, there was at least one person working North High Street who held an opposing opinion.

After the paper hit the streets, David called me from a pay phone and, to say the least, was not happy.

"Goddamn you. What the fuck are you doing putting all this shit in the paper? You're going to ruin my business," he screamed.

"David, you're HIV-positive. You shouldn't have a business. You need to find a new line of work."

"I don't need you to tell me what to do, motherfucker. I shouldn't have talked to you in the first place. And besides, I don't have no damn HIV disease, like you say in your story. All I have is the virus."

"But, David, the virus is the . . . never mind."

"You just best keep your distance from me," he yelled, and hung up.

I made it a point to do just as he said. Still, I would occasionally see David working North High Street. He would look at me, but there was never any sign that he remembered me. And I wasn't about to reintroduce myself.

David died of complications from AIDS on Friday, May 11, 1990. He was twenty-five.

TWENTY-ONE

❏

Never Knowing

As tragic as it is to lose a loved one, there are, at the very least, conclusions to most cases. Even when a person becomes the victim of a random act of violence or a drunken driver, those left behind have an explanation or an understanding of how the death occurred. The explanation may seem just as senseless—Mark Anderson being shot for the $8.44 in his pocket—but at least it was there.

There are, however, survivors who will live their lives without an answer. A loved one is lost—to a known tragedy or disappearance—with no logical explanation. I always wondered how these people go on with their lives with such a void. Eventually, I would move on to other stories. I might check with them at anniversary dates to do follow-up stories, but I did not have to live with the pain of never knowing where a missing loved one had gone, or how he or she had died.

Beth Wagner

On the evening of Wednesday, August 25, 1982, Beth Wagner and some friends went dancing at the Gold Rush, a popular east-side nightclub. They danced into the early Thursday morning hours.

Just before 2 A.M., she disappeared from the Gold Rush. A few minutes later, the twenty-one-year-old Bowling Green State University senior suddenly materialized in the middle of the eastbound lanes of I-70, where she was struck and killed by a tractor-trailer.

No one saw how she left the nightclub; no one saw how she got out to the middle of the interstate. Police investigated several theories, including the possibility that someone pushed her out of a moving car, or that she was fleeing someone and ran out to the interstate to escape. Ultimately, they remained just theories. No one saw anything. It was as if she suddenly materialized on the interstate.

According to one trucker, Wagner was on her knees and waving her hands, as if trying to stop the oncoming traffic.

One tractor-trailer swerved to miss her, but the semi that followed it struck her. The trucker who hit Wagner didn't stop and was never identified. Police said it was possible that the offending driver didn't even know he had hit her. (I never bought into that theory. Of course, he or she knew.) I always believed the police floated that theory in case the trucker was local and bothered by a guilty conscience. That would enable him to contact the police and say, "I found some blood on my bumper. I don't remember hitting anything, but I guess I could have."

No one ever came forward.

Reports surfaced that Wagner had been seen climbing a fence near the accident scene. That report was later discounted.

An autopsy showed her blood-alcohol level to be .11, barely enough to be considered legally intoxicated. Her father said it was "rare for her to even go out drinking."

When I interviewed Wagner's father about six months after the accident, he had hired a private investigator to look into the case, though he admitted the chances of solving the mystery were slim.

It remains unsolved.

Jane, a.k.a. Mary Rose

Then, there was Jane. When I wrote about Jane, in September 1984, she had been lying on a stainless steel gurney in a walk-in freezer at the Franklin County Coroner's Office for fourteen months. A police investigation and subsequent autopsy revealed many things about Jane, except for the two most important: Who killed her and who was she?

Jane came to be a resident of the cooler on July 2, 1983, after two fishermen found her body near Hoover Reservoir on the far north side of the city at 1:45 A.M. In life, Jane had been about twenty-six-years old, five-foot-four and 102 pounds. She had some expensive dental work, leading investigators to believe that she might have come from an affluent family. That was the extent of what they knew about the living Jane.

When the fishermen discovered the body, it was already badly decomposed. The body had been lying in the June-July heat, the coroner estimated, for a week. Jane had been strangled and at the time of her death had a blood-alcohol level of .32, which is considered extremely intoxicated. She was wearing blue jeans and maroon slip-on shoes; a multicolored shirt was wrapped around her neck. Perhaps she had been murdered where she was found. Perhaps she had been dumped there.

Columbus police sent out a nationwide teletype and received about fifteen inquiries. None panned out. After that, the body stayed in the freezer until the coroner performed a disarticulation, a process in which the jawbone and teeth are removed, against the remote chance that anyone ever inquires. The body was to be remitted to a local crematory for disposal.

After my story appeared, a priest at Sacred Heart Church got a local funeral home to donate a $250 coffin, and St. Joseph Cemetery donated a plot for the woman, whom the priest named Mary Rose. As thirteen Sacred Heart parishioners looked on and maintenance workers from the cemetery acted as pallbearers, Mary Rose was buried on October 26, 1984.

Twenty years later, Mary Rose's true identity remains a mystery.

Sandra Blythe and Princess Doe

On the other end of a similar situation were Elmer and Virginia Blythe. When I interviewed the Blythes in January 1984, their daughter Sandra had been missing for nearly three and a half years. I interviewed the Blythes after I saw this ad in the classified section of the *Dispatch*:

> *Happy 17th Birthday*
> *Sandra Kay Blythe*
> *We love you, Mom & Dad*

Sandra had been just fourteen when she disappeared from their west-side home. At the time that I interviewed her parents, Sandra had been missing longer than any other Columbus teenager.

Elmer and Virginia posed for a photo holding Sandra's baby doll, Chrissy, which they continued to display on a table in the living room, along with a grainy, enlarged snapshot of their daughter.

Sandra Blythe spent the morning of August 13, 1981, helping her mother clean the house. Afterward, the mother and daughter sat down together on the living room couch. Sandra got up and said she was going to the bathroom. Instead, she sneaked out the back door.

Virginia and Elmer Blythe's daughter Sandra was just fourteen years old when she disappeared from their west-side home in August 1981. She has not been seen since. (Courtesy of the *Columbus Dispatch*)

It was not the first time Sandra had run, but it was the last time either parent saw her. Columbus police spent hundreds of hours on the case and could not turn up a single solid lead. The last tip they had put Sandra either heading toward or living in Rochester, New York.

"I've done everything I know to do," Elmer said. "We still hope, but that's all we can do. People ask us, 'Do you think she's dead?' We don't know. We hope not, but it's been almost four years since we've even heard from the girl. She's made up her mind she doesn't want to live at home. She obviously can fend for herself. All we want her to do is write us a letter or call and let us know she's alive."

More than a year later, April of 1985, the Blythes thought they had learned the fate of their daughter after seeing a composite photo of a young girl whose body was found along Route 94 near a cemetery in Blairstown, New Jersey, a resort town near the Pennsylvania border. The young girl in New Jersey had been bludgeoned beyond recognition, and authorities were forced to construct a composite drawing and a model in an attempt to learn her identity. A police officer in Blairstown who had investigated the case had the body buried with a tombstone that stated:

Princess Doe:
Missing From Home
Dead Among Strangers
Remembered By All
Born ?—Found July 15, 1982

The body of "Princess Doe" was found less than a year after Sandra left home and just a few months after she was reportedly last seen in Columbus. (Although police never documented any evidence that she had remained in Columbus, there were "Sandra sightings" for months after she left.)

There were several similarities between Sandra Blythe and "Princess Doe"—age, height, weight, reddish-brown hair color, double-pierced ears and facial structure. Although the New Jersey authorities had retained dental records and a blood type, Sandra's parents could supply neither. Sandra had visited the dentist only once in her life. The dentist had died when Sandra was ten years old and the records that had not been claimed by patients had been destroyed. Sandra's parents did not know their daughter's blood type, either.

Columbus police still list Blythe as missing.

George Mosko

George Mosko was a delusional man who had finally reached the end of his mental rope.

Or George Mosko was cunningly portraying a delusional man who had finally reached the end of his mental rope to avoid going back home and into business with his older brother.

Either way, it was a fascinating story.

Mosko's brother, John, had contacted Columbus attorney Pat Smith because he needed help in the bizarre disappearance of his brother, who had vanished while traveling through central Ohio. I got involved investigating the case after talking to Smith, who was looking for some publicity to help generate attention to the case.

On June 25, 1987, George Mosko packed his pickup truck and left Loveland, Colorado, for Lima, New York, to take a sales job in John's computer firm. George was forty-three, twice divorced, and had been living in New Mexico and Colorado for thirteen years. George told friends that he did not want to return to New York, but felt pressured by his older brother to do so. The day before he left Colorado, he and John argued on the phone because George wanted to delay the trip by two weeks. "I screamed at him," John told me in a telephone interview. "But I scream at everyone. I had screamed at him before. It didn't seem to affect him."

At 9:30 P.M. on June 27, George was traveling east through central Ohio on I-70 (a most indirect route between Loveland and Lima; the more direct route would have been via I-90 across the northern part of Ohio) towing a U-Haul trailer behind his pickup truck. East of Columbus, George pulled off the Interstate and drove north to the Jacksontown Bar & Grill at the intersection of Routes 40 and 13. From a phone at the bar he called a local fire dispatcher and said he needed help. He claimed that he had been chased by truckers for 200 miles. George claimed to have been listening to the CB banter between the truckers who were chasing him. (Oddly, he had stopped to buy gasoline at a truck stop near London, Ohio, west of Columbus, and did not ask for help or call police.)

When a sheriff's deputy arrived, he could find no truckers, just a wild-talking Mosko who had defecated himself. The deputy took a report and suggested that Mosko take Route 40—a parallel east-west route to I-70—to Zanesville before getting back on the interstate.

Mosko agreed to the suggestion and the two parted company.

About twelve hours later, Mosko's truck and trailer were found in a ditch along Brushy Fork Road, about fifteen miles east of Jacksontown. The clothes he had been wearing in the bar, two sets of keys, the U-Haul contract, and an empty pistol carrying case were found in the truck cab. The state patrol had the truck towed.

At 5:45 A.M. the following day, Mosko walked up to the home of John and Marge Goodin near the village of Toboso, a half-mile from where the abandoned truck was found. He was wearing tan pants, a blue and white pinstripe shirt and cowboy boots. He told the Goodins a wild tale of someone burning his truck and stealing his guns. In fact, he claimed, someone was trying to shoot him. There was a gash on his face, which he said was the result of his pistol recoiling when he returned fire.

He claimed to have been hiding out in the woods for three days. Mrs. Goodin knew that was not possible, because Mosko was clean-shaven and "crispy clean." She urged him to call the sheriff's department, but he claimed he could not because they were on the side of the gunmen who were after him.

About two hours later, a man matching Mosko's description surfaced three miles away at a home on Texas Road. He asked for directions and complimented the owner on the appearance of her home. He was on foot, Mosko told the woman, because "your people are after me."

He was never seen alive again.

John reported his brother missing on July 6.

My story about George Mosko and his brother's efforts to locate him appeared on September 28. By that time, attorney Pat Smith had hired local private investigator Lois Colley to help solve the mystery. Colley searched for weeks, looking for people who might have seen George Mosko. She checked out his friends in Loveland, Colorado, and New Mexico. No one had seen him after he headed east on June 25. He had simply disappeared.

In November 1988, nearly sixteen months after George Mosko left Colorado, his skeleton was found in the woods of Licking County by two hunters. His pistol was lying beside the bones. A single gunshot wound was found in the skull, and the death of George Mosko was ruled a suicide.

TWENTY-TWO
❏

Predators and Survivors

The Name Game

WE LOVED ASSIGNING NAMES TO OUR CRIMINALS. DURING THE time I covered the police department, we wrote about the Bandana Burglar, so named for the colored bandana he wore over this face; the "Grandview Rapist," the "Copycat Grandview Rapist," and the "Rt. 33 Rapist," so named for the territories that they stalked; the Friendly Robber, who profusely apologized for robbing his victims, but claimed his family needed the money; and the Sorry Robber, who turned himself in a few hours after robbing a bank because of the overwhelming guilt. (After receiving probation for the offense, he apparently became the Not-So-Sorry Robber ten months later when he robbed another bank.) We covered the "Screen Burglar," who was robbing homes in the Ohio State University area by removing screen windows; the Fat Gunman, an obese robber who targeted motels. (the Fat Gunman, aka the Beer-belly Bandit, turned out to be Columbus Police Officer David H. Baisden. *Dispatch* reporter Bob Ruth wrote about Baisden's arrest in one of the most sadly amusing vignettes I had ever read in the paper. Following his arrest in January 1983 on eight counts of aggravated robbery and one count of attempted robbery, Baisden told police investigators that he hoped his arrest didn't adversely affect his career as a police officer. One police investigator read the quote and said, "I don't think David fully appreciates the gravity of the situation." He eventually pled guilty and was sentenced to six to twenty-five years in prison.) And finally, there was the Talkative Burglar, who broke into homes with no apparent motivation other than to talk to children in their bedrooms. In one instance, he talked to a sixteen-year-old girl for more than an hour.

That one creeped me out.

Some children would awaken in the morning and tell their parents about the man who had come to visit and chat during the night. Some dismissed the claims, assuming that the visitor was simply a product of their child's vivid imagination. That was, until they found a bedroom window pried open or a damaged door.

Reynoldsburg police had been searching for the Talkative Burglar for seven years when, forty burglaries later, they apprehended and charged Howard S. McCardle in January 1983. Police began investigating McCardle in connection with as many as one hundred other felonies. He was convicted in June 1983 of aggravated burglary and rape. He remains a guest of the Ohio Department of Rehabilitation and Correction.

Grandview Rapist

For more than four years, police had searched for the "Grandview Rapist," who police believed was responsible for as many as one hundred rapes in a section of northwest Columbus that was bordered by the suburbs of Grandview Heights and Upper Arlington. Occasionally, he would slide into the suburbs looking for victims. The rapist preyed on women who lived alone and who were careless enough to leave a door unlocked or open a window for fresh air. He was thorough and intelligent. He struck only at night and in all the years he had stalked the area, he had left few clues. And he took great delight in admonishing his victims for their carelessness, as though he justified his attacks as their punishment for allowing him such easy access to their homes.

By the early '80s, police were growing even more concerned about the "Grandview Rapist." He was becoming more violent, now choking his victims into unconsciousness before he left. In several cases, it was believed that he nearly choked them to death. Women told of being choked unconscious, then awakening to find the rapist reviving them with CPR. It was only a matter of time, police believed, before he choked a woman to death and was unable to bring her back, or decided not to bother.

In the late summer of 1982, I began doing interviews and conducting research for an in-depth story on the "Grandview Rapist." I started the research after Upper Arlington police had arrested a rapist they at first believed was the "Grandview Rapist." I wrote a story for a police news roundup under the headline:

ASSAILANT MAY BE 'GRANDVIEW RAPIST'

It was one of several instances where police believed they had apprehended the rapist. But, as had been the case in earlier reports, the arrests had no connection to the serial rapist.

My first interview was with Detective James Rothwell of the Upper Arlington Police Department. I had gotten to know Rothwell when he was investigating the Fritz Herder murder in 1981. Rothwell was an atypical detective, funny, always laughing, but serious about his job. He had been investigating the "Grandview Rapist" for several years. Over a two-hour interview, Rothwell shared with me the rapist's techniques, tendencies, and tactics. Rothwell said that the rapist wore surgical gloves, sometimes used surgical tubing to tie up his victims and used knots often found in medical procedures. After choking a victim into unconsciousness and reviving her, he would check her pulse on the inner thigh or neck. Rothwell's speculation was that the "Grandview Rapist" was somehow connected to the medical profession.

He didn't know how right he was going to be.

On Labor Day night, 1982, just as I had sat down with a bowl of popcorn and a beer, I received a telephone call from Mike Martin, the Columbus police vice cop with whom I had worked on several stories about undercover operations. "Hey, they caught the 'Grandview Rapist,'" Martin said.

"Mike, every time you guys catch a burglar in the area, you think it's the 'Grandview Rapist.'" It's never him."

"I'm tellin' you, it's him this time. Go check it out. He's a doctor and they set the bond at some outrageous amount. They caught him in a house up around Graceland Shopping Center."

I remembered Rockwell's suspicion that the rapist had a connection to the medical field. I left my beer and popcorn, got dressed and went to the Franklin County Clerk of Courts office downtown. I had gotten to know the night staff at the Clerk of Courts during my nightly visits to check the day's arrest records. They were good guys who usually pointed out the good arrests to me on my nightly visits. "Do you guys have someone locked up on a burglary with a real high bond?" I asked.

One of the boys plucked a sheet from his desk. "What's the deal on this guy?" he asked, handing me the file. "They're holding him on $75,000 bond for a burglary?"

I shrugged, not wanting to give too much away; other reporters checked in with them, too. "I heard he might be connected to some other burglaries." I copied down the information from the slate sheet: Edward F. Jackson, 38, 2525 Stafford Place, Columbus. A quick check in the city directory showed that he was actually Dr. Edward F. Jackson. The slate sheet also listed an alias of Michael Remington Jackson. According to the arrest record, a witness saw Jackson prowling around a north-side apartment complex and called police. Jackson was caught in the kitchen of an apartment and surrendered without incident. According to police records, he was carrying a flashlight, ski mask, rope, gloves, pry tool, and a plastic bag.

Captain Harry Dolby, head of the Columbus police detective bureau, happened to be walking down the hall of the bureau when I arrived.

"Hey, Harry, I hear you caught the 'Grandview Rapist.'"

Harry Dolby didn't like me and the feelings were mutual. He whirled, his face reddening, and said, "That's '*Captain* Dolby' to you."

"Harrrr-eeeee. You don't see a badge on this shirt, do you?" I afforded most cops the respect of addressing them by their rank. With Dolby, I returned the respect he showed me, which was none. "What's the deal with this Dr. Jackson you arrested? I hear you think he's the 'Grandview Rapist.'"

"I don't know anything about that."

"Uh-huh. Really? You're holding a burglar with a $75,000 bond and the commander of the detective bureau just happens to be in the office on Labor Day night, yet he doesn't know anything about the biggest arrest in years? Come on, Harry, whatta ya got for me?"

"No comment."

"Okay, Harry, that's fine," I said. "I've already got several sources who say that you think Jackson is the 'Grandview Rapist' and you'll be going after indictments on a series of rapes. And, that's what my lead is going to be tomorrow."

"Do that and you'll ruin our investigation. I'll never give you any information again."

"Harry, you never give me any information, anyway, for God's sake. What have I got to lose?"

He stormed down the hall and out of sight.

The copy desk edited out any reference to the 'Grandview Rapist' in the next day's story; I was livid. They wanted more confirmation. A prominent Columbus internist is arrested and they were afraid to connect him to the rapes committed by the "Grandview Rapist." I still believe the fact that Jackson is African American played into the decision. I think they were afraid of the potential criticism from the black community if we linked Jackson to the serial rapist. This was evidenced by the fact that I did not have trouble getting the 'Grandview Rapist' reference in previous stories about other arrests. We were able to get the reference in the paper the following day after Mary Yost, who covered courts for the *Dispatch,* was able to get a source in the prosecutor's office to confirm police suspicions.

On Friday, we ran a copyrighted story that police had found a list in Jackson's handwriting that contained the names of sixty-five women, many of whom had been victimized by the "Grandview Rapist."

"Why would you keep something like that?" I asked one detective.

"It's his trophy list," he said.

Jackson was tried on one set of charges in a trial in Akron, where he was convicted of 60 felonies, including 21 counts of rape, and sentenced to 191 to 665 years in prison. He also was convicted of an additional 15 counts of rape in a separate trial in Cincinnati. (A 1978 law change forced prosecutors to put Jackson on trial twice, once for crimes committed before the law change and once for those committed afterward.)

Dr. Edward F. Jackson Jr. and William Bernard Jackson were linked by name, likeness, and, unfortunately, Dr. Jackson's crimes. (Courtesy of the *Columbus Dispatch*)

I covered the first part of the trial in Akron, though Jackson would never consent to an interview. I followed Jackson and his lawyer down the street one day at lunch and peppered him with questions. He ignored me except to flash me a condescending look of distain, as though to say, "What a pitiful profession you have chosen." Which was fine. I returned a look, as though to say, "You're going to prison for the rest of your life. I'd rather be a reporter."

After his conviction in Akron, the judge asked him if he had anything to say before sentencing. Jackson said only, "You may fire when ready, Gridley," reciting the order to open fire given by Commodore George Dewey at the onset of the Battle of Manila Bay in the Spanish-American War.

He will never get out of prison. He has never agreed to be interviewed.

Innocent Jackson

William B. Jackson became known as "Innocent Jackson" or "Other Jackson" after authorities discovered that he was in prison serving time for two rapes committed by Dr. Edward F. Jackson. Investigators spotted the error after looking at the list of victims Edward Jackson had kept and found two familiar names. They remembered the cases and knew William Jackson was in the penitentiary for the rapes. In fact, during the trials, the two victims had identified William Jackson as their attacker.

When investigators went to the prison to interview Innocent Jackson, they said, "We don't think you did it."

"I told you that when you arrested me," he said.

After being transferred from a state prison to the Franklin County Jail, Jackson was released at 3 P.M. on September 22, 1982. An hour later, photographer Kenny Chamberlain and I tracked him down at the home of his Aunt Middy, who, eerily, was a patient of Dr. Jackson. We managed to get Jackson in the press car and away from his aunt's home. We bought him a couple of packs of cigarettes and a twelve-pack of beer and took him to the home of an old friend. Our mission was simple. We knew every other media outlet in town was looking for him. We wanted to get our story, but do so while keeping Jackson hidden until the *Citizen-Journal*'s deadline had passed and it was impossible to get him on the eleven o'clock news.

Jackson, who was known to his friends as "Billy Jack," was an affable sort who sipped his first beer in five years and began telling his story of life in prison. He said he wasn't bitter about his wrongful imprisonment, though I figured that tune would change after he had an opportunity to talk to an attorney. At that moment, however, he was just glad to be out. I had everything I needed within an hour. However, that was still five hours before the *C-J* deadline. I continued to ask him questions, essentially asking him to recount his entire life. We had been at it several hours; I was out of questions and he had plowed through a host of beers and cigarettes when he asked, "Man, how much more do you need?"

"Just a little. You hungry? We can send Kenny out for food. You'd probably like to have something besides prison food."

He smiled. "Yeah, well, food isn't all I missed. I got people I want to see, you dig?"

"Cool. So, you're not going back to your Aunt Middy's?"

"What? Hell, no. I've been in prison five years, man. There're some ladies I want to see a lot more than my Aunt Middy."

So, he and his friend Leroy went out looking for women. And, for that night, he went unfound by the rest of the Columbus media.

Jackson was eventually compensated $717,500 by the State of Ohio for his wrongful imprisonment. However, that money was soon gone. He continued to have scrapes with the law—drug abuse and carrying a concealed weapon. He was twice charged with domestic violence, but both charges were dismissed. In 1992 he was sentenced to a year in prison for theft and carrying a concealed weapon. In a 1997 interview with *Dispatch* reporter Steve Stephens, Jackson said he had spent big on "cars, a house and a marriage that lasted less than a year." At the time of the interview, he was living on a $484 a month disability payment and his cable had been cut off for nonpayment.

Penny Wolfe

When they asked Penny Wolfe to identify the man who had raped her, she calmly stood, left the witness box and walked to the defense table where she looked hard into the eyes of Dr. Edward F. Jackson. She slowly raised her arm and shoved a finger into the face of her attacker.

Jackson had tied her up, raped her, and nearly choked her to death. I thought she was the toughest woman I had ever met.

When I interviewed her after the Akron trial and after Jackson had gone to prison, she revealed the torment she had gone through after the rape. It had been horrendous. While she was viewed as a hero around central Ohio, she says the years after the rape made it difficult for her to think of herself as such. She had suffered through a bout of anorexia and later gained eighty pounds. She sought psychological care, began drinking, installed five locks on her door and attempted suicide by driving into the path of an oncoming car.

"Obviously, you didn't get killed. Did you get hurt?" I asked.

She shook her head. "I missed." Even she had to smile.

It wasn't until Jackson had gone to prison that she felt she could go back out in public. Once that happened, she went shopping.

She said she didn't feel like a hero and she said she didn't feel tough.

I thought she was both.

Welcome to Fantasy Island

I had gotten a call from Assistant City Editor Jerry Tebben at 1:30 P.M. "How do you feel about Louisiana?"

"Is this a trick question?"

"We've got you booked on a flight for Monroe, Louisiana, at four o'clock. Let's get moving. Stop by the office and pick up your tickets and some cash."

My son was about four months old. I handed him to my school-teacher wife as we passed in the driveway. I told her what I knew. "I'm flying to Louisiana."

"When will you be back?"

"I don't know. I'll call." She was not amused.

There is a degree of unpredictability about reporting that is difficult for those not in the business to appreciate and understand. I didn't know if I was going to be gone two days or two weeks. All I knew for sure was that I wouldn't return until the story had played out.

Jon Barry Simonis had been arrested in Lake Charles, Louisiana, and accused of being the "ski mask rapist." He had already confessed to at least seventy-seven crimes in eleven states, including Ohio. One of the crimes he had confessed to was a rape near Lancaster, Ohio, the county seat of Fairfield County, southeast of Columbus. When Simonis was told that another man was already in prison after confessing to the rape, he reportedly said, "What the hell did he do that for? I did that rape."

Simonis had graduated from Bloom-Carroll High School, a rural school in the village of Carroll in the northern part of Fairfield County, in 1969. He had committed the rape in 1979 while he was back in the area for a ten-year class reunion. He told authorities that the husband and wife were watching *Fantasy Island* when he sneaked into the house. He came up behind them with a gun and, using the show's signature line, said, "Welcome to Fantasy Island."

He then tied up the man and raped the woman.

Bradley C. Cox had confessed to three rapes and was serving a prison term of up to two hundred years. Cox had confessed to the crimes after days of intense questioning by Lancaster police—and hours hooked to a lie detector.

This struck me as odd, as I didn't see why anyone would confess to something he hadn't done, particularly a first-degree felony.

The newsroom secretary had my tickets. I was to fly to Atlanta, catch another plane to Memphis, and catch another to Monroe, where I had to get a car and drive to Baton Rouge.

"Where's Monroe?" I asked, looking at the tickets.

"You'll have to find it on a map," Tebben said.

"What state is it in? I've never even heard of it."

I grabbed an atlas and found it in the northern part of the state, about thirty-five miles from the Arkansas border. "Good God! You can't get me any closer than this?"

"That's the best we could do," Tebben said.

"My plane gets in at 11 P.M., and you want me to rent a car, drive the length of Louisiana and have a story for tomorrow afternoon?"

That seemed to be the newsroom consensus.

Fortunately, I had been in contact with Lt. Ronnie Jones of the Louisiana State Police, who was the agency's public information officer and extremely helpful. I called Jones from a pay phone in the Memphis airport. He updated me on a new list of confessions by Simonis; he had copped to committing seven rapes in Ohio. Jones said that authorities in Louisiana now believed that in 1979 and 1980, Simonis had raped as many as 130 women. This information gave me my story for the next day.

I could have called the newsroom and dictated the story, but I didn't. I would wait until the next morning. During my time covering the police department, I had developed an acute understanding of how the city desk worked. If I called in the story that night, they would expect even more details and new information for the next day. However, if I didn't call it in until the morning, they would be thrilled with the details.

After I got off the phone with Jones in Memphis, resigned to driving all night, I happened upon one of the most spectacular strokes of luck of my career. As I was walking back to catch my plane, I passed another Southern Airlines gate with a plane leaving for Baton Rouge ten minutes after my plane was to leave Monroe. There was one man at the gate and only a few passengers. "Is this flight full?" I asked.

"Naw. Hardly anyone on it."

I showed him my ticket. "Can I exchange this ticket and get on this plane?" I asked. He looked at it and said, "Yeah, get on," he said. "I'll take care of it for you." The flight to Baton Rouge was ten dollars more. He said not to worry about it. I spiffed the guy twenty bucks and ended up in Baton Rouge a day earlier than I had expected. (Why our crack travel agency couldn't locate the Baton Rouge flight remained a mystery.)

The most interesting aspect of the trip to Baton Rouge was watching the dynamics between the Fairfield County sheriff and the Lancaster detective who had won an award for getting the confession out of Cox. Although peace officers will talk about the "brotherhood" of law enforcement, there is tremendous competition between police and sheriff's departments. In Columbus, the cops condescendingly referred to the sheriff's deputies as "Lock Keys," because deputies were responsible for operating the county jail. In the case of Simonis and Cox, the police believed they had done everything properly, though it was evident that the wrong man was in jail. The sheriff seemed overly interested in freeing Cox and seeing that justice was done. And, if that happened to rub a little salt in any open wounds in the other department, so be it.

Simonis pleaded guilty to armed robbery and burglary charges in LaSalle Parish and was sentenced to 231 years in prison with no chance of parole. At his sentencing, Simonis said: "I am guilty of these crimes. I knew extremely well what I was doing beforehand, while I was doing it, and I know now."

Cox was freed from the Ohio prison.

TWENTY-THREE
❏

Sad Deaths

Tim and Becky Rogers

SHORTLY BEFORE ELEVEN ON A SUNDAY MORNING IN MAY 1982, George Fraley's car was on fire in the street in front of his west-side house. His neighbor, Tim Rogers, saw the car burning and ran up onto Fraley's porch to tell him. There had been some bad blood between the two, but Rogers wasn't going to let his neighbor's car burn.

"George, George, your car is on fire."

There was a slight pause in the conversation. From next door, Becky Rogers could not hear what Fraley was saying to her husband.

"I didn't start the fire, George," she heard her husband say.

Then, a shotgun blast came through the door and into Rogers's torso. He staggered out into the yard, collapsed, and said, "Oh, God, he shot me." Then, Tim Rogers closed his eyes and died. He was just twenty-four; they had a one-year-old son and Becky was pregnant with their second child.

Becky Rogers ran to her husband. As she did, Fraley came out on the porch and leveled the shotgun at her. "I've got one left," he said.

George Fraley gunned down Tim Rogers with a shotgun while Becky Rogers looked on. When she ran to her husband's side, Fraley leveled the gun at her, but did not shoot. (Courtesy of the *Columbus Dispatch*)

I interviewed Becky Rogers on May 25, 1982, in her Terrace Avenue home. It was the day after her husband had been killed. She was more angry than distraught. Columbus police had confiscated the shotgun used to kill her husband about two weeks earlier after Fraley used it to threaten Tim. The police kept the shotgun for just three days, then gave it back to Fraley. When Becky questioned the rational thinking of giving Fraley back the weapon, the police told her that she was needlessly worrying. "They told me I was just hyper," she said.

Tension between the Rogerses and Fraley had apparently begun a few weeks earlier when Becky asked Fraley if she could borrow a few bricks to build a hothouse for her tomato plants. She said a sober Fraley gave her the bricks. However, a few days later, she said a drunk Fraley smashed the glass roof of the house. When he was confronted by Tim Rogers, Fraley aimed the shotgun at him and said, "I'm dying of cancer, and I'll take you with me."

A week later, he did.

Tim's death was another strike in what had been a tough twenty-seven years for Becky. Her mother had died during breast cancer surgery when Becky was just nine. She went to live with her grandparents, but they both died a short time later and she lived in foster homes and Franklin Village, the county children's home, until she was eighteen. She then met Ricky Widner—the father of her eldest son—and they were living together when he was shot and killed during an argument with another man.

Fraley went to trial on October 27, 1982, a day that would have been Tim and Becky Rogers's third wedding anniversary. She gave birth to their daughter, Amy Nicole, a month before the trial.

Fraley was convicted of murder and was sentenced to fifteen years to life. His claim of dying of cancer apparently was bogus. He was convicted, sentenced and paroled in August 2000.

I interviewed Becky just before the trial. She was trying to raise three children under the age of five.

"Every time I love someone, [God] takes them away. It isn't fair. If I'm faithful [to Tim] someday I can have him back. God will have to give him back to me. I can wait. Life doesn't last that long."

Twice a Widow

When I arrived at the Leonard Avenue carryout, David Murib was lying in front of the store, dead. Blood covered the front of his shirt. It was March 2, 1984.

A few feet away, sitting in the front seat of the police car, was his four-year-old son. There was still blood on the little boy's arms where he had embraced his fallen father. Only minutes earlier, Murib had been shot to death after he attempted to frisk a customer he believed had stolen something from the store.

"I told him about that one time before," James Collier, a sixty-four-year-old employee who ran the carryout's lottery machine, told me. "I told him he's got no right to pat people down."

After the customer purchased a felt-tipped pen, Collier said Murib followed him outside and began patting him down. Collier heard the man say, "Man, I didn't take nothing out of your store." He then pulled a gun and shot Murib in the chest. Murib's brother, Ahmad, ran to his brother's aid and was shot in the wrist.

That is when little Yasser ran from the store and hugged his dying father.

The following day, Ted Wendling and I co-wrote a follow-up about David Murib's widow, Loretta. It was the second time she had been widowed, both times to Murib brothers. In October 1973, Loretta's husband, Mohammad Murib, was stabbed to death outside of a west-side bar. Following an Arab tradition that allows an unwed man to marry his brother's widow, Loretta married David. Both men, who were Palestinian natives from Jordan, were twenty-nine when they were slain.

In November 1984, James Austin, thirty-five, was convicted of voluntary manslaughter and felonious assault in the death of David and the shooting of Ahmad Murib. He was sentenced to eight to twenty-five years in prison for killing David and three to fifteen years for the shooting of Ahmad. He was paroled in June 1999.

Janice and Brandon Beidleman

Janice Beidleman, twenty-one, and the diaper-clad body of her twenty-month-old son, Brandon Lamar Beidleman, were found floating in a foot of water near the shoreline of Alum Creek on September 14, 1981. Janice had been beaten, raped, sodomized and strangled. Her son had been suffocated with a pillow that police found near his body.

 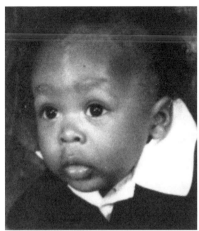

Janice Beidleman and her infant son Brandon were found murdered in the summer of 1981. It was the first big homicide case that I covered for the paper. Their murders remain unsolved. (Courtesy of the *Columbus Dispatch*)

The dead woman's mother, Helen Foster, drove a few miles from her home to where the police had set up the crime scene tape. They hadn't yet identified the woman and child in the water, but Helen instinctively knew it was her daughter and grandson. She had been at home when she heard a radio news report of a young woman and an infant being found in the creek.

"I hoped I was wrong," she later told me. "I hoped it wasn't them. But when I got there, it was."

Helen said she had last seen her daughter at 11:30 A.M. the previous day, a Sunday. The daughter and grandson had stopped for a visit.

I interviewed Helen near the intersection of Sunbury and Agler roads. Down the hill, blocked by trees, were the two bodies and the detectives. The Crime Scene Search Unit was just arriving. As I interviewed Helen, a *Citizen-Journal* reporter stood off to my right, listening, waiting to ask a few questions. I asked Helen if she had a photograph of her daughter and grandson that I could borrow. Her hands were shaking. I remember watching her fingers shake so badly that she could hardly get the photographs out of the plastic sleeves in her wallet. She had about seven photographs in all, some of Janice, some of Brandon, and a few of them together. I held them in my hand for a moment. The *Citizen-Journal* reporter was Alfred Lubrano, a transplanted New Yorker who was politely waiting for me to select the photos I wanted, so he could then take one of the remaining. I folded them into a neat stack and said, "You know, Mrs. Foster, I'm no photographer, so I'm going to have someone in the photo department take a look at all of these so we get the best photo in the paper."

"That's fine with me," she said. "Just make sure I get them back."

"I will. I promise." I flashed Alfred a wink, then locked the photos in the glove compartment of my press car.

(I returned the photos two days later. Did I feel bad for taking all the photos? No. Alfred was a nice guy, but a competitor, nonetheless. I realize that some might read this and ask, "How could you be so dispassionate as to be concerned about your competition while interviewing a woman who is going through the most traumatic hours of her life?" It's the nature of the beast. Did I feel bad for Helen Foster? Absolutely. I find it hard to imagine anything worse than losing a child and a grandchild. But I still had a job to do, which was to accurately report the incident and deliver a better story than the competition. Photos were part of the equation.)

The next afternoon, I received a call from Charles Rawlins, who lived about a half-mile from where the bodies were found. Rawlins said that he and his wife were awake about 11 P.M. the night before the bodies were found and that he had heard a woman screaming and being beaten, a baby crying, and the muffled voice of a man who said, "shut up" and "keep him quiet." They heard the woman say, "Don't cry, baby." Another neighbor, Zenora Kenley, heard the screams, which she at first thought to be a domestic argument.

The Rawlinses attempted to call the police, but inadvertently called the Mifflin Township Fire Department. (This was before the 911 emergency system was implemented.) By the time the fire department arrived, realized the mistake and contacted Columbus police, which responded with a helicopter, the man, woman, and child were gone.

This turned out to be my breakout story on the police beat. I had been on the beat for four months and had been struggling up to this point. The difference between the leisurely pace of the state desk and night police was overwhelming, and I was worried that I was going to get fired. There were big expectations of the night police reporter and I had to produce quality stories. Ned Stout was waking me up every morning at 6:10 AM with questions about the previous night's story.

Stout called me the next morning after I had filed my follow-up story on Janice and Brandon Beidleman and said, "Well, even the blind pig finds an acorn once in a while, eh, Yocum?" At this point in my police reporting career, it was as close to a compliment as I would get.

The story ran under the headline:

SCREAMS HEARD HALF-MILE
FROM LOCATION OF BODIES

I went back and interviewed Helen on the one-year anniversary of the deaths. For awhile, she had gone to the cemetery every Sunday after church. She had stopped the practice and was trying to go on with her life. "They [detectives] gave me hope," she said. "They said there isn't a day that goes by that they don't work on the case. They said they want to find out who killed my daughter and grand-baby. They think they got away. But it will all come out . . . someday."

Homicide detectives said they had a suspect in the murders, but they never had enough evidence to convict him. No one was ever charged in the murders.

Don's Burgers

I loved Don's hamburgers.

Donald Manson ran Don's Hamburgers, a little carry-out hamburger joint on Sullivant Avenue on the Hilltop, a couple of miles from my house. Don's burgers were widely recognized as the best in town. They came with a mustard and onion spread. There were only two things that could make my mouth start watering just by thinking of them: DiCarlo's Pizza—Sicilian-style pizza from Steubenville—and Don's hamburgers.

He also owned Grandpa's General Store, which was in the other half of a duplex from his hamburger joint. I only knew Don to see him in the restaurant and speak. He was always friendly and a favorite of the neighborhood kids because he would give them a free hamburger if they brought in a good grade card.

Don was murdered on October 19, 1981. He was shot once in the back while he worked at Grandpa's.

I tried to talk to Don's son-in-law, Darrell Storck, but he waved me off and shook his head. My rule for interviews was pretty simple: If you were an elected official or a public figure, then I had every right to badger you for an interview. If a crime victim or a relative didn't want to talk, I would say thanks, hand them a business card, and say, "If you change your mind, give me a call."

David Yost was a reporter with the *Citizen-Journal*. Yost went up to Storck and started asking questions. When Storck gave Yost the same treatment that he had given me, Yost asked, "Why not? I just want to ask you a couple questions."

Storck was a big man and you could see by the look in his eyes that he was getting ready to unload on Yost. I reached out, grabbed Yost by the sleeve of his leather jacket and pulled him back.

"Are you trying to get yourself killed?"

"I wanted to ask him some questions."

"I don't think he's in the mood."

Yost started saying something about his rights as a reporter and I just walked away. At that moment, the First Amendment wasn't high on the family's priority list and I didn't want to be guilty by association if he decided to badger the son-in-law again.

TWENTY-FOUR

❑

The Characters

James W. "Jimmy" Loughridge

James W. "Jimmy" Loughridge was a horrific drunk who for twenty years had been using the police station to flop after his drinking binges.

Columbus police had so many arrest cards on Loughridge that they could not tell for sure when they first arrested him, although they believed it to be July 1964. By 1985, he had been arrested about 700 times. He had 507 arrests for disorderly conduct, 60 public intoxication arrests, 100 arrests for being a pedestrian under the influence, and a host of other charges, including aggravated menacing, resisting arrest, and escape.

Loughridge would get drunk, then wander into the police station and pass out on one of the church pews in the downstairs hall, or crawl into one of the stalls in the men's restroom and sleep on a commode. Most of the drunks who used the halls of the police station as a flophouse smelled bad. Loughridge, however, raised that bar to new heights. If he was sleeping in the restroom, you couldn't go in. I have been around week-old corpses that did not smell as bad as Jimmy Loughridge.

In the years I covered the police beat, he never once asked me for money, which was odd. If he was vertical, he would sit on the bench, hands in his pockets, rocking. One morning he was sleeping on the bench and rolled off as I was walking by. His face hit the floor like a dropped watermelon—splut. He never moved. I nudged him with my toe and said, "Jimmy. You okay, man?"

Nothing.

Deputy Chief Robert Kern came out of his office and asked, "Is he dead?"

I shrugged. "How would I know?"

Kern shook his head. "I've never seen him sober," he said. "He's been sleeping around here for about twenty years. He's a nuisance."

A couple of uniformed officers drew the unfortunate assignment of hauling him away. None of the cops wanted Jimmy in their cruiser because they had to get it disinfected afterward. He was charged with criminal trespassing. The routine had started again. He would be released from jail that afternoon. He would fail to show up for his court appearance and would get arrested again and sentenced to thirty days in jail.

Mark Huffman

Covering bank robberies was a pain. You had to do it, but the police would never tell you how much money had been stolen and it was simple record-keeping journalism. In my years at the *Dispatch,* there were only two bank robberies of note.

In the early 1980s, federal authorities were looking for a gang of bank robbers who had been hitting banks in Kentucky and Ohio. They suspected the same men were responsible for the robberies because of their method of developing clever ruses to keep police occupied while they robbed the banks. They introduced their techniques to the area when one of the robbers went into Mary Rutan Hospital in Bellefontaine, Ohio, and planted a fake bomb—a clock, road flares, and wires neatly tied together to look like an explosive. One of the men then called the hospital and told the operator that a bomb had been planted and exactly where to find it. When the device was found, every cop in the area was called in to help evacuate the hospital. While law enforcement officers from the area were busy with the evacuation, the robbers went to a small bank in nearby East Liberty, Ohio, and cleaned it out.

Columbus's most famous bank robber was Mark Huffman. In a way, like much of the rest of Columbus, I wanted to see him get away with it. Anyone involved in the day-to-day grind of the corporate world has probably fantasized about pulling off the perfect bank job, getting away with it, and using the ill-gotten money to sail the world. So, part of me was pulling for Huffman to become the B. D. Cooper of Columbus, Ohio. On the surface, it looked like he was going to get away with it. Ultimately, like so many other criminals, he got sloppy.

On December 18, 1982, twenty-five-year-old navy veteran Mark T. Huffman reported to his job as a service technician for Bank One. Huffman's job was to stock the ATMs at the twenty-five Columbus-area Bank One branches. On this day, he began work at 8 AM and worked a fifteen-hour shift, turning in his keys at 11 P.M.

He would be thousands of miles away before anyone knew he had stolen $409,000.

It was not until the next afternoon that the first warning signs began to surface at Bank One. The computer system that monitored the ATMs was showing that some machines were out of money and others were low on cash. Huffman had partially filled the machines with just enough money that no one would realize there was a problem until he was long gone.

Police would later discover that he had rented a white Ford Pinto the week before the heist. It was found in the parking lot of a north-side motel. Authorities found a room he had rented under an alias. Inside they found a box of hair dye. In the sink were the remains of his beard and moustache.

We talked to his neighbors, who said they hoped he would get away with it. This, of course, infuriated the police and Bank One officials. (Years later, when I took a job in public relations for Bank One, I pretended to have been outraged at Huffman's thievery.) The neighbors said Huffman grew tomatoes and shared them with his neighbors, helped a neighbor with a bad back take her trash to the curb, and house-sat for vacationing neighbors. "He would be the last person in this neighborhood that I would think would do all that," one neighbor said.

A month after he disappeared, I did the obligatory one-month follow-up story. Huffman and his brother, Richard, thirty, who was suspected of helping with the heist, had not been seen. Edwin Billman, who was head of security for Bank One, said, "I've done an awful lot of research on those two boys. I know them like the back of my hand. But I haven't talked to anyone who has seen the whites of their eyes since they disappeared. Maybe they're a little smarter than we thought."

Huffman was captured eleven months later in Australia. Using the name and stolen passport of an old U.S. Navy buddy, Steven Janney, Huffman had bought a thirty-eight-foot yacht—the San-poi—for which he paid $100,000 cash, and had been sailing be-tween New Zealand, New Guinea, Australia, and Timor. When he had docked in Darwin, Australia, Huffman went on a shopping spree, buying a Ford Escort and a motorcycle. He also began spend-ing too much time in the casinos. This all caught the attention of local authorities.

Police said Huffman "was quite surprised" when they boarded

his yacht and asked if he was Mark Huffman. Huffman and his brother both received ten-year prison terms after pleading guilty to four of the twenty-six counts of embezzlement.

Ed Compton and His Two-point Buck

The best stories are the ones that simply write themselves. On a Saturday morning in November 1983, I spotted a Honda motorcycle hanging by a noose from a tree next to Compton Roofing and Siding on West Second Avenue. A hunting arrow was stuck in the motorcycle's tank and next to it was a sign that read, "Public Nuisance."

The motorcycle belonged to Matt Rackman, who had been storing the motorcycle in the Compton Roofing and Siding garage for three years, over the complaints of Ed Compton, who owned the garage and had for years asked Rackman to remove it from the premises. A little scouting around the area led me to a local watering hole and Ed Compton, a good-natured fellow with an obvious sense of humor. Compton was the primary suspect in the cycle lynching.

Like I said, sometimes they just write themselves. The following exchange ran around a photo of Compton standing beneath the motorcycle and holding his bow.

I was told you hanged that motorcycle in the tree.

"Me! No. I don't know who did it. All I know is that it was found guilty."

Found guilty?

"Oh, yeah. We had a trial for it. It was all done real legal."

A trial?

"Uh-huh. We had a trial, found it guilty of being a public nuisance, and decided it should be put to death. Shooting was too good for it, so it got hanged. We almost ended up in a hung jury. Get it?"

Ed Compton is standing in front of his "two-point buck." Ed strung up the motorcycle when a buddy refused to get it out of his garage. (Courtesy of the *Columbus Dispatch*)

I get it. I get it. But why is there an arrow sticking out of the gas tank? What really happened?

"Really?"

Yes. The truth.

"OK, the truth. I thought it was a deer and I shot it."

A deer?

"Yep."

How did it get in the garage?

"I don't know, but I would have sworn it was a two-point buck. I saw those handle bars sticking up, and I thought they were antlers."

So how did it get in the tree?

"We put it up there to gut it."

You mean to clean out its insides?

"Right. Well, when we got it in the tree we found out it was a motorcycle, so we ran."

Why did you run?

"What if the game warden comes around? I don't even know if those things are in season."

In season?

"Sure, you can get in trouble for shooting motorcycles out of season. Besides, did you ever try to gut a Honda?"

AFTERWORD

THE TRUTH IS, I JOINED THE *DISPATCH* HOPING TO MOVE EVENTU-
ally to the sports department. I had been the Associate Sports Editor of
the *Times Leader* in Martins Ferry, Ohio, before joining the *Dispatch* on
the state desk in early 1980. My plan was to bide my time reporting
news until there was an opening in sports. After a few months of covering news I lost all desire to cover sports, having fallen in love with the
thrill of tracking down a big news story. I loved the chase.

When I was reporting for the *Dispatch,* I linked my very identity to
my job. I loved being a newspaper reporter, and I loved being Robin
Yocum of the *Columbus Dispatch.*

I covered the police beat for more than four years and, by the summer of 1985, was ready to leave. I was tired of writing stories about dead
people. I was tired of knocking on doors and talking my way into
homes for interviews with grieving relatives. And I was tired of always
battling with the cops.

The relationship between reporters and cops is always going to be
tenuous. They have completely separate agendas. Cops will always look
at reporters with disdain, and reporters will look back with suspicion. A
juvenile officer once said to me, "Don't take this personal, but I would
never, ever want to be a reporter. It's such a scummy job."

My guess is that she was simply expressing the views of most cops.
They do not like scrutiny. Police want to work in a vacuum, free of judgment by the press and, ultimately, the public. Generally, reporters will re-

port the successes of the department, but they also will expose the misdeeds and botched investigations. This is when the relationship gets ugly.

After four years of this, I'd had enough and wanted to do something different. The *Dispatch* was starting a special projects team and I wanted to be a part of it. I always believed my forte was in long-term, investigative projects. There were few opportunities to do long-term projects on the police beat because of the daily responsibilities, such as doing the rounds, making calls, and monitoring the scanner.

Bernie Karsko was incredulous when I told him I was leaving the police beat. As a former police reporter, he could not believe that I did not want to keep covering the police. I was the first reporter hired by Jim Breiner, who headed the special projects team. As much as I liked the police beat, the years I spent on the investigative team were my most fulfilling at the paper. I learned a great deal from Breiner, who was the best editor I ever worked for, and he gave me a great deal of latitude to chase down stories.

Despite this, on a late spring afternoon in 1990, I knew that my newspaper days were numbered. As I sat at my desk working on a story for the next day's paper, I realized that I was more concerned about another obligation than about my deadline. My mind was already at a baseball field in Grove City where my nine-year-old son's team was to begin play at 6 P.M. My eyes kept drifting from my computer screen to the clock on the wall. I realized that I was infinitely more interested in his game than I was in writing the story at hand. That was a first, and that afternoon I realized that being Robin Yocum of the *Columbus Dispatch* was not nearly as important as being Coach Yocum.

The party was over and it was time to go.

I worked at the *Dispatch* for eleven years—1980–91. Leaving the paper for a job in corporate public relations was by far the most difficult decision of my professional life. For the most part, the transition has been smooth. There are times when I miss being a reporter. I miss the camaraderie and humor of the newsroom and the direct, nononsense manner of reporters.

Most of all, I miss the thrill of the chase. And I'm certain I always will.

Index